THE CRINKLE CRANKLE WALL

SABINA OSTROWSKA

ASIN B08FP8Q65R

ISBN 9798674344056

Painting on the cover by Alison Cole @RosieTileArtsandCrafts

Formatting by www.antpress.org

For updates about new books and to read free stories, subscribe to my website or follow me on social media:

www.sabinaostrowska.com

Facebook @sabinawriter

Instagram @cortijob

Published by: textworkshop.org

WHAT READERS AND AUTHORS SAY ABOUT THE CRINKLE CRANKLE WALL

"I enjoy expat books and this is one of the best ones I've read. The trials and tribulations of beginning homeowner issues, not to mention, completely rebuilding the place had me cheering for them every step of the way. Everyone should have neighbors as helpful and wonderful as the author's. I'm eager to read the next installment!" *Kathy H. Hobbs* reader

"How brave, or was it foolhardy? Sabina and Robert set off to a country they didn't know and a language that they didn't speak - could this be a recipe for disaster or an amazing adventure? I gasped and laughed and almost cried at various points in their story. Do read it you won't be disappointed and the good news is that there is more, as this is only the first year!!!" *Marian Quick* reader

"At first, I was appalled by the concept of anybody who, knowing nothing about the area they are moving to, would buy a fixer-up cortijo while relying on Grand Designs (tv programme) as the guide on how to accomplish a nice house and letting apartments. However, I ended being greatly amused by language difficulties, looking for paella for dinner in the mountains and other daft situations. Clearly, they have been accepted and liked by their neighbours. A true picture of moving to Andalucia." *C. Saunders* reader

"I could not put this book down and despite a mountain of jobs to do I kept convincing myself 'just one more chapter'. I am not going to give any details away - let the author do that. I enjoyed the honesty of the many blunders and whilst we can sit smugly and think 'how stupid I would never do that' the chances are all these rookie mistakes are repeated time and time again - even if we have read the books! I hope there is a sequel." *Amazon reader*

"I have read an inordinate number of books by people starting a new life in France, Spain, Outer Womberbumboojah and for the most part, they are not well written and seldom as amusing as their authors think they are. This book is different. First of all, the writer is Polish and writes exquisite English that makes me weak both in admiration for her and shame for the rest of us. Secondly, it is hilarious. The vicissitudes of Sabina and Robert's first year living in Andalusia make one both wince in sympathy and fall about laughing. If this sort of book is your sort of thing, you will love it too. Highly recommended." *Mrs. Olga A. Danes-volkov* reader

"Sabina Ostrowska has a sharp eye for the eccentricities of British ex-pats (including those of her English husband) and an even keener eye for the customs and foibles of her new rural neighbours in rural Andalucia. In this delightful memoir of the trials and tribulations, she and Robert endure as they attempt to convert a set of farmyard buildings into a comfortable home and attractive guesthouse, the author captures not only national characteristics with wit and flair but reveals all the missteps they make with humour and self-deprecation. Readers who enjoy reading about the entertaining and inevitably frustrating efforts of ex-pats struggling to settle into a new life in Spain, will read *The Crinkle Crankle Wall* with pleasure. After rapidly smiling my way through this, Sabina Ostrowska's first book, I look forward to her second." *Ronald Mackay* author of *The Kilt Behind the Curtain: A Scotsman in Ceausescu's Romania*

"A truly fabulous memoir on Sabina Ostrowska's relocation to Spain from living in the middle east. Would you move to another country without any research, without speaking the language, without anything other than a feeling it may be a good place to live? This is what Sabina and husband Robert did. Consequently, her tales of relocation, readjustment and reawakening are superb. Written in wonderful prose with a great sense of humour the book had me glued to its pages wondering what would be their next pitfall, their next mad idea. I think they only survived (just) thanks to their wonderful neighbours who must have shaken their heads and decided that if they did not step in then something truly disastrous would befall them." *Louise Davis* author of *Hideaway Hotel: Secrets of a Mediterranean Celebrity Retreat*

"What happens if you take two city dwellers, living in the UAE, and transplant them to a ruin in rural Andalucía? Answer: *The Crinkle Crankle Wall*. Sabina Ostrowska's first travelogue memoir is full of those ouch moments of a duck out of water scenario with hilarious language mistakes, dodgy builders and a rapidly greening swimming pool but Sabina and husband Robert buckle down and get stuck into fitting into the local community with aplomb. Although I live 1000km north of Sabina in a totally different part of Spain, her descriptions of rural life and the characters which populate their tiny rural town struck a strong chord. Language problems, fitting in with the neighbours and renovation nightmares all struck home and I enjoyed following a similar yet very different story of moving to Spain." *Lisa Rose Wright* author of *Plum, Courgette & Green Bean Tart: Seeking la vida dulce in Galicia*

To my husband, Robert Ryan, who has always been my biggest supporter.
xxx

"I went to the woods because I wished to live deliberately, to front only the essential facts of life, and see if I could not learn what it had to teach, and not, when I came to die, discover that I had not lived. I did not wish to live what was not life, living is so dear; nor did I wish to practise resignation, unless it was quite necessary. I wanted to live deep and suck out all the marrow of life, to live so sturdily and Spartan-like as to put to rout all that was not life, to cut a broad swath and shave close, to drive life into a corner, and reduce it to its lowest terms."

HENRY DAVID THOREAU, WALDEN

CONTENTS

PROLOGUE

BEFORE WE SET OFF TO THE WOODS

I t's a freezing cold February evening of 2016. If you peek through the open garage door, you can see a giant wooden box lying on its back in the middle of an improvised carpentry workshop and a couple dressed in winter jackets. They are surrounded by random pieces of recycled pallet wood and engaged in a heated debate as to which piece should go where. The wooden box looks like a monstrous coffin made for a two-hundred-kilogram giant. This cold and uncanny tableau is not an opening scene to a Scandinavian crime drama, however. In fact, we are in sunny Andalusia, and the massive 'coffin' is a wardrobe that we are finishing in great haste for our next paying guests who are arriving in three days.

We had opened our small rural guesthouse two months earlier, on the New Year's Eve of 2016, and had since been struggling with the harsh winter weather and an equally severe lack of funds. As I was standing next to the pile of recycled pallet wood with a nail gun in hand, I realised it was Friday night. In my previous life, I would be making my selection from the cocktail menu at a five-star hotel bar in Al Ain. I would be sitting by a glistening swimming pool and laughing my dizzy life away with equally tipsy friends. As it was, I was bemusedly searching through scraps of second-hand wood. Our first two years in Andalusia were a lesson in perseverance and self-reliance. I contemplated the journey we had made, from the glitz and glamour of the Gulf expat lifestyle to this unforgiving place one thousand metres above sea level and with no soul in sight – a place where there is little room to escape from nature and its fierce elements and where a steady supply of water and electricity cannot be taken for granted.

Robert and I came to our little cottage in the middle of nowhere in August 2014 with a dream of living a more profound life. Tired of the expat lifestyle in which we were stuck for several years in the UAE, we hoped to support ourselves financially by writing textbooks, translating, and opening a small rural guesthouse. We were very familiar with doing the first two jobs — I had been writing textbooks for several years, and Robert began translating and editing academic texts when he was still at university. But it was the third job, the renovation of a country house and opening a guesthouse, that turned out to be the most exhausting task of our lives. By February 2016, we had our first paying guests, our first online reviews, but no more money to properly finish the guest apartments. We managed to escape the gilded cage that many teachers in the Gulf don't dare to leave, but little did we know how hard it would be to live on the other side of the cage.

This is a *story* or a *memoir*, as an editor might want to call it, of our first year in the Andalusian countryside. There might be moments in this account when you will gasp at our naivety and lack of experience. You may wonder why we did not make more considered plans, learn more Spanish, or just were more careful with our finances. Still, the reality is that to change your lifestyle as dramatically as we did, you probably won't have time to think it over. Instead of planning, you plunge into it and hope for the best. Why did we decide on such a dramatic lifestyle change? In philosophical terms, I would say to escape Dubai's hyperreality; in layman's terms, we wished to escape the ultimate dissatisfaction we felt from excessive consumerism and endless consumption. Let me explain.

By August 2012, Robert and I had lived and taught in the UAE for seven years. By then, we were past the honeymoon stage of living in one of the wealthiest countries in the world. The novelty of spending weekends in five-star hotels and travelling on holidays to exotic places had worn out. Between 2005 and 2012, we had moved from a cramped and very basic two-bedroom student apartment in a working-class Swedish suburb to a villa with two living rooms and a maid's room. The idea of having two living rooms and a maid's room was one that I had never entertained before we arrived in Al Ain, but once I got used to it, I couldn't live without them. The second living room was, in fact, intended to be the *majlis*, a private area in the house with a separate entrance where male members of the family could entertain their male friends. Robert and I turned the *majlis* into our everyday living room, where we would watch TV, play games, eat, smoke, and drink wine — an echo of our student life. The other living room was never used by us alone and thus remained presentable for pop-ins and ready for impromptu parties. As we did not have a live-in maid, the maid's room served as a storage room; I use the term *storage* loosely here since this room functioned more as a purgatory for items that we did not use anymore but were not sure whether we should throw them away. In 2014, when we finally moved out, the scale of our pointless hoarding was embarrassing.

Most of the items that we *stored* there went straight to the bin, like the tatty plastic Christmas tree that I bought for Christmas 2008 when Robert broke his leg and my family came to visit. Being an atheist and generally averse to religious celebrations, I could not imagine myself ever using the tree again. So, it went to the bin together with: a vacuum cleaner that stopped working a few years back, some broken reading lamps, electric cables of unknown use or origin, a punctured air mattress, some esoteric exercise equipment, an air pump and other bits and bobs of indefinable use. We loaded it all onto Robert's trailer parked outside the house and drove it to the bins a few metres outside the compound's wall. Being good and conscientious (non-)citizens, we put the first load inside the rubbish bins, but I realised our mistake when we returned with the second load. Most of the things that we had thrown into the bins a few hours earlier were gone. They were taken, not by the rubbish collectors, but by the Bangladeshi and Pakistani workers who lived in cheap accommodation on the other side of the compound wall. Even the Christmas tree had disappeared

— which I thought was odd in a country where so few people celebrate Christmas. Realising that there was some interest in the tat we had hoarded, we left the second load outside the bins for easy collection. It, too, was gone within hours.

The items that we decided to keep were reminders of our past experiences and hobbies in the UAE. An almost endless range of camping and snorkelling equipment from the time when we enjoyed spending weekends in the desert in Liwa or on the beach in Fujairah; various tennis rackets from the days of our Hilton Hotel club membership; an electricity generator for our camping trips; an American-style fridge-freezer and even fishing nets from our numerous holidays on Masirah island in Oman, where we would spend a week or two on the beach in isolation from the rest of the world

These were all splendid times which we would have never experienced if we had remained in Sweden working part-time at the university. But the truth is that there is no long-term future for expats in the Gulf. You can't buy a little house in the oasis and settle there and become a member of the community. No matter how long you work for your sponsor, you will never get a pension or job security. Your friends come and go. Every September, as the new academic year began, a parade of newcomers would arrive in town. Every year, we would make new friends only to see them go away either because they'd been fired or they'd tire of the unacceptable work conditions that they were subject to.

After five years in the UAE, a sense of despondency had set in. I stopped paying my membership at the club, we stopped playing tennis, and even camping on the weekend had lost its appeal. Every day that passed seemed depressingly the same, with little hope for the future. Once so proud of my varied and colourful desert garden, I filled it with aloes that needed no care. The garden was let to look after itself. We lost interest in maintaining our rented house and only repaired things when they were deemed essential, but even then, with great delay and a marked lack of enthusiasm.

One day our oven gave up the ghost. Instead of having it repaired, I simply stopped baking. A year later, while calling the landlord's assistant to come to fix an air conditioning unit, I asked him to send someone to fix the oven too. It was an easy job, and the oven was working again in a matter of minutes. But in those days, 'getting things done' wasn't on the agenda. For years before we left the country, we had a dripping AC unit in our lounge. It would occasionally get better — usually after being cleaned — but instead of insisting on getting it fixed properly, I left a small plastic bucket underneath the unit to collect the dripping water and continued watching *American Idol* and drinking wine.

For years, we watched termites eat away the wooden door frames around the house. The termites' nests were easily visible, and the holes left by their appetite, in some cases, went as far as the base concrete of the walls from which the house was built. We had to evacuate everyone out of the house and into the garden during one Friday night party because the termites decided to migrate that very night, and they all evacuated their nests. A black cloud of insects covered all the surfaces in our living room and kitchen. In hindsight, our gloom was overwhelming. If we did not have our trusted Filipino maid, Marvie, come in once a week to clean the surfaces and do the ironing, our living conditions might have become catastrophic. Every Friday morning, Marvie and her friend would arrive with their umbrellas in hand (shading them from the relentless sun on their journey to our house) and would start cleaning and scrubbing. It would have been embarrassing to sit on the sofa, read a book and watch them clean, so we would drive to the club, position ourselves by the pool and read until it was time for lunch. My friend Theresa would often join us by the pool, and we would sit under the palm trees, drinking mojitos and gossiping until late afternoon. Then we would go to *Lulu Hypermarket* for the weekly grocery shop and back to a sparkling clean house. With Marvie and Jenny out of the way, we could go back to our shameless TV watching and general decadence.

We were not unique or alone in this hopeless lifestyle. The writing was on the wall, and it was then that I started to understand the expat urban legends of people who 'go over the edge'. George, a friend of mine, told me a story of one of his colleagues from an institute in Abu Dhabi who got fired after a cascade of empty cans of beer fell out of his car as he opened the door to go to work at 7.30 a.m. in the morning. Not a good impression to make in the car park in front of your colleagues. Another legend was of a female teacher at another institute who came to class one day and put a bottle of wine on her desk and proceeded to open it in front of her Muslim students. These are reports I heard of people who had lost the plot; the poor souls who could not bear another minute in that most gilded of cages. Two years after I had left Abu Dhabi, a close colleague of mine became the 'stuff of legends' when she was found half unconscious and slurring on her office floor. She had to be escorted home by her kind-hearted boss, who had to walk her, semi-catatonic, across the campus, hoping to avoid any higher-ranking managers on his way to the car. I often wonder that had I stayed, it might well have been me. And so, it was time to say *masalama*!

ONE

THE ITALIAN JOB

In August 2012, after several months of daydreaming and fantasising about different Spanish cottages, farmhouses, and ruins that we'd seen online, we decided to contact some real-estate agents online and travel from Abu Dhabi to Spain to view some properties. We had the idea of buying one. We'd never been to Spain before, and neither of us could say much in Spanish. Before we arrived in Andalusia to look for our dream house, we pronounced the city name *Jaén* as one would say *jam* or *Jane* in English, and we had heated disputes about the meaning and the pronunciation of *cortijo*, a word that featured on all the adverts that we selected.

People often ask us why we chose this part of Spain to live in, and there is no good answer to this question. Since we had never been to Spain, our only guide was Google Earth images. We had some vague ideas about the region from documentaries and movies that fed into stereotypes. We chose the area between Granada, Cordoba, and Malaga because of the charming photographs of the cottages posted on the real-estate websites. With olive groves stretching as far as the eye can see, grapevines shading the patio, pink oleanders in front of white cottages and never-ending blue skies, we fell in love with Andalusia. And we were not disappointed.

As we drove from Madrid to Jaén province for the first time, the stunning Andalusian nature, its vast landscapes, and quirky white villages took our breath away. For me, Andalusia's true beauty lies in its natural open ruggedness; in the secret narrow cobblestoned streets of tiny villages where neighbours keep their doors open most of the day to let in fresh air but also to keep tabs on village life. Its beauty is in the colourful make-shift curtains that locals hang over the front door to protect the entrance from the sun. It's in old wooden chairs strategically positioned on the pavement outside a row of houses. It's in recycled paint buckets that are used as flower pots to decorate a busy street. It's the old, unattractive men sitting by sun-scorched plastic tables, playing cards and smoking cigarettes. It is a beauty that is not immediately attractive or polished since it is not self-edited or idealised. It's honest. And that's why I felt that it was a perfect place to start a new life.

After our lengthy search for a Spanish country house, we made a shortlist of several properties and contacted the agents in Spain. We selected houses that had a little bit of land and some olive trees. Some of the adverts claimed that future owners could support themselves by harvesting their own olives, so Robert spent endless hours researching olive farming.

Instead of reading about how to purchase a property and what pitfalls to look out for (since we were both first-time property buyers), we dove right into a number of Arcadian fantasies. We watched hours of online videos on olive farming and sun-drying tomatoes. We spent all our free time discussing the details of the bucolic life that awaited us. Were we not so preoccupied with our impractical daydreaming, we might have considered it strange, if not ominous, that the one particular agent whose advertised houses we liked the most resided in Germany. He promised us by e-mail that this was a normal state of affairs and that his trusted associate would meet and show us the houses that we were interested in buying.

Once we arrived in Andalusia, we arranged to rendezvous with the trusted associate outside a small church on the outskirts of Illora. A 4x4 car arrived on time and we were greeted cheerfully by a group of people consisting of an older Spanish man — the associate — a slovenly seventeen-year-old English girl, and her chubby Spanish boyfriend — the son of the associate. We were soon informed by the English teen that the Spanish' estate agent' could not speak any English, and so he had sought the assistance of his son's girlfriend, Amy. When I asked Amy whether she often helped her boyfriend's father with his real-estate business, she seemed unsure whether the old man was an estate agent or just a friend of the German guy who ran the real-estate website.

Fortunately, I had printed out the information sheets for the different houses that we wanted to see and showed them to the 'agent'. We did not question neither the strange assembly of people who had arrived to help us find a house nor the fact that the agent himself did not live in Spain. In fact, we were quite anxious to see (what we hoped) would be our future dream home. We showed José, the 'estate agent's' proxy, the printouts and explained that we were looking for a country house situated away from its neighbours. We wanted some space for a woodworking workshop and a little bit of land to grow fruit and vegetables. José nodded and seemed to know where the properties that we wanted to see were located. So we all got into our cars and followed him into the *campo*, or the countryside.

The first house was not far from our meeting point. It was a tiny stone cottage on a steep hill. It was pretty, but it was so small that we would not have been able to fit just our clothes in one of the two teeny bedrooms. The thing about looking for a dream home is that you often start convincing yourself that this could be it. You imagine how you might fit your life and your possessions into the house you are viewing at the moment. It's a tiring exercise and one that has never ended in a happy purchase.

Robert and I examined this miniature house that had no place for a vegetable garden and boasted one of the smallest patios ever built on top of a cliff. No matter how hard we tried to rationalise our interest in the house, we realised that we could never compress our lives to a size that would fit inside it. And so, we proceeded, onwards and upwards. The next house was much closer to our dream. It truly was a charming Spanish cottage, with giant cacti and aloes growing by its walls, surrounded by olives on flat land. Inside there was an old Andalusian-style fireplace and weathered dark wooden beams. There were even handcrafted tiles on some of the floors. The only downside was that it was a complete ruin with no water supply and no electricity. This shortcoming did not stop us from dreaming and imagining how beautiful it could be and where we could have our bedroom and the kitchen, and how wonderful our life would be there.

Our entourage seemed to encourage this mad thinking. The house owner, who came to meet us, said that the electricity could be connected from his current house, which was just a mere two kilometres down the road.

Amy stopped snuggling up to her boyfriend for a minute and suggested that her dad renovate the whole thing for us.

'You'd be better off knocking it down and starting over,' she recommended. Even a seventeen-year-old could see that this house was a complete wreck. It was nothing like the photos that advertised it. The internet listing featured only a few interior details, which fooled us to believe that the cottage was ready to move in. The listing mentioned that some renovation may be necessary depending on the buyers' tastes. As we were in Spain in August 2012 during the terrible financial crisis, the owner was willing to sell us the house at a very low price. His very low price was, in fact, close to our whole budget. We realised that if we bought the house and then knocked its ruined walls down, we would be left with nothing but a pile of rocks surrounded by giant cacti and aloes.

Sensing an opportunity for some caravan-based negotiations, Robert suggested that we buy a caravan and live in it on this beautiful site surrounded by the olives. I reminded him that we would have no money left, even for the most derelict of caravans. As we whispered the pros and cons, keeping all our cards close to our chest, Amy kept on telling us what a wonderful job her father would do with this old ruin. We announced that we'd think about it — and no, we never thought of it again — and proceeded on to see the next dream house.

The next house was one that we really had fallen in love with when we viewed it online. The estate agent called it *The Italian Job* — a strange name, yes, but it did capture the imagination. I couldn't understand why it was *Italian*, since it was located in the heart of Spain. The name was explained in more ways than the estate agent thought possible, but as I looked at the photos online, I could not find a single fault in *The Italian Job*. It was such a beautiful property. A few weeks before we left for Spain, I had shown the house photos to my friends at lunch. The first photo featured a Mediterranean white gate. Through the gate, you could see a stunning house with wooden shutters and lots of large windows. The white walls shone like a white jewel surrounded by fruit trees and olives. The listing mentioned four bedrooms, two modern bathrooms, a large kitchen, and an open plan living room perfectly appointed in the pictures. I loved how rustic and enchanting it all looked in the photos. The house came with lots of land and hundreds of olive trees. The price was also reasonable. As I showed this property's photos to my friends, they too started to fantasise about the pastoral lifestyle that I would live there. One friend suggested that, with this lovely property, we could set up an agritourism guesthouse where people from around the world would pay us to stay at the guesthouse, pick the olives, and experience the Spanish countryside. What a dream!

Now it was time to see the dream house in reality. As Robert followed José's car on the way to see *The Italian Job*, we were both excited. By then, we'd already forgotten the other ruins that we had been shown and again set our expectations high regarding this amazing property.

We drove through wheat and barley fields for quite a long time, and then we started to climb a dirt track up a rather steep and commanding mountain. One-third of the way up the mountain, José parked his car and we stopped our rental sedan next to him. Amy explained that it would be better to continue in José's 4x4 because the road got even steeper from this point on. Amy and I squeezed into the backseat next to her chubby boyfriend and Robert took the front passenger seat. The road not only got steeper and steeper, but it also became narrower and narrower.

When I peeked through the window to my right, all I could see was a massive drop. It did not seem like a road designed for a dramatic car chase and so the name of the property remained a puzzle. As we drove up and up, the road got worse and worse and I stopped thinking of cars as a means of transport and started to think of helicopters. 'Would they be able to land a helicopter on top of this mountain in case of a medical emergency?' I'm rarely concerned about health and safety, but this place made me think about different emergency rescue vehicles. I have driven a 4x4 in the desert in the past, but that was for leisure. I struggled to see the appeal of driving up or down this road, especially if it was raining or if parts of the road were washed away. Since Robert was sitting in front and I was stuck in the back, we could not really discuss the state of the road in front of José. It seemed rude to make negative comments since the man was clearly concentrating quite hard on staying on the road and wringing every single horsepower from his little Mitsubishi's engine. I sat in silence, waiting for a little paradise to greet me at the end of this road of death.

The property took me by surprise. I kept straining my eyes, trying to find the charming gate with fruit trees I had seen in the photos. The house was built in a small clearing on the very top of the mountain that we'd just scaled in José's car. We parked the car at the back of the house on the dirt track. What should have served as a foreboding omen was the white plastic one thousand litre water tank abandoned in the 'parking' space. We should have appraised that water tank and ran back to the car screaming in horror, knowing what we know now. A plastic thousand-litre cube is a clear sign that a house has no water or a very limited water supply. It means that the owners have to transport water on the back of a trailer from a communal source in the nearest village or from a shared *fuente*, a natural spring in the mountains. But we did not know any of that then and did not read much into the presence of the white cube. We walked past it and around the house to the main door.

While José was fiddling with the keys and doors, Robert and I paused to admire the stunning views. We were truly on top of the world. The views were so spectacular that I decided not to mention the howling wind and lack of any flat land for a vegetable garden. The listing was correct in that there was a lot of land, but it was suitable only for Pyrenean mountain goats and not for growing tomatoes. The soil was rock hard and too dry to bear any vegetation. The hundreds of olive trees we were planning to cultivate would require a team of experienced Nepalese Sherpa to harvest them. But ever the optimists, we swiftly changed our life ambitions.

José and Amy joined us in our stroll around the steep olive groves and told us that, with so much land, we could get a hunting licence and hold hunting parties. Yes, this new image fitted well with what we were seeing in front of our eyes. Robert got sold on the idea of becoming a hunter and before I knew it, he was ironing out the details of future hunting expeditions and speculating the types of rifle and shotgun that he could get. Even though I did not like the new idea of hunting, I was still convinced that the Italian Job could be our new home. The house itself, we read in the online listing, was newly built and so, unlike the ruins that we saw earlier that day, would not require much work. With new visions starting to blossom in my mind, I turned my head away from the stunning views and went to inspect the house inside.

As Robert and I stepped over the threshold, we saw José running around the living room with a broom. At first, I thought he was doing some last-minute cleaning of the room, which appeared strange. From the speed with which Robert left the house, I realised that something was amiss. As I watched José dance with the broom around the dilapidated room, Amy explained that he was chasing away some rats.

I did not need to hear more to abandon the building at a rapid pace. We stood outside and waited for the green light from José while Amy took position at the main entrance, ready to convey the message. We looked silently into the distance. The hoard of rats may have rendered us speechless, but the general feel of the living room and the interior was more than disappointing. It reminded me of a room from a crime reconstruction show, where the detective talks the viewer through the scene of the crime and deconstructs the gruesome fight and subsequent murder step by step for the viewer's voyeuristic pleasure. 'The victim's decaying body was found in the wardrobe by the landlady, who was concerned by the rancid smell and the flies circling the main door,' the narrator would explain. 'The blood splatter pattern shows that, before he died, the victim had been thrown over the coffee table and had his head smashed several times against the tiled floor. The victim was then dragged to the hall and hidden inside the wardrobe. The over-turned bookshelves, broken mirrors, and smashed chairs suggest that the perpetrator tried to stage a robbery,' the narrator would continue.

I really did not need to spare this room another look, but seeing José's friendly face peeking out of the door, we were too polite to say anything. So we entered Dr Lecter's kitchen — cautious not to touch anything in case Interpol found our fingerprints there in the future. Inside the open-plan kitchen and living room space, there was nowhere to look to without offending the eye. Nothing nice could be said about it. I kept staring at the real estate advert that I had printed out, but no matter how hard I tried, I could not match the photos with what was in front of me. I scanned the detailed description of the property and saw that it mentioned a 'modern bathroom'. To resuscitate our hopes and dreams, I asked José about the said 'modern bathroom'. José pointed to a filthy door leading off from the kitchen and opened it for us to have a look inside. To say that the bathroom was unusable would have been an understatement. I have seen better bathrooms at petrol stations in the middle of the mountains in Oman, which were tar-black inside the toilet bowl and had layers of crispy yellow piss all over the floor and walls. The bathroom in *The Italian Job* was on a whole new level entirely. I closed my eyes, fearing that I might vomit, and retreated to the crime scene area.

'There are three more bedrooms upstairs, but they are not completely finished,' prompted the quick-witted Amy. The girl was clearly becoming adept at the subtle craft of selling houses. We did not inspect the downstairs bedroom since I really did not care anymore, assuming that more horrific crimes may have been committed there. José, for some reason, did not insist that we view the downstairs bedroom at all. According to Amy's interpretation, the upstairs was really what we were looking for.

'It has not been finished, and so it has a lot of potential,' she chirped. And, as we were reminded again, Amy's dad could renovate it for us because he's done a lot of attics. While we waited downstairs for José to search for a ladder, there being no staircase to the second floor, Amy brought us up-to-date on the history of this house.

It transpired that the piece of land was purchased a few years back by two lovebirds; a Spanish woman and her Italian boyfriend. In a romantic haze, they settled on the top of the mountain and built this house. But then they split up from each other and were now trying to get their money back. However, because they had bought the land at the peak of the Spanish real-estate bubble, they were unlikely to break even.

As I listened to this story, I could not help but wonder whether the house itself and its treacherous location did not contribute to the failure of their relationship. From what I had seen so far, the house and its land would have required at least several hardy Andalusian farmers to look after it. It needed the sort of farmers whose parents had spent decades in caves hiding from Franco's persecution. They would hibernate in the winter and work like donkeys throughout the warmer months, bringing water from secret *fuentes* and growing *habas*, or broad beans, in tiny garden patches high in the mountains. In the lean years, they would devour acorns and prepare almond soup to survive.

This was not a life fit for two Mediterranean lovebirds. I imagined them meeting on the beach on Costa del Sol, getting drunk on sun, sea, and hormones, and two weeks later deciding to stay together forever. I was confident that buying this piece of unforgiving land was a rushed decision made by them on the spur of a romantic moment. While things may have looked idyllic when subject to frivolous discussion at a beach bar, I wondered how they survived their first year here. I imagine that, for the first few weeks, the couple stayed somewhere in the village and visited the site every day to walk around and make plans for the future. It must have been summer when they bought the land and started to build because I cannot fathom anyone wanting to live there in winter.

This, of course, is my hindsight; I would have been just as naive. If you visit Andalusia between May and October, then the stark blue skies and the endless sunshine seem to suggest that this is the weather all year-round. However, the winters in the Andalusian mountains are some of the most unforgiving and unbearable that I have ever experienced. I've witnessed horizontal rain that hits the front door so hard that the living room floor is covered in a creeping puddle of muddy water. I've watched rain soak the house's external walls so much that the walls start to seep water down to the skirting boards causing patches of black mould to artfully decorate each damp room. I've observed torrential rains that wash away whole cliffs and hillsides, causing landslides; hurricanes that break roof tiles away and lift whole sheets of steel from barns; hailstorms the size of golf balls that destroy your plants and fruit trees, and even snow that can crush young olive trees under a white blanket.

I believe that the weather here may seem harsher than anywhere else because there is no shelter from the elements. In a city and at lower elevations, you are always protected by other buildings that help break the wind and rain. But in an Andalusian cottage on top of a hill, there is nothing to shield you from the wind or torrential rain. You are forced to face the full brunt of Mother Nature and all her fury. With this in mind, I imagine the two sweethearts in the middle of an Andalusian winter carrying bricks against the wind and rain, and seeking refuge from the weather in their barely finished first floor. Were they even able to get to their house through the muddy dirt track? How disappointing it must have been to see their dream slip away as every night became colder than the night before. Listening to the wind howling outside, could they even look each other in the eye?

I don't know what caused these two to give up. Was it a particularly cold winter, or was it the summer drought? But I know for sure that the *Italian Job* was not built with love. I often imagine the young Italian smashing a chair against the wall and leaving the house for good, not even looking back or locking it up. This is all wide speculation prompted by my own experiences. The omens were present at the site of the *Italian Job* — if only I could have deciphered them at the time.

By now, José had brought a ladder and we carefully clambered up to the second floor. Whilst the first floor was the setting of a crime scene, the second floor was a scene of unfulfilled ambition. The un-rendered, bare brick walls revealed poor construction techniques and amateurish electrical wiring. Even to the untrained eye, the whole setup looked particularly dangerous. The newly-built walls had giant cracks in them, and the brickwork was based more on Kandinsky's freestyle approach than on Mondrian's strict geometry. On closer inspection, Robert pointed out that the bricks were only five centimetres thick and resembled those you might use to build a flimsy chicken coop. It clearly was an Italian job, but more so with reference to the modern Italian economy and the country's politics, and decidedly less so regarding its great ancient architecture.

Since there was not much further to say at this point, we left the house. I don't like immediate confrontation with people and prefer to digest any injustice done to me in silence and then vent about it to my friends at parties. Both Robert and I were astounded by the derelict properties we had been shown and the consequent waste of time that this whole day had been. There was nothing to argue about, especially not in front of an assembly of complete strangers. Once we were taken back to our rental car, we said goodbye and that we'd be in touch, even though we knew that we wouldn't be. As we were to learn in the weeks to come, José and his team were not exceptional or unique in their lack of professionalism.

During that summer, we inspected our fair share of ruins that had no water supply and no electricity. It seemed that whenever we informed an estate agent that we were looking for a country house surrounded by nature and with a little bit of land, they immediately translated this specification into 'an abandoned ruin with a lot of land'. The one thing about ruins is that they hardly ever put you right off. In fact, they draw you in and allow your imagination to run wild. A pile of misshapen stones densely covered in grass and weed transforms itself into a lovely Romanesque patio with well-established palm trees and grapevines providing plenty of shade. A jagged hole in a wall becomes a window from which you can look out every morning to gaze at blue skies and olive hills. You start to believe that decrepit wooden doors can be easily repaired and brought back to their glory; that rotting beams scattered on the floor can be restored and put back up to hold the rustic cottage roof. A ruin located in the middle of the Spanish olive groves is a siren call for romantics and optimists.

It's impossible to overlook the allure and beauty of an abandoned *cortijo* since it is a folly both in the figurative and literal senses. There is something in a Western mindset that is immediately attracted to a ruin. We travel to the European capitals to admire ruined buildings. We hike up mountains to see ruined monasteries, and when we have a little bit of money, we travel to Spain and fall in love with an old ruin that turns out to be a folly and a financial downfall.

TWO
THE SEARCH CONTINUES

After a few weeks of searching for our dream home, I got tired and weary and started convincing myself that I could live in whatever dump the real estate agent was showing us at the moment. Every evening during the house hunt, Robert and I sat down, drank wine, and crossed off more items from our dream specifications.

'Well, maybe we don't need to grow vegetables,' I would suggest.

'These dogs can't be that noisy at night. I'm sure,' Robert would delude himself.

'I don't think that river ever overflows,' I would state an obvious lie.

'Do we really need a fireplace? It's hot in Spain.'

'Maybe we won't hear the highway on the other side of the house.'

'Who needs two bedrooms? It's just the two of us,' we went on cutting things out and making compromises, until one day, we found ourselves standing in a one-bedroom apartment located between the parking lot of a Carrefour supermarket and the Granada-Cordoba motorway. We were confronted with a collection of empty bottles of cheap whiskey and at least ten cats rubbing themselves against the drunk owner's blotchy varicose legs and the real estate agent's freshly pressed power suit.

Whilst ruins tend to trigger your imagination and make you believe the impossible, a depressing apartment inhabited by a widowed alcoholic makes you worry that you are catching a glimpse of your own future; a parallel universe in which you made only bad choices. During our house hunt, we saw a good number of places inhabited by lonely old men. As we entered one cottage, the owner and his brother were positioned at a filthy kitchen table drinking homemade red wine. Their lips purple from the day's intake. The facial marking reminded me of my high-school French teacher who smoked so much that part of his moustache was permanently discoloured. Unlike the rest of this hair and moustache, which were jet-black, the spot where he held his cigarette was the colour of wet hay and mud. Many other teachers at my school had the inevitable orangey-brown spots on their index and middle fingers and tawny front teeth. They used these body markings to warn us against smoking, and it did curb our appetite for nicotine a little bit, but not for long.

Observing the two drunken brothers, it became clear to me that if you drink a lot of cheap red wine, your lips can become permanently discoloured, similar to a gentle uneven application of lipstick. These two macho men seemed somewhat incongruous wearing surreptitious makeup.

Most of the kitchen space was taken up by a large dining room table and a TV set. It's a setup that I have seen in many country homes inhabited by older people in Andalusia. Usually, there is an imposing dining table in the middle of a small kitchen. By the table, you will find sofas and armchairs facing a TV set that is often hidden inside a locked cabinet. The lifestyle suggested by this furniture arrangement is very obvious and one that, I have to admit, is particularly appealing to me. As I watched the brothers comfortably lounging on their sofa in the kitchen, watching TV, and guzzling glasses of red wine, I could easily see myself enjoying this very same lifestyle. This, of course, raised internal concerns about my future.

'Is this going to be me in 20 years?' I wondered. 'Is this how I will spend my last decades on earth?'

What was appealing about the whole setup was that you could not call the two men' couch potatoes' because they were sitting at the dinner table. The simple act of placing the couch in front of a proper table made the whole tableau more acceptable. I could not compare this pair of free-livers to slobs who spend all day watching telly on the sofa with an ashtray on the sofa's arm and an assortment of empty beer tins on the floor. These guys had their paraphernalia neatly arranged on a rustic wooden table; the wine came from a massive jug and a giant leg of *jamon* that rested on the counter ensured that they were fed protein and fat at regular intervals. All this made me like and even admire the inebriated house owner. Even though we could not envisage ourselves living in his house, we obediently followed him around the different rooms and outbuildings and acted as prospective buyers.

In retrospect, the tour of his *cortijo* was precious because it was the first time during our search that we actually got to see a real, functioning Andalusian cottage and come to appreciate the lifestyle of a seasonal olive picker. Our latest agent, a tiny Basque girl called Amaya, explained that there was no work for the old men in the summer because the olive season starts in late October.

I struggle to classify him as a farmer. He did have some chickens living in the same enclosure as his guard dog, and he had prepared a small vegetable patch at the back of the house, which was protected by a minuscule pug that barked at us throughout our visit. But these arrangements were just for his own use and pleasure.

The house etched itself in my memory because of the overwhelming sense of sadness that it left me with. In stark contrast to the kitchen that was inhabited almost permanently by the two brothers and their jugs of red wine, the living room was in pristine condition. There was a traditional Andalusian cabinet displaying decorative plates and framed photos of the family. Some of the photos were black and white and showed doe-eyed brides and bewildered grooms. Others were from more recent decades and showed big-headed babies and stiffly posed relatives in their Sunday best. Under each photo, there was an embroidered serviette that indicated that someone had once loved and cared for this place.

It was clearly the formal dining room. The big table was covered with white linen with crochet borders. Fading red plastic flowers constituted the centrepiece. Gaudy religious ornaments on the shelves and an assortment of Virgin Marys in pink and blue tones decorated the walls. They brought about a sense of sacred sadness to any visitor. This formal dining room was a place of solemn remembrance of times past and not a place for joyous family festivities. A wooden cross hung over the doorway with an accurately impaled Jesus who was clearly uncomfortable holding two miniature bouquets of plastic flowers in his arms. Had better days suffused this room with joy and happiness? I imagined the first communion of a loved child with family members gathering from far and wide with expensive gifts paid for by their hard-earned money: a gold necklace, a pair of silver earrings, a leather-bound prayer book? A little girl in a puffed meringue dress proudly sitting at the head of the table with her gifts generously displayed in front of her. Her uncles and aunts drinking coffee and eating cream cakes, and surreptitiously comparing the gifts each had brought for the occasion. Or perhaps an Easter celebration — *Semana Santa* with the pair of living room doors flung open to the garden to let in the spring air, providing the visitors with a glimpse of bearded irises in full bloom next to a rusty chicken-feed bucket. The competing odours of fried *roscos*, sugar-coated festive doughnuts, and *croquetas de bacalao*, cod croquettes, would drift tantalisingly from the kitchen, causing the visiting family members to cast furtive eyes to the stove in anticipation of long-awaited sustenance.

Another time, we may find a small group of burly men sitting and drinking their *cervezas* and snacking on *salchicha*, or dried sausage, and bread, while the women fuss around and don't dare to sit down until all the food is ready. I hope that these were the happy days for this house, but I did not want this living room. It was brimming with memories and ghosts that were not mine.

As one of the old men showed us upstairs, the empty despair of his life became even more evident. Upstairs there were three little bedrooms with no signs of life. It looked as if the owners of these rooms just left them in a hurry; their books and some personal belongings were still neatly arranged on the shelves but clearly untouched for decades. Adjacent to these rooms was a cold store where traditionally one would cure giant legs of *jamon*, store meats, and other preserves made in the summer. The ham and other cold meats would be hung on hooks from the ceiling and drip fat slowly for several months, permeating the polished concrete floor with indelible splatters of grease. The room, which is a feature of any genuine *cortijo*, was so cleverly built and positioned that it stayed cool even throughout the hottest summers. Amaya suggested that it would make a great master bedroom. She said that we could connect it with one of the adjacent bedrooms and make it into an *en suite*. I turned around not to look at her and rolled my eyes.

'Honestly!' I thought. I could see myself lying in bed in my cold store bedroom and staring for hours at the empty ceiling, expecting to see the spectre of *jamons* past, hanging from the rusty hooks. I might as well buy an abandoned abattoir and try to make it into a cosy home. We followed the owner downstairs to have a look at the patio and the outbuildings. Since I had not seen a recently occupied bedroom, I assumed that there was another room adjoining the kitchen where the owner usually slept.

'Or did he just slumber on the sofa in the kitchen?' I wondered, but I did not ask. The outdoor patio revealed the incredible vitality of Andalusian nature. Despite the despair and anguish that shrouded this semi-abandoned abode, the outdoors revealed life and cheerfulness. The doorframe was guarded by pots of lively red geraniums, and the patio was surrounded by a fantastic array of gladiolas, hollyhocks, and dahlias. Stunning roses framed the picturesque view of the olive hills and a brilliant pink bougainvillaea climbed from the base of a white wall. Massive green and red grapes were hanging over our heads, creating a secret garden. This was a slice of paradise. I looked at a piece of paper that contained the details of the listing and noticed that it mentioned a swimming pool. I asked the estate agent about it and she directed my sight to a cylindrical concrete water tank flanking the house. It was placed there to collect the rainwater throughout the winter. I decided to give the 'swimming pool' a closer look even though I started to question her mental abilities. As I stood next to this two-metre-tall rainwater tank, I wondered how on earth would anyone ever get in and out of it. Another nagging issue was the notion of swimming in the same water that you would wash your dishes with. These two activities could not be reconciled.

'Well, let's see,' I thought as the owner brought out an old wobbly ladder so that we could inspect the content of the rainwater tank. I clambered up to take a peek and saw a thick layer of green sludge encrusted with moths, mosquito eggs, and dead wasps. It was a cesspit in the making. Seeing my befuddled expression, Amaya explained that it was an Andalusian custom to jump into such water reservoirs to cool off on hot August days. How she got from the monstrosity that confronted us to call it a swimming pool was beyond my imagination.

Seeing my disbelief, she started to suggest sites around the property where a proper swimming pool could be built. With the owner optimistically chipping in with ideas, we passed another half an hour making plans and modifications for a house we did not want to buy in the first place.

You might think that it was all a waste of time, but looking at homes that you don't want to buy and discussing how you would fix them is part and parcel of spending time with an estate agent and viewing properties. And the estate agent is usually quite aware of this. It gets you warmed up and ready for the real deal.

THREE

DO YOU LIKE TO SING?

In the summer of 2012, when we were searching for our dream home, we rented a small house in a hamlet outside Priego de Cordoba. The cottage was very basic, and the village reminded us of a ghost town or, more accurately, a zombie village. Whilst we never saw anyone during the day — the only signs of life were some pieces of laundry hanging outside and noisy chickens in the gardens — at night, swarms of people would emerge from behind the colourful curtains that protected the front door of their houses. They would socialise with each other on the streets until late into the night. This experience of village life did not entice us into buying a house in a village. But after almost three weeks of looking, we were quite low-spirited and did not really know how to find a suitable house in the countryside.

Out of desperation, we drove to Priego, which was the biggest town in the area, and decided to find a proper estate agent, one that worked out of an office. The main drawback of this expedition was that neither of us had a clue what 'estate agent' was in Spanish, and we had left our faithful dictionary at home. As Robert navigated his way through the one-way system of the medieval town of Priego, I hoped to see a familiar shop with house adverts displayed in the shop window. We drove three or four times around Priego, a town whose one-way traffic system confuses us to this day because it forms an impossible maze of one-way roads that have a tendency to narrow down from a normal size road to a bicycle path.

On our third drive through town, I spotted a photocopy of an estate agent's listing in the window of a shop. We drove around some more, looking for parking and trying to remember each new turn so that we could walk back to this ephemeral estate agent's office. Our determination to buy property in Spain had to be admired. We set out from the car to the estate agent's office armed with twelve words of Spanish between us. I knew *casa*, numbers from one to ten, and *comprar*. We still were not confident about the meaning of *cortijo*, so we felt it was for the best that we did not use this word. While *casa* and *comprar* were pertinent to the dialogue that was to come, the numbers that I managed to learn were useless unless our dream house turned out to cost between one and ten euros. I decided that we would delegate any discussion of house prices to write them down on a piece of paper. As we were on our way to the estate agent's shop, a more astute reader may ask a myriad of questions, like: *Why did you not learn more Spanish before coming to buy a house in Spain? Why Spain and not another Mediterranean country? Were you not giving up by now?* These are all great questions, and if I could answer them, then we would not be heading to an estate agent's shop in the middle of Andalucía planning to buy a cottage in a country where we had never lived in or even visited before. We might still be sitting in our living room in Al Ain planning and strategising our future; dreaming about a bucolic future in nature, but being too afraid to venture out because we don't have enough language skills or enough experience, or enough money. Even though I can't explain why we were so poorly prepared for this adventure, I know for sure that, as we walked the stone streets of Priego, we were determined to stay in Andalusia.

When we entered the office, it became clear that the woman, Mari Carmen, did not speak any English. However, it did not stop her from kissing each of us on both cheeks and welcoming us as if we were her dear friends. After this emotional introduction, we sat down and went silent. I was the designated speaker since I was much quicker at finding English words with a Romance etymology that could be used in conversation with Spanish people. Since I was not going to get far with *baguette* and *bizarre*, I decided to revive some of the Italian that I had learned in my youth but since forgotten. And so, it went:

'Casa?' I said with a questioning intonation.

'Si, si,' followed by lots of fast spoken Spanish that I did not understand, but we seemed to have established a common interest.

'Comprar casa?' I wanted to make sure that we were on the same page.

'Si, claro!' followed by some more Spanish, but this time she appeared to be asking us a question. Robert guessed what she wanted and gesticulated for a piece of paper and a pen. On this paper, he drew a stick drawing of a cottage.

'Casa, si?' he made sure she understood his drawing.

Then he drew a circle around it and proceeded to fill it with stick-figure trees.

'We need some LAND,' he emphasised the last word because foreigners find it easier to understand English when such emphasis is placed on certain words. 'To eat vegetables, fruit. EAT,' he supplemented his drawing with a gesture of a person eating an apple. I could see that Mari Carmen was getting confused, so I tried to translate the best I could.

'Casa, tierra. Mucho tierra,' this put a smile on Mari Carmen's face.

'Si, sin problema,' she said and then asked a question in Spanish, but this time we guessed she was asking about how much land we would like attached to this cottage. Since we needed more than ten square metres, I had to resort to writing it down. We never thought about the exact size of our prospective land and, what was worse, we did not have a clear idea of how much one thousand or ten thousand square metres would look like. So, we pulled a number out of thin air and Robert wrote *10,000 m²* between the cartoonish house and the trees.

'Olivos?' Mari Carmen came down to our level of linguistic ability and ditched the grammar. We had no idea whether we still wanted the *olivos*. It looked like hard work. As we struggled to find words in our very poor Spanglish, Mari Carmen decided to abandon the topic and started to question us about the *casa*. We wrote and drew all that we could think of. I became slightly overwhelmed with all the Spanish, and so Robert elaborated on his drawing by enunciating the keywords in English as if Mari Carmen was a lip reader. But I could see from the confused expression on her face that we were going nowhere. As we learned later in the afternoon, the only two words she knew in English were *Seven Up*.

Not wanting to lose a potential client, she started to make phone calls and appeared to be shouting at someone. Watching her making a series of frantic phone calls provided a great respite for Robert and me since, by then, we were exhausted from stretching our brains to find words in a language that we did not know. Finally, Mari Carmen smiled and got off the phone and wrote '20 min' next to our drawings. At this stage, Robert and I decided to forsake any attempts at communication and waited in silence, not knowing what we were waiting for.

As we sat there, an elderly lady strolled in. Both women started kissing and squealing, which is a typical form of greeting in Andalusia. We were then introduced, or so we guessed we were since our names were mentioned, and the old lady proceeded to shake our hands. The women kept on talking to us and repeating the word that sounded like *cantar* in Italian. In my smugness, I took it upon myself to translate to Robert the one word that I thought I understood and told him that the old lady was asking him whether he liked to sing.

'*Cantar*, no? Play guitar,' Robert decided to engage in that topic. 'How do you say *I play the guitar*?' he asked, looking at me. I don't know what gave him the impression that I would know this. Still, it has subsequently become a particularly endearing habit of his to ask me to translate complicated English phrases while in the middle of a conversation with Spanish speakers.

'I have no idea,' I responded in a tone that told him that he was on his own with this topic, and so he continued to entertain the ladies on his own.

'I have GUITARS. GUITAR,' he mimicked played the guitar as he enunciated the word. The old lady and the estate agent nodded their heads, and both gave us a smile reserved for mentally ill relatives who have convinced themselves that they are Napoleon.

'Yes, sure you are. Now go and take your pill, please,' the smile said. It took me another year before I figured out that people in Andalusia were not asking me whether I liked singing whenever they met me. I have to admit that I started to wonder why people who have just met me kept on bringing this topic up, but I assumed that they must really love music very much. I don't remember the exact moment when I found out what the word really meant, but it revived my memory of the discussion about music in the estate agent's office and made me feel quite stupid. What they were saying was *encantada* which means *Nice to meet you!* and not *Do you like to sing?*

After we waited for almost an hour, a young man appeared in the doorway of the agent's office. His name was Pedro, and he was Mari Carmen's friend's son. He was also an English teacher. We spent a whole day with them and saw a good number of beautiful ruins. But by then, even we were running short on nostalgia, and despite Mari Carmen's great efforts, we did not contact her again. We reported our house hunting adventures to the owner of the cottage that we were renting, and he set us up with some trusted realtors who did not deal with ruins. On a few occasions, our host even accompanied us and assisted in translating our questions. Andalusian generosity is something that truly has no bounds. Eventually, with José's help, we were making some progress and were able to view several houses that were not romantic follies.

A week later, we finally found a house in which we could both imagine ourselves living. It did not look like much on paper. It was well over our budget, so I don't know why we even bothered to see it. But that's the agent's job. They show you homes that don't fit your brief until you find something, and then you will bend over backwards to get it. The agent, Tony, told us that the owner might accept a reduced price, so we agreed to view the house. We were driven in her car for about twenty-five minutes outside Alcalá la Real on what, in comparison to all the other places that we had seen, was a very well maintained and reasonably broad asphalt road. The road was winding, but with views of the mountains on the left and olive trees as far as I could see, it was a picturesque drive, and we did not regret getting into the car. As we came to a sign for the village of Lojilla, I noticed an older man standing on the side of a small bridge. The man was wearing a worn-down straw hat and farmer's pants. Toni stopped the car next to him, and after a brief exchange, we followed his car, which was parked under a tree a few metres ahead.

'Is he the owner?' I asked.

'No, his name's Gabi. He's the owner's father,' she replied. 'Look at the beautiful asparagus.' I looked at a field on my left of what looked like dill or some sort of exotic herb.

'Did she say *asparagus*?' I asked Robert as Toni was busy changing into second gear to attack the very steep hill ahead of us.

'She must mean something else,' Robert was as sceptical as I was about the crop, which could be seen in many of the open fields in the area. It looked nothing like the asparagus plant that we were familiar with.

'No, no. It is *asparagus*,' Toni must have overheard our debate. 'You eat the root,' she explained. Nothing of what she told us at the time made sense until a couple of years later, in the month of April, we noticed green asparagus spears shooting up from the ground. She was right, after all. Distracted by all the chit-chat about asparagus, we arrived at the gate to the house. The house was a very cosy looking cottage in the middle of a south-facing hill. We drove up to the house, parked under an ancient Iberian oak and greeted Gabi, who then proceeded to show us around the house and the garden.

After the inspection, we sat on the patio of our future home. Shaded by the grapevines, I looked at the stunning views of the olive hills and the mountains stretching from left to right, listened to the water shooting out from the swimming pool jets, and gazed at the pink hollyhocks. I fell in love with our future home almost instantly. The house had everything that a dream home should have: an ancient oak tree in the driveway, an open fireplace in the living room, a vegetable garden, fig and apple trees, walnuts and almonds, a grapevine and a bay leaf tree shading the patio, an impressive gate, stunning views all around, neighbours seen in the distance but impossible to hear, and lots of potential.

As we sat down, Gabi told us that it was his childhood home. He loved telling stories about the house. He had a definite sense of pride in the property which his ancestors had built by hand. The *cortijo* was built from stone brought by donkey wagons from Granada because the local stone is not suitable for building. The walls are seventy centimetres thick, and only when we had to knock some of them down did we realise the massive enterprise that it must have been to build the house from stone. The reason why these farmhouses have such thick walls is to protect the inhabitants from the scorching heat of the Andalusian summer and to keep the heat generated by a fireplace inside the house in the cold winter.

Over the years, we learned a lot from Gabi, or Old Gabi as we call him now, to distinguish him from his son, Young Gabi. The estate agent translated for us that Old Gabi and his sister, Mercedes, were born in this house and grew up in this valley with his grandparents. In fact, Old Gabi's whole family lived in this valley. I liked the idea that we might become part of a small community. Old Gabi pointed to an aged wooden bench on which he was sitting and told us that in the past, it was used to slaughter pigs. I'm not sure which part of the process required a wooden bench; I can only imagine, as I have never attended the *matanza* or the pig slaughter that takes place every December.

I quickly warmed to the old man who was chatting away and telling us all about the oaks, the fruit trees, and the soil on which we stood. As we walked around the property, he often picked fruit from a tree and would taste it to see if it was ready to eat. I admired a family that knew how to kill a pig to make food that would last a year. I liked that they had kept the old killing bench, even though it was of little use to them anymore. His children and grandchildren all lived in the city and had no interest in making their own *salchichón* or *morcilla*, the delicious blood sausage.

The idea to use an old killing bench as a decorative piece of patio furniture is simple but one that reflects the Andalusian spirit. Nothing ever gets thrown away here. Things that lose their ability to fulfil their original purpose are simply assigned new roles: empty paint buckets become flower pots, a rusty bed frame becomes a supporting wall in a greenhouse, a broken fridge can be used as a storage cabinet in a garage. Everything goes through a multitude of lives and reincarnations. They are not always pretty solutions, but they don't cost anything. I like this principle because it goes against the mindless consumerism that informed my life in the UAE, where my closets were filled with unused but fully functional objects. In contrast to their counterparts in the Andalusian countryside, the objects that are stashed away in the drawers and cupboards of city dwellers have no chance of ever seeing the light of day ever again. On saying this, the Andalusian principle of never throwing anything away became a curse the following year when we finally moved into the house.

After the first visit, Robert was not convinced about the property. While I loved the house, he was not a fan. We both liked its position in the middle of nowhere, the access road, and the big vegetable garden. However, the main bone of contention was the low-hanging wooden beams on the first floor. The whole first floor, namely half of the house, was inaccessible to him due to his six-foot-four height. Despite this setback, I was brimming with ideas about how we could develop the house into holiday apartments or a B&B — I wasn't sure which one then.

In the morning after our first visit, I presented Robert with my vision and explained that we could renovate parts of the house to rent for tourists. This would give us a source of income in Spain in addition to the free-lance writing and editing that we both did. Hearing this, Robert agreed to see the house one more time. This time, I took on the role of a pushy estate agent. We went through different rooms and I outlined to him my idea of having self-catering family apartments with private bathrooms, kitchens, and separate patios.

'OK. But we need to raise the roof of the whole house.' Robert had agreed to make an offer.

We decided to make a conservative offer by offering what we initially planned to spend and hoped for the best. We figured that if our offer was rejected, we would simply come back the following year and keep on looking. We got an answer a day later, well after midnight; we were entertaining José and his family at our rented house when we received a text message from the agent. Young Gabi was willing to accept our offer. We felt like new parents. We had so many hopes and dreams for this property. Because the house sale was going to take several months to finalise, we flew back to Al Ain, excited about spending the next summer in our own Andalusian cottage.

FOUR

A LITTLE HOUSE ON THE HILL

We returned to our dream home the next year. We were going to spend the summer cleaning and finalising ideas for the future before finally moving in the following year. On the way from Granada airport, we stopped by the Englishman who was looking after the house while we were away, and he handed over the keys. It was a strange feeling to hold the keys to a house that you had only seen twice before and which constituted the biggest purchase of your life. With keys in hand, we went off to spend the summer in our new home.

As we arrived by the gate, I felt that the property looked somewhat different, but I could not put my finger on what the difference was. I got out and started to search through the dozens of keys that were handed to us. I eventually located the key that fit the gate's lock, but even unlocked, it would not budge when I tried to move the gate.

By then, Robert had switched off the car engine and got out of the car. We tried pushing the gate together, but it was stuck fast. We fidgeted with the lock for several minutes and argued vehemently about the right way to open a gate, but none of this seemed to help. We shook it, kicked it, and even shouted at it. By now, we were both dripping with sweat and could barely see what we were doing. Since our soon-to-be neighbours did not know us from Adam, I was worried that someone might call the Guardia Civil and have us arrested for an attempted breaking and entering. Fortunately, it was siesta time — the hottest time of the day in Andalusia — and so no one was out and about. We started to think that Andy, the Englishman who looked after the house, must have given us the wrong keys.

Robert decided to brave it and climb over the gate to the other side to inspect the lock mechanism and to see whether it was jammed. The gate is over two and a half metres tall and crowned with metal spikes. As you can imagine, climbing it did not put Robert in a cheerful mood. Especially that all that his exploratory mission managed to ascertain was that the lock was fine and worked perfectly well. What we figured out by the process of elimination was that the metal gate must have expanded in the direct sun and was now jammed inside its frame. Thus, Robert went over the gate again, and more kicking and thrusting pursued, but this time with confidence that it was the right procedure. Finally, the gate gave way and opened. We left it open for the whole summer because we were too anxious to close it again.

As we drove up to the house, I realised what was different about the property. The year before, when we viewed the house and the land, it had a lovely vegetable garden with watermelons, squashes, tomatoes, and peppers. Now, the land was covered by two-metre-tall grass and weeds that were half dry and yellowish but dense and thick nevertheless. Most of our beautiful land was now completely inaccessible because the vegetation was so dense and high. It was a rookie mistake made by people who had never owned land before and who had spent the previous eight years in the Arabian desert.

One positive thing was that, in his foresight, Andy had trimmed down the weeds in the driveway throughout the springtime, and we were thus able to drive right up to the house without any problems. We got out of the car and I started fumbling through the bunch of keys once again. The house and its surroundings seemed somewhat lifeless now that we were there alone. Inside, everything was in place, but it felt as if we were staying in someone else's house. The rooms were full of other people's stuff. There were kids' toys, a crib, blankets, pillows, and some old clothes left in an ancient wardrobe. It was all a bit creepy, if not uncanny.

We unpacked our clothes and put some groceries in the fridge in complete silence; both of us were re-evaluating our decision to buy this house, but neither was willing to say anything out loud. To cheer ourselves up, we decided to sit by the pool, which was clean and sparkly. Sitting on the edge of the turquoise water with glasses of wine in hand definitely lifted our spirits.

'So, we bought a pool with a house,' Robert summed up our predicament. Surveying the house, I thought that it had somehow shrunk in size over the year and had lost its charm and beauty. Not being one to ever give up, I set up a plan on how to save this bad situation.

'Tomorrow, we will get a skip and throw everything out. Then we will scrub the rooms from top to bottom,' I announced. Robert agreed with me, and since we had a good plan in hand, we topped up our glasses and decided not to think about it all too much and focused our attention away from the house and onto the rolling hills. The next day, I searched my English-Spanish dictionary for the word *skip*, but because it was a basic learner's dictionary, they did not have it.

'Try *dumpster*,' Robert suggested.

I tried all possible variations from *skip, dumpster, rubbish container* to *giant bin*, but I could not find anything of use. Obviously, the authors of the dictionary wrote it with tourists and travellers in mind and did not foresee a backpacker walking around the gardens of Alhambra and asking for a skip, or a dumpster. This was not going to make things easy.

After we had bought the house, I made a sincere effort to learn

Spanish, and during my daily commute to work, I listened to several Spanish audio courses. The problem with learning a language when you have no chance to experience it in real life is that it's difficult to make any real progress. You feel like you're memorising the pronunciation of alien words that have no meaning to you. They are just clusters of arbitrary sounds. With each new lesson, I paced myself through greetings, colours, food, drink, and numbers — words that I had come across on our first visit to Spain. However, I struggled to remember any new verbs or useful nouns.

Because the new words that I was trying to memorise whilst driving to work had very little meaning to me, I had to use a complex system of mnemonics, a system that the reader of this text may find difficult to comprehend. Thus, the Spanish word for *car* — *coche* — sounded to me like the Polish word for a *kitten* — *kocie* — uttered in the vocative case, as if you were calling a kitten. The word *gordo* — used when describing a fat person — reminded me of Greta *Garbo*, who was skinny, so a system of mnemonic antonyms was used in this example. Following the same logic, I knew that *delgado* meant *skinny* because it sounded like the surname of the chubby son, Manny, from the comedy show *Modern Family*. As you can see, great effort was put into memorising just a few words.

I had no idea how to use any of these words in a sentence. I simply repeated whatever the actors in the audiobooks were saying.

'This is a big house,' the teacher would first say in English and then translate to Spanish: 'Es una casa grande,' I repeated the Spanish in a robot voice.

'This house is yellow,' the teacher continued making sentences out of the few words that we were taught so far. 'Es una casa amarilla,' I repeated while cruising on the modern highway past the rolling sand dunes of the Abu Dhabi desert. I spent hours repeating these types of sentences but never had any time to check how these words were spelt. The Spanish, or Andalusian, pair of /b/ and /v/ allophones was something that I found the most confusing. I heard it for the first time when my audio teacher said: 'This is a green dress. Es un vestido verde.'

'*Bestido berde?*' I blinked in confusion as if I had heard this word for the first time.

You can imagine my surprise when I finally got to see some of these words in writing. Whilst Spanish is relatively straightforward to read, a lack of awareness of even the most basic pronunciation rules may confound a beginner. I remember seeing the word *coche* for the first time and being blown away by it.

'This is not how I would have spelt it,' I marvelled at the letters <*ch*> in the middle of the word. The more complex issues of the pronunciation of <*g*> and <*j*> were a complete mystery to me at that time.

Because my reading skills in Spanish were so poor, I couldn't trust my phrasebook. Robert's Spanish was even worse. He didn't listen to any of my audiobooks because they distracted him whilst driving the car, and he found the one coursebook that we bought the year before in Madrid to be too difficult. Since I myself only managed to persevere to *Unit 3 Estoy en España*, I did not blame him. It feels futile to solve endless conjugation exercises when there is no one to correct them for you or guide you as to pronunciation. Despite these limitations and not having a clue what *skip* was in Spanish, we left the house that morning with great optimism.

We first drove to the town of Alcalá la Real. Whilst the village of Montefrio is much closer to our house, we developed a certain affinity to Alcalá and found it much more suited to our needs and wants than other towns and villages around us. The main reason for this fondness was the fact that Alcalá has a big expat community. The unofficial centre of this community was a shop run by an Englishman, Fred, called *A Little Bit of Britain*, or as most people referred to it, *Little Britain*. Because of our limited knowledge of the area and ability to speak Spanish, we found that *Little Britain* had a soothing and calming effect on our nerves; mostly, I suspect, because there was no language barrier. With Robert being British and me an English teacher, we could communicate without having to search the dictionary for any new word.

Fred's shop sold second-hand goods and anything else that a Brit abroad might find indispensable, such as Heinz baked beans, Dettol soap, Marmite, HP sauce, English birthday cards, and frozen steak and kidney pies. As we entered the shop, we saw a small woman in her late fifties sitting on one of the second-hand sofas. She had short sun-bleached hair and a red face; a countenance coloured by the sun and good living. Wearing just a spaghetti top and loose-fitting shorts, she seemed quite at home on the worn-out sofa.

'Are you all right, love?' Robert greeted her in what sounded like a mix of Scouse and Brummie. Born in Liverpool, but without the Scouse accent, he likes to mimic it, usually when meeting fellow Brits abroad. The lady did not seem deterred by the accent and replied.

'I'm waiting for me rice,' she explained, revealing a missing front tooth. I'm always taken by surprise by English people's eagerness to engage with total strangers when outside of their little island. The last time I visited those pleasant pastures alone, the only person who would speak to me was the girl at the till in Tesco. If I did not have to do any shopping, get train tickets, or get on the bus, whole days could go by without anyone ever speaking to me. All I got on the street and in cafés were cold shoulders and blank stares. Yet, as soon as the English check-in at the airport and wander into a departure lounge, they become the most jovial, forthright, and exhilarating of people you have ever met. When in Spain, they take over bars, parks, and beaches and turn them into one cheerful and sociable space.

It was the same with *Little Britain*. There were always Brits in Fred's shop and they were always ready to chat, give advice, and share their experiences — usually about their construction and renovation projects, since this is the main pastime for the expats in Spain. So, it was not unusual that an English woman would be sitting in the shop and conversing with strangers. What I was puzzled by was that she was waiting for a bag of rice.

'*Rice*, you said?' I checked my understanding. English dialects can be very misleading sometimes.

'Yes, English rice. I've been here since 10.00. I dunno where he is, the van, you know, they don't have it in Spain. Not even on the coast. They bring it for me from home.'

'English rice?' I was confused. Whilst my knowledge of English geography is not the best, I was curious about these English rice paddies. 'Did they grow rice in the Lake District?' I wondered. 'It must be truly wonderful rice since it was already noon, and she has been waiting for it for two hours,' I thought to myself. But I did not have time to ask her more questions about this bag of rice because I wanted to catch Fred between his customers. As soon as he was free, I asked him how to get a skip.

'Hmmm? A *contenedor*?' Fred reiterated our query and paused to think. This was great progress for me because now I knew the Spanish word for a *skip*.

'It will cost to have it delivered to your place from Alcalá. You'd better get one from Montefrio,' he explained.

'But where do we get it from?'

'Go to a brickyard. They will have them there.' As Fred was explaining this in more detail, a new obstacle occurred to me: *How were we going to explain where we wanted it to be delivered?* In fact, it was a worry that had been at the back of my mind for a while by then. With the planned house renovation, I imagined trucks full of bricks and other building materials driving around the twisty country roads and searching for our cottage. Whilst I knew the Spanish words for *left, right*, and *go straight*, I did not know all the other words that would make these three into a coherent sentence to give instructions on the phone. I resigned myself to the idea that we would have to fetch anyone who ever wanted to visit us or deliver anything from the local olive mill by the crossroad, about four kilometres from the house.

As we were about to leave the shop to go to Montefrio, a van arrived and parked outside the shop. The driver opened the sliding side door; inside the van, I could see neatly arranged boxes of Tetley tea, Bisto gravy, Smash instant potatoes, and bags of Tilda basmati rice. 'The foundations of the great British cuisine,' I smiled as we walked out of the shop.

FIVE
CENTURIES OF CLUTTER

Following Fred's advice, we went to Montefrio. We visited a brickyard and saw some skips in the back, but the place was locked, and neither of us had enough confidence in Spanish to even suggest calling the number on the gate. Because it was getting close to the siesta, there were only a few cars on the roads, and we did not see anyone walking the streets. Suddenly, Robert saw a builder's pick-up parked on the street and decided to seize the opportunity. He parked behind them, and as Robert was leaving the car, he asked me, 'What must I say?'

'Necesito contenedor,' I stammered.

'Nesito contedor,' my linguist husband repeated and went off. Cutting out whole syllables and shortening long sentences into a few words is an English habit. Whilst Spanish requires careful articulation of all the syllables and consonant clusters, the English tongue skips over everything but the stressed syllables. Instead of *buenas* for *hello*, an Englishman shouts out *buens*; when he wants to buy a fridge instead of *frigorífico*, he asks for a *frigofico*, and when discussing his *construcción*, he shortens it to *construcion*. As a result, only the most devoted Spanish listener can understand a beginner Englishman. Knowing how bad Robert's pronunciation was, I was positively surprised when he came back to the car, clearly pleased with the exchange of information that must have taken place.

'He'll show us,' he pointed to the driver of the pick-up who was about to drive off. He followed the driver for a minute — Montefrio is a tiny village after all — and we saw the driver wave his arm in the direction of a hardware shop. Then he sped up and disappeared over the hill. We assumed that the elusive skip was to be found in the hardware shop, so we went there. Inside, Robert announced to the shopkeeper, 'Nestocontedor.'

Seeing the shopkeeper's baffled expression, I reiterated, 'Necesito contenedor.'

'That is what I just said,' Robert whispered indignantly. The shopkeeper seemed to understand my paraphrase and started to ask questions about the size and the purpose of the skip. Using gestures, body language, and the faithful pen and paper, we established the dimensions and the types of things that would be disposed of in the skip.

'Cosas de casa,' *things of the house* I summed up. Alfonso, the shopkeeper, made some notes and started to make phone calls. A few minutes later, a young man named Salvador arrived. Salvador spoke some English and explained that he could rent us a skip but that he would prefer to see the site first and the types of things that we planned to put in his skip. This could not have been a better idea because, as you may remember, I would not have been able to explain to Salvador where exactly we lived. Even the English version of the directions was still incomplete in my head. The first two steps from

Montefrio to our house were somewhat easy to follow; if you drove slowly and kept on a lookout for two green rubbish bins by a bridge over a dry river bed. There was, however, a crucial turn from the paved road to our house that I struggled to explain. It was marked by a ruin on top of a hill and a withered oak tree. Since both ruins and oak trees abound in our area, I was not convinced that anyone would ever be able to find us by following these instructions.

Ignoring this problem did not make it go away because we were faced with the same dilemma two years later when we opened our little guesthouse and had to send directions to our first guests. Fortunately, by then, we were country savvy and were able to establish a clear set of instructions for visitors and provide them with a hand-drawn map.

As we drove with Salvador to our house, I wondered about the names given to Spanish children in Andalusia. I don't know whether Salvador knew much about Dali or liked his art, but he seemed bemused to see my excitement about his name. The delight to meet someone called Salvador was only superseded when we met our neighbour, Mercedes, and then later her friend, Tiny Mercedes — we added *tiny* obviously to distinguish between the two Mercedeses. In fact, Mercedes derives from *María de las Mercedes*, Mary of Mercy, as we learned one afternoon while driving through the town of Alcalá la Real and wondering about all the banners and flowers celebrating 'Nuestra Señora de las Mercedes'.

Maria de las Mercedes is the patron saint of Alcalá and not the name of a very popular car dealership. The names given to children in Andalusia are wonderfully old-fashioned and almost extinct elsewhere. Many were used in other parts of Europe centuries ago but have since been replaced by more catchy versions. Andalusian names, on the other hand, carry a mix of Christian Apocrypha and mediaeval chivalry. They also provide a good exercise in Spanish pronunciation. You know that your Spanish is getting better if you can talk about *Jorge, Georgina,* or *Jaime* with confidence and your listeners know who you're talking about. Not coincidentally, all three names derive from the Greek word *georgos* which describes *an earth-worker*, a profession known in modern days as *a farmer*.

But the names not only test your tongue's adeptness to the

phonetic intricacies of the Spanish language, but also give you a good insight into the country's religious past. In Andalusia, you will find yourself surrounded by Gabriels, Miguels, and Rafaels — the somewhat vengeful but reassuringly holy threesome of God's archangels — we have all three for our neighbours. Alfonso, Alberto, and Isidro sound like mediaeval knights or heroes of a long-forgotten legend. None of these is a popular boy's name in other European languages. It's a shame because Alfonso means *noble and ready for battle*, Alberto is *noble and bright*, and Isidro is *the gift of the Egyptian goddess Isis*.

My favourite Andalusian name is *Loli*. I'd never heard it before, but since we moved to Andalusia, it seems that a third of the female population in Cordoba, Jaén, and Granada provinces is called *Loli*. First, I thought it was short for Lolita and felt positively surprised at the literary taste of the Andalusian farmers. But then I was told that it was not *Lolita*, but just *Loli*. I associated it with a pink lollipop for simple mnemonics. As I later discovered, Loli has little to do with being fun and sweet. Like *Lolita*, it is a diminutive form of the name *Dolores* — the queen of pain and sorrow — or Maria de las Dolores, as she's formally known. I could see why a parent would not want to call a kind and adorable four-year-old girl — *Pains*.

'Pains, stop bothering me! – I need to finish the laundry. Go out and play, Pains. Look, here're your cousins Nobel, Ready, and The Gift of Isis, and take your sister Mercy with you,' I imagined a busy mother talk to her girl. Or an Andalusian family at dinner:

'Pains, if you don't eat your blood sausage, you won't get any quince marmalade for dessert!'

I could see why *Loli* is perhaps a more popular name than *Dolores*.

By now, we had arrived at the house and Salvador — or our Saviour — had ascertained what we needed. The next morning, he appeared at our gates with a skip the size of a Spanish galleon. He skilfully offloaded it from the back of his truck and said to call him when the skip was full.

'It's too big. It will never be full,' Robert said jokingly as we were saying goodbye to Salvador. As soon as the truck was out of the gate, we started a two-week-long Herculean labour of clearing out the house, the garage, and the old barn. Getting rid of the unwanted objects from the house was pretty straightforward, but it took endless trips from the house to the skip in the scorching heat.

The garage was a mixed bag; we found a whole assortment of farming tools that we hesitated to throw away. There was a whole set of equipment that would be used for a *matanza*, or the pig slaughter, that I had ambivalent feelings about. There were baskets of various shapes and sizes, ancient wooden sticks for knocking olives off the trees, and nets for collecting olives from beneath the trees. We've kept many of these items as we both entertain a wistful fondness for old working tools; even though we never planned to use them ourselves.

All of the other items that filled the garage to the brim made me question the future of humanity: old bicycle tires, boxes of odd mismatched ceramic tiles of varying sizes and thicknesses, paint buckets with at least a cup of dried-out paint stuck to the bottom, broken chairs, broken window frames, broken glassware, some bricks, boxes of books, bags of rotten clothes and shoes, and hundreds of bits and pieces that someone found difficult to throw away. Since all these were booby-trapped with mice and spiders, I was left alone to get rid of these items while Robert threw away stuff from the main house.

It took me three full days to clear the garage, and during that time, I had a good long stare into the mind of a hoarder. I promised myself then and there that I was never going to keep useless lumber and that I would throw unused objects away with vigour and enthusiasm. Of course, other people's trash is far worse than your own, and so I never kept that promise.

Whilst clearing out the garage was gruelling, and at times, an adrenaline-inducing activity — with field mice jumping out at me from different dark corners and random small birds flying by my head from the nests in the garage ceiling — the cleaning out of the old barn was a true Herculean labour. Even the mice had abandoned it because it was too cold, stinky, and miserable for any respectable country mouse to set up home in.

The old barn, or, as we referred to it, *the animal house*, is a common feature of most old *cortijos*. Traditionally, there would be a door leading from the kitchen in the main house to a small stable where goats, sheep, donkeys, pigs, and chickens slept together at night to shelter from the cold and rain. I would not call this place *a stable* because *stable* has a certain dignified ring to it. This was, in its true meaning, *an animal house*.

The previous owner of the house, Young Gabi, did not keep animals there; it had been used for that purpose for several decades before him. As a result, the first fifty centimetres of the floor's surface consisted of layers of dried animal excrement that had been laid down over different epochs. The place stunk to high heaven, and, as we started to excavate the shit, thousands of disturbed flies and maggots joined us in our labour. We took wheelbarrow duty in turns so as to give each other time to breathe and regain consciousness while wheeling the debris away.

We continued in this way for several days; the reason was that we could only endure a couple of hours a day of this work. It was difficult to find the motivation to shove dried manure mixed with odd cola and beer bottles and other random bits and pieces in forty-degree heat. We often found ourselves sitting outside the animal house and discussing the job at hand for long hours. My admiration for Hercules and how he persevered at cleaning the Augean Stables was never greater.

On lazy days, we would find excuses to go to town and buy things like work gloves, spades of different sizes and shapes, rakes, cutters, shears, and anything really just to stay in the hardware shop until it was too late to start digging. Shopping for tools gave us a clear and tangible sense of achievement. Since it was the hottest month of the year, our workday was limited to the early morning hours. Usually, by one pm, we were spent and ready for a cold beer. This would lead to tapas and more cold beers, which would inevitably carry us into siesta and then an obligatory afternoon by the pool. We were, after all, two sedentary university teachers. Before we arrived in Andalusia, the most physical labour that we would do in a week would be a couple of laps at the club pool and a game of tennis. Because we lacked the necessary stamina, cleaning the animal house seemed interminable.

The first milestone was when we finally cleared the front room of the animal house and discovered that there was a second room behind it. As I walked through a tiny opening in the wall, I saw a dilapidated sofa and a brewery's-worth of beer crates. This was a puzzling sight on many accounts. The sofa was much bigger than the wall opening, so we could not fathom how someone got it inside. This became apparent when we tried to take the sofa out and dump it onto the skip. Unless the walls were built around the giant sofa, we were at a loss to explain how it got there. The second question was why someone would want to sit there and drink a seemingly endless supply of beer. How would they get there through the mountain of debris that used to be in the front room?

On further archaeological exploration, the animal house transformed itself from being the scene of a Greek myth to an underground horror movie. As I stood, gazing at the sofa and trying to make sense of its location, I noticed a wooden ladder leading up to a hidden half attic. I encouraged Robert to go first since I did not fancy encountering any more mice in my lifetime. He went up and called me to follow. In the tiny attic, there was a miniature studio apartment, like an uncanny dollhouse. It was evident that someone must have lived there at some stage. There was a foldable couch, a small cabinet with clothes, a straw hat on a tiny table, two miniature chairs, and a corner that served as a kitchen with a few plates and pieces of cutlery scattered around. It would have made perfect sense as a London apartment, but here, in the vast countryside, we could not understand why someone would live there. The small round window in the attic did not even have glass, and there was no running water or electricity.

Thinking that some poor soul had spent his days there was disheartening; finding a young girl's clothes in the cupboard was creepy and mysterious. 'Did a child live in this space? Was it a family?' My imagination was going wild and my secret interest in the supernatural was awoken. Mystified, I shared the findings with some expats who frequented *Little Britain*. They were of the opinion that the space must have been used by olive pickers.

'During the olive picking season, you'll find them sleeping everywhere,' said one informant.

'Some work just for shelter and food,' chimed in another.

'They use garages and sheds, even well houses, and put the labourers there during the olive season,' continued the first interlocutor. This was unsettling information. Since we had not lived in Spain during the olive season, which starts in late October and can last until the end of April, I could not validate any of these stories. In those days, I trusted my informants. The information that was given to me created a picture in my mind of desperate, hungry, and overworked labourers roaming the olive hills outside our house until they could find shelter from the rain and cold.

Suddenly it made sense why every little space outside the house had a lock, even our well house, and why, when we arrived, we were handed a veritable bunch of keys — most of which I have not managed to match with a working lock until now. I imagined two friends in straw hats and with dirty canvas sacks over their shoulders. They were hungry and cold, sharing a piece of dry bread and drinking nasty red wine from a metal beaker, shivering on the concrete floor of our well house and seeking respite until the next morning when their ordeal would start over again. Thinking of the two poor souls sleeping on the floor in the well house made me think better about the living conditions in our animal house. Perhaps, whoever lived there had their life sorted after all. I, for one, would rather sleep in a dirty attic than in a well house.

Since we moved to Spain, I have experienced the olive season every year and no one has ever knocked on our door asking for shelter. The stories that were shared by the local expats may have been true decades ago, but they did not seem plausible now. The mystery of the phantom attic dweller and his young daughter remains unsolved. I could have asked Old Gabi about it, but now that the animal house has been knocked down and rebuilt from scratch, it would require some complex Spanish grammar and vocabulary to ask about it. I could see myself pointing at the second floor of the new structure and asking him in Spanish, 'There is a man and a child. Why?'

He would look at me and nod, 'Good. Do you have new guests? Where are they from?'

'No, not guests. A man lives there. There is a hat on the table and a bed. And in the kitchen, there is a knife and fork. And a dress of a girl. Why?' I would try to explain our past findings, which would help me develop a reputation of being a loopy lady. And so, I let it all rest, choosing the ghost of a young girl to dwell rent-free in the guest bedroom over the possible spectre of a crazy foreign lady.

SIX

GRANDISH DESIGNS

As the house began to relieve itself of abandoned objects and decades-old rubbish, our imaginations started to soar. We could now see the potential hiding behind the old bed frames, worn-out tables, and cheap plywood cabinets. The house became a blank canvas and we had new ideas for it every day. Considering that neither of us is a qualified architect or a designer, the source of these, mostly fantastic ideas, was the British TV show, *Grand Designs*. To say that we've been avid viewers of the show would not give justice to the enthusiasm with which we have watched it for years.

The show is about the titular *grand designs* that are undertaken by regular people. I still remember the first episode of the show that we watched in the early 2000s. It was about a family in the UK who wanted to build an eco-friendly house based on Scandinavian eco-principles. We watched transfixed as the poor man, the husband of the family, wracked his brains and went through the most stressful time of his life: balancing finances, builders, materials, designs, deliveries, and trying to keep his family together all at the same time. It looked like a dream come true. I could not think of a better way to spend my time than walking around a construction site with a hard hat, a pair of wellingtons, and a clipboard clenched to my chest.

In the years to come, we were to watch every episode of *Grand Designs* several times — during some particularly testing times, we palliatively binge-watched whole box sets. For some strange reasons, I found doing this comforting and reassuring, even though many of the grand designs were never completed. Despite the hours of viewing, all I seemed to absorb from the show was the prospective builders' enthusiasm and naivety that allows them to disregard common sense, finances, and reality, in search of a dream. I feel that the other themes that were addressed in the program did not come through to me strongly enough until it was too late, and we were knee-deep in mud on our own construction site, carrying bricks in the cold rain and arguing over dwindling finances. I blame Kevin McCloud and his optimistic personality for making us believe that building your own house was fun.

In each episode, an innocent couple decides to build something amazing and unique; that's when Kevin, a seasoned architect, comes in and tries to wrap his brain around the design. Patiently and with the help of computer graphics, he explains the problems related to the build to amateurs, like us, on the other side of the screen. After all these hours spent watching *Grand Designs*, what seemed to escape Robert and me were some common motives or themes. The titular *grand designs* are hardly ever finished during the generous timeframe within which the show is filmed. The most common reason why projects are incomplete is because the owners underestimate their budget and don't have enough money to finish the project. That's when the computer-generated graphics come in really handy and help the viewers understand what the giant hole in the ground was supposed to look like if the design had been completed.

In the most common scenario, digging the said hole costs the couple their whole project budget, and from then on, they borrow from distant relatives, sell family heirlooms, move onto a converted barge and do everything, short of begging, to finish their dream. Most of the time, they have to learn the trades themselves and start building in their free time; and, if they are lucky, they manage to enlist the help of friends and family. In some cases, to save money and to make progress with the build, the families move onto the building site and live in caravans or in make-shift rooms inside the unfinished structure. This inevitably leads to nervous breakdowns and deep fissures in marital life. In one of the episodes, Kevin seemed surprised when he popped by on one of his periodical visits and saw that nothing had been done on-site in six months. Questioned about the slow progress, the wife reported not being able to get out of bed for months.

'I just can't face what my life has become,' she admitted, almost in tears. 'We used to have friends and parties, and now it's just this. It's endless,' pointing to the unrendered walls and electric cables hanging over her head.

'I can't do it anymore,' she pleaded as she wandered away to her make-shift bedroom, an inflatable mattress on the floor of an unfinished living room.

In another episode, we saw an elderly English couple who had decided to renovate a house in France. It was evident that they had clearly lost their mind completely because they didn't even blink when they told Kevin about the husband's six-metre fall from a crude, hand-made scaffolding platform inside the house. They reported on this potentially life-changing event over cream cakes and tea served in their caravan while shoving their over-fed cats away from the plates on the camping table. It was evident that hope and optimism had left their lives. In hindsight, I could see the cracks, but back then, all I could see was a happy couple building their dream home in France. I was so jealous of their life.

In many situations presented in *Grand Designs*, the owners of the property that is to be built are so deeply in debt to the banks that they pay thousands of pounds a month in loan fees before the house is even finished. One unfortunate man was paying six thousand a month in bank loan fees on top of the mortgage for a castle that was — clearly — never going to be completed. In all the mayhem that unfolds in each episode, Kevin McCloud acts as if it's all normal. He ends each episode by visiting the grand design, and you have to admire the skilful camera work and careful staging. Suddenly a rustic table with some strategically arranged sunflowers and a glass of wine convince the viewers that the living room is ready and in regular use, even though we only get to see a wall and a single window and never the full view.

A few decorative cushions scattered around the bedroom and a book on a side table are there to convince you that people actually sleep in a house that has no toilets or running water. The last shot is always of Kevin — usually on top of a rolling green hill at sunset with the blurred view of the house and some uplifting music to wrap it all into a perfect fantasy. He admits that he had no hopes for this project from the beginning but that now he's convinced that the couple will finish it very soon and live in their dream home forever after.

This reassuring message must have been compelling because it was all that I remembered from binge-watching over a hundred episodes. We were excited about having our own grand design to focus on and spent every day walking around the house and making plans. Robert insisted on a stained-glass window with the motive of San Francisco to decorate our staircase. This idea must have remained in his mind after a church conversion episode. Whilst I disapproved of the holy motive, I admitted that we should utilise the warm afternoon sun that lit the staircase window. Then we thought of knocking a hole behind the old fireplace to install a double glassed firebox that would simultaneously heat two rooms.

This idea blew our minds and opened a Pandora's box of extremely expensive and impractical ideas that we must have seen somewhere in the past — we just could not remember where. We spent hours discussing a spiral staircase, circular windows on the second floor, converting a bathroom into a sauna, a bar instead of a kitchen counter, secret doors hiding behind bookcases, wine cellars, and many more impractical ideas. In our mind's eye, we knocked down walls, built new ones, covered old doorways, installed new ones, and radically redesigned the house's general layout. It became evident that we needed an architect.

As always in time of need, we set off to *Little Britain* to ask for help in finding an architect. We entered the shop and noticed that the toothless lady was there again — this time she was chatting to Fred, who did not seem very busy. We all greeted one another as if we were long lost friends with kisses on both cheeks and animated *How are yous.*

'Hi,' I heard another voice from the street. We all looked in the direction of a man smoking a cigarette and leaning against the open door.

'Don't mind him,' Lindsey, the toothless lady, said. 'It's my husband, Pete. He's stinking, so he can't come inside.'

'Oh, that's all right,' Fred waved his hand. 'He can smoke inside. I don't mind.'

'No, he's stinking; he hasn't showered in days,' Lindsay clarified as if it was a perfectly normal occurrence. We all looked at Pete, and he gave us all a grin and a nod.

'It's perhaps for the best that he stays outside,' I thought to myself, not that excited about the possibility of catching a whiff of mature August B.O.

'Anyway,' I said. 'We're looking for an architect.' This was not a problem. Fred gave us phone numbers to three different architects and I spent an afternoon composing a text message to all three. I was confident that I would not be able to conduct a Spanish phone conversation, especially one of a technical nature. Two days later, one of them answered in what looked like Google-translated English, but the gist of his message was that he was interested and could come over to our house in a couple of weeks to view the project. Even though the financial crisis and high unemployment were still evident in Spain in

2013, it was August, so he felt compelled to go away on his annual summer holiday to Almeria.

Whilst we were waiting for this dedicated professional to come back and discuss our grand design, we noticed that our swimming pool water had turned green. The slow, inexorable process of a swimming pool taking on a verdant tinge is very difficult to spot when you watch it every day and spend endless hours by its side. It's like watching a close friend or relative try to lose weight. They tell you that they follow a diet and exercise regime, but it's impossible to see the difference because you see them every day. Only until they come to a party in their old jeans that are now two sizes too big and need a belt to keep them up, do you realize the transformation that occurred in front of your very eyes. When we first arrived that summer, the water in the pool was sparkling and crystal clear. You could easily distinguish the glimmering tiles at the bottom of the pool. Every afternoon we would sit by the pool to relax after hours of cleaning the house or hacking through the jungle of vicious weeds that covered our land. We never noticed the water changing its hue from a pleasing hue of Mediterranean turquoise to a rather sinister Prussian green.

If you are not familiar with oil painting, Prussian green is the darkest and the deepest green pigment on an artist's palette. The colour is, supposedly, akin to the foliage of the Black Forest. The morning when the pool had finally turned a robust and boisterous Prussian green, I could not believe my eyes. I put my hand in the water and my fingers immediately disappeared from sight. Visibility was down to about one centimetre, a crisis situation. The thought that we should be doing *some* pool maintenance did occur to us once or twice since our arrival, but because we were busy with other things, we put this task low on our list of priorities. Now, it was too late — the stew was burnt and the pot was black, well, at least very green.

Not having any idea what to do, we went to the pump house, a tiny and uncomfortable space below the pool. Robert switched on the pool pump to 'skim' the water and spotted an abandoned bucket containing some chemicals. I took the bucket out into the sunlight. Inside, there were hefty chlorine tablets for the pool. I took three or four of these and went back to the pool. Robert hauled the floating chlorine dispenser to shore with a long stick, and we filled it with the tablets. What I expected to happen was for the chlorine to start killing off the greenness like a powerful antibiotic in a Petri dish. I hoped that we would soon see a halo of clear water around the dispenser. Silent minutes went by as we looked at the chorine dispenser, but nothing happened.

'Let's give it a couple of hours,' I reassured Robert. 'In the afternoon, the water will be clear again.' We went back to work on the house. Each time I walked past the pool, I took a peek to see whether the water was undergoing a miraculous transformation. By noon, I felt that it was losing its aggressive Prussian hue and turning a decidedly soupy Sap green. However, this may have been my mind playing tricks on me or the change in the sun's inclination, causing different angles of refraction and reflection. When we finally finished our day's work and wanted to sit by the pool to cool off, the pool was still as inviting as an Irish bog.

Because we did not have the internet at home or on our phones, I could not Google this problem. Not knowing what else to do, we turned the pool pump on and went inside the house. The next morning the pool was a deep Cobalt green, a fetid primordial backwater. On closer inspection, I noticed several squadrons of black, cockroach-like creatures swirling around in it. They were having the time of their lives, it seemed. I tried to fish them out with a net whenever they came to the surface for air, but they would quickly dive back in strict formation into the emerald abyss. They did not seem to mind the darkness. In fact, they appeared to be thriving in the putrid water. As neither of us had any idea what to do, it was now time for us to trudge back to *Little Britain* and ask for advice. The pool had, so far, been the biggest positive highlight of our adventure. It was pleasing to look at and gave us encouragement that we have achieved something in our lives after all. It's a silly status symbol and a folly which announces to the world that you own enough land to dig a giant hole, fill it with water, and enjoy your life.

Being able to sit by your own private pool gives you a definite sense of accomplishment and satisfaction; I am surprised it doesn't feature quite high up on Maslow's hierarchy of needs. For a pool to fulfil its social function, the water has to be crystal clear. You can't sit at the edge of a green cesspit and think that your life is on the right track. As we entered Alcalá, my mind was filled with dark thoughts. This perspective didn't improve when we saw that *Little Britain* was closed. We sat in the car outside the shop and scratched our heads. Asking a salesperson at a hardware shop was out of the question because I could not even imagine the amount of Spanish grammar and vocabulary needed to explain the situation. Even if I managed to convey *piscina aqua verde*, I was certain that I would not have been able to understand any of the inevitable follow-up questions or instructions or any of the advice given. And I was not in a mood for charades.

'They must have the internet at the library,' my genius husband suggested. As it was our second summer in Alcalá la Real, we had noticed a beautiful renaissance building in the middle of the town square with a calligraphed sign indicating *biblioteca*. We parked the car by the park and rushed to the library full of high hopes for the future. Inside the library, we were welcomed by the cool air of an ancient stone building and a neat row of PCs. We asked the genial librarian for permission to use the internet. He was very obliging, and he seemed happy to see inquisitive faces in the public library in the middle of August. Once we logged on, we went straight to Google search. It turned out that *green pool water* was a very common search phrase. I was surprised that I'd never heard of this problem before. According to most 'pool bloggers', the first step is to understand why your pool has turned green. Unfortunately, the explanation involved some rudimentary chemistry.

Chemistry has always been my least favourite subject. I remember that once, at high school, the chemistry teacher asked me whether I wanted to retake a chemistry exam so as to avoid lowering my GPA. I looked at her in horror.

'NO, thank you!' I answered and rushed off. I was happy to take a 'D' in chemistry for eternity rather than spending another evening in front of the periodic table calculating moles.

My distaste for the subject has not changed since then. Whenever I hear anything remotely related to chemistry, like checking the pH level or adding *x grams of chlorine*, all I hear is white noise.

I skimmed through the bloggers' advice, hoping to find a piece of information that did not contain any chemistry or require doing litmus tests. I searched through different blogs and pages, but they were all in unison that the first step was to test the water in your pool. Because I had no idea how we would go about testing the water, I did not bother to read past the first step. Some bloggers advised draining the pool and refilling it again, but after quickly thinking about it, we knew that we wouldn't have enough water in the well to fill it up again. Since Andalusia is one of the driest places in Europe, even newbies like us knew that we would not score many points with our farming neighbours by throwing away tons of water in the middle of the summer just to improve the colour of the water in the swimming pool. We needed a quiet solution that did not waste water.

Robert, on the other hand, was engrossed by this literature. He refused to scan or skim or skip the passages and read every single word as if it was the last chapter of a crime novel. Most of the advice was not applicable at this stage. For example, they recommended scrubbing the tiles with a brush to remove the algae. This was obviously pointless when the pool water was a deep, opaque green. The only useful piece of advice was that green algae is not harmful to our skin.

It was evident that we needed to buy some more chemicals and start to use them. Not knowing who else to ask where one could buy these items, I asked the friendly librarian. He recommended that we go to the supermarket Mercadona. I was doubtful that a supermarket would sell them, but we stopped there on the way home anyway. The swimming pool section was hidden in the back. It had obviously been there before, but because I was oblivious to our pool's needs, I had never noticed it.

As I perused the shelves, I was smitten. It seemed that whoever stocked them had thought of everything. I was quickly drawn to a bottle with a photo of disgusting green water and *aqua verde* clearly stated on the label. I grabbed two bottles and kept on reading the labels on the other containers. Since I had left my dictionary at home, I was unsure what some of the other products were for. Still, we filled the trolley with everything that looked like it would get the job done: chlorine *choque* powder, anti-algae liquid, flocculent liquid, chemicals against murky water, against black mould, chemicals to fight green algae, to make the water translucent, to remove a green water-line, and many more. Most of the products had their job description in the title and a photo illustrating the problem that they were intended to solve. We also spotted a tiny box called an *analizador* which we presumed to be a device to test the water. I put it on the top of the other products, and we went home armed with a trolley full of powerful chemicals and optimism.

On seeing our deep green pool, I exercised great restraint in not throwing all the chemicals into the pool all at once. We lined them up on the patio table, and I brought out the dictionary. Whilst before we were confronted by simple chemistry, we now faced some primary school maths.

'How many cubic metres are in the pool?' I asked my husband, who has a fondness for maths.

'I don't know.'

'It says here to put one hundred milligrams per cubic metre,' I read the label of one of the products. After a short debate, we agreed that we needed to multiply the pool's width, length, and height to get the volume. Because we did not have a measuring tape, we used the age-old method of counting our steps. Robert walked the length and I did the pool's width, but it quickly became apparent that our steps were not of equal measure. In fact, we both had a fundamentally different idea of how much one metre might be. As we stood by the pool arguing and stretching our arms to compare each other's understanding of a metre, we realized that measuring the pool's depth was going to be an even bigger problem. Since the pool had a shallow end and a deep end, we were not certain how we were to measure the total volume. The simple maths problem was too much to handle in the heat of the summer.

We decided to ignore the exact measurements indicated on the labels and treated them more as gentle suggestions rather than fast rules based on science. We threw a little bit of each of the chemicals into the pool, hoping that none of the products would counteract each other. We added a good amount of anything that looked powerful (a yellow triangle or a skull and bones on the back was a good indication of the stuff's potency) and a dash of the other liquids and powders. I still hoped that the next day I was going the witness a miracle. I hoped that I would rise and be greeted by the sparkling clean water.

This never happened. We spent the rest of the summer fighting the green algae. When we were not cleaning the animal house, fighting the weeds, and revising our grand design, we were cleaning the pool. By then, we were so desperate for any relief from the scorching heat that we did not mind swimming in the green water. It's an uncanny feeling not to be able to see your arms or legs as you swim and one that I don't wish to experience again.

It was only when I decided to employ the *analizador* that I found out what our problem was. According to the instructions inside the box, we were supposed to keep a fine balance between the water's pH level and the chlorine level to keep the water clean. When we eventually tested the water, which turned out to be a very simple test, we found out that our pool's pH level was extremely high. This meant that the water was very hard and did not allow the chlorine tablets and powders that we've been chucking in on a regular basis to work properly. After one more visit to the supermarket, we purchased the most important of the chemicals, which was the pH *reductor*.

Once we poured the whole bottle into our ailing pool, it made all the difference. The green broke within hours, and day by day, we watched our pool move through shades of light green to a milky blue. It did not regain its original sparkle that year, but I was happy to be able to see my arms underwater, although my feet remained somewhat blurred at the bottom of the pool in a dark milky cloud. As the water became cloudy instead of a healthy organic green, the strange swimming cockroaches decided to relocate. I never found out what they were or where they went.

Two days before our scheduled departure, an architect arrived and we spent a few happy hours in his company walking around the house and making plans for our future home. After that, we left for another year while the architect drew up the project and worked with the municipality and other offices to get all the necessary permits for our own grand design.

SEVEN

TWO CATS IN THE AIR

The following spring, our paperwork was ready, and we had all the necessary documents to start the renovation. As soon as we heard this, we both resigned from our jobs in the UAE and started packing. We could only leave at the end of July, but — in our excitement — we started packing and planning our move in March. That whole spring, we spent our weekends wrapping our possessions in sheets of newspaper and bubble wrap and labelling boxes.

When we first came to Al Ain, we had our books and a few belongings shipped to us in a small container. After nine years in the Emirates, we had three bedrooms, two living rooms, and a storage room packed with stuff. We would have needed two shipping containers to take everything with us.

To avoid the expense of two shipping containers, we spent the spring selling things online. We sold most of the furniture, a lot of kitchen appliances, unwanted gifts, Christmas decorations, gym equipment, roller blades, shoes, motorbikes, unused electronics, and a gazillion other bits and bobs. A lot of our life's clutter was also given away. Anything that we could not sell or gift, we left behind. Despite our best efforts to minimize the amount of stuff we had, a great deal was still left to ship out to sunny Spain.

When the moving company arrived on a hot July morning, there were many things that we hadn't decided whether to keep or leave behind. A giant container arrived from Dubai and was parked outside the compound because it would not fit through the main gate; it was going to be the exact container that would travel to Malaga. Throughout the day, six young Indian men worked tirelessly packing the remaining items and filling the container box by box until the behemoth was full at dusk.

Even though the container was full, there were still boxes and furniture items waiting in the middle of the almost empty living room. The biggest of these items was a king-size mattress that we definitely wanted to take with us. Robert took it upon himself to turn this problem into a challenge for the workers. He told the movers that if they managed to fit everything into the container, they would get extra cash then and there.

That seemed to be enough of an encouragement. With renewed energy, the guys worked like a teenager cleaning her room before her mum's inspection. They abandoned their earlier approach of stacking the boxes in a neat and orderly fashion. Instead, they forcefully shoved our items inside the container and squeezed them into every nook and cranny that they could spot. The aim was to fit everything inside and close the doors of the container. To this aim, they disassembled some boxes that they had prepared previously and stuffed individual household items into any small space that they could find. They squeezed and bent whatever they could until —with a lot of persuasive kicking and pushing — the container doors eventually closed and were locked. It was clear to me that if a customs agent in Malaga were to inspect the container, the metal doors would fling themselves open, and all our junk would fall out on top of the agent's head. But by then, it was late at night, and I did not feel that it was my problem to worry about. We waved the container goodbye, gave the movers generous tips, and went off to make some final arrangements.

With the container out of sight, I felt strangely relieved. It had been months of sleepless nights planning what to take and not to take. Thinking how our furniture and stuff would fit in the new home. For months before the final packing, I hardly slept at night. I would fall asleep quickly but then wake up at one or two a.m. and have my mind spiral out of control in endless worry, trying to anticipate any possible problem that we may come across during or after the move. My mind would focus on one tiny problem and would chew it over and over with no possible solution in sight until it was six a.m. and time to get up and go to work. The strange thing is that I did not worry about big problems, like how to renovate a cottage or set up a guesthouse in a foreign country. It is peculiar how one's mind works in times of worry.

Instead of stressing over the big picture, during many a sleepless night, I obsessed over small details. 'How are we going to get the internet,' was one of the worries. The house was not far from the village of Montefrio, around twelve minutes by car, but it was separated from the village by numerous hills. I was certain there was no internet cable near our house. Then I worried about the post. 'How were we going to get our post delivered?' My mind was stuck on this conundrum for many weeks. On the last summer visit, I did not see any post boxes near our neighbours' houses or anywhere near the main road. My concern about the lack of a post box made me worry about our address. I realized that, in fact, we had no address that I knew of. The deed had the plot number and the property number, but I could not recall seeing an address. There was no street name or road number because our new house was in the middle of the olive groves. Small problems like these were creeping up on me and keeping me awake all night.

It's common knowledge that moving home is a very stressful experience. According to several self-help bloggers, moving home is at the same stress level as losing one's job or having health problems. Moving home across different continents, I would assume to be even more stressful. As I was soon to find out, moving two cats across continents is an entirely new type of anxiety that psychologists have yet to identify and name.

Unlike all the other goods that we wished to ship and restore to their glory in our new home in Spain, our two house cats, Twiggy and Whitey, refused to remain static. This created a great deal of apprehension in the days leading up to our final relocation. I expected that the night of our departure, both Twiggy and Whitey would wander off and hide in the neighbour's garden or decide to hang out with the strays that lived by the municipal bins. In order to prevent the cats from disappearing during the night preceding our departure flight, I had them both on complete lockdown weeks before we left.

Because I had no clue about the procedure that shipping feline pets involved, I started by reading advice on the internet. While I bless Google for providing me with its wisdom in times of need, there are occasions when Google provides a little too much, too quickly. My initial idea was to give the cats sleeping pills prescribed by the vet so that they would drift away into kitty Neverland throughout the ordeal entailed by the long flight. This, I found out by reading the internet, was a common practice in the 1980s and, like most transport practices from that era, is now highly frowned upon. Modern veterinarians do not endorse a dose of sleeping pills because, in the event of air turbulence, the animals often get hurt inside their cage by being thrown from side to side if they are unconscious. Many pet bloggers recommended travelling with the cats on board as the safest option.

Here I had to disagree. Our younger cat, Whitey, has a nickname: 'Whiny', since he tends to whine mercilessly to get attention. And that's him on a good day. When transported anywhere in his cat box, he meows continuously and with great vigour and determination. Once, I was fortunate to spend three hours with him in the car on the way to get a series of vaccinations and had the opportunity to experience his whole repertoire of cries and screeches. His performance commenced as soon as the door of the pet carrier was closed. I almost gave in and started to think that maybe his vaccinations could be postponed until another year.

As we drove from Al Ain to Abu Dhabi — the only vet in Al Ain at that time was under investigation — Whitey realised that his ordeal may take some time, and so he paced himself. The tone and frequency of his cries decreased, but the duration of the individual yowls extended. He now uttered long wails, each akin to the cry of a Roman legionnaire who, upon his return home from the war with the barbarians, finds out that his whole family has been slaughtered and his beautiful villa has been burned down.

I switched off the radio. For the next hour, we travelled in bleak silence, which was shattered at regular intervals by the cat's wailing. I started to ponder other dark periods of human history. Remembering this experience, I was determined that I would not sit on the plane with this lamenting diva squealing for eight hours. The cats were going to fly in the cargo compartment as excess luggage.

This was not an easy decision to make. Most American pet bloggers, who can be quite judgmental and self-righteous, were in agreement that transporting your pets in this way is dangerous and negligent. They recounted numerous stories of pets who were found dead after landing or who passed away shortly after landing. From reading these blogs, it would appear that most American airlines were in the business of live freezing dogs and cats. Maybe some tough Siberian cat would be able to withstand -50°C when up in the air in an unpressurised compartment, but not our Arabian friends, who were more accustomed to +50°C.

After days of reading the tales of horror, I decided to just call our airline. They reassured me that they have state-of-the-art animal pens in pressurized holds in the plane's cargo area and that the pilots keep an eye on the temperature and the pressure in these areas throughout the flight. They also informed me that only falcons (with a valid ticket and assigned seat) were allowed to fly in the passenger cabin and that all other animals had to be assigned to 'animal class'. Since there were no other options, we reserved space for our cats in the hold on the same flight that we would be on. I thought that it may be an interesting experience for Twiggy and Whitey to hang out with some high-class racehorses for a few hours. I remembered seeing a programme about Dubai sheikhs flying their purebred Arabian horses to England with the same airline. I imagined the whole animal hold as some kind of a comic Noah's ark where different species got a chance to exchange world views, share experiences, and moan about their travel arrangements.

'When are we going to take off?' Whitey would moan to Twiggy in the next box. 'I hope they serve us some fresh tuna soon.'

'I don't think they will,' Twiggy, who is a more mature and seasoned traveller, would reply in a lacklustre tone. 'They only serve fresh tuna in the passenger cabin, First Class, I believe.'

'It's my first time travelling abroad,' a fluffy Pomeranian in the next box would interject. 'We're going to Monaco for the summer. Where are you off to?"

Whitey would snub the cheerful Pomeranian and pretend that he's reading an inflight magazine.

'Well, we're leaving the Emirates for good — we have a new home in Spain,' Twiggy would feel obliged to explain. 'We bought it two years ago, but we had to wait for all the permits to come through. We'll —'

'How exciting!' the Pomeranian would interject. 'I have friends in Spain; they live in Marbella. Have you been there? They're Ebony and Chico; you should give them a call when you are nearby. They have a gorgeous house near the marina. I love the sea …' While the Pomeranian would drone on, Whitey would overhear two Arabian horses behind them whispering.

'I really don't know where this airline is going,' one Arabian would mutter to another. 'When I started to fly, they did not allow all this riffraff in the hold. You had to be a thoroughbred to be allowed here.'

'I see your point,' the other Arabian would mumble with a slight lisp. 'Last month, I flew to Manchester with four cats, two dogs, and a chinchilla.'

'A chinchilla?' his friend would repeat indignantly. 'What's next — a ferret?' They would both start to giggle incessantly and take another bite of the fresh hay that had been thoughtfully provided by the live cargo steward.

Following the pet blogger's advice, we were supposed to prepare our cats for the ordeal of the journey. The cats would spend more than eighteen hours in their pet carriers in total. First, there was a two-hour drive to the airport, then three hours at the airport, the eight-hour flight, and then a five-hour drive from Madrid to our house. To prepare them for the long trip, the internet-based cat whisperers recommended leaving the cat boxes in the middle of the living room for several weeks before our departure date. We were supposed to keep the carriers' doors open so that the cats could explore the boxes and get in and out freely. In this way, they would lose their anxiety about the containers. I even put some blankets and things with familiar smells inside the boxes to encourage the little rascals to explore. That was the theory. Needless to say, the cats avoided the boxes as if they were made of plutonium and preferred to walk across the living room in large circles to avoid the pet carriers.

Desperate to get the cats to like their temporary shelters, I followed another blogger's suggestion. This person recommended putting the cats in the boxes for short periods of time and then going about your day as if nothing had happened. It sounded like a good idea. I got the quiet one, Twiggy, first by tricking him with a fresh prawn placed strategically at the back of the carrier. As I locked the door behind him, he was still too confused to warn his buddy and just stared at me, uncertain whether to eat the prawn or start fighting for his life. As he chose to be reasonable and began working on the seafood buffet at the back of his new (temporary) lodgings, I commenced enticing Whitey with the same trick. I was full of hope that this may actually work … until Whitey spotted his pal stuck behind bars and shot out like a firework. I did not see him for the rest of the evening.

The next day, I decided to focus my efforts on getting Whitey into the carrier. I tried a fresh piece of prawn, but he was not a fool. Since I could not convince him with a treat, I had to resort to the old ambush technique. While Robert calmly distracted Whitey with a feather on a piece of string, I quickly covered him with a towel and shoved him into his carrier, locking the door in one swift motion.

The ambush and the subsequent incarceration did nothing to

change Whitey's attitude towards the box. He started yowling and wailing as if we'd poured hot lava on him. This had a terrible effect on Twiggy, who had been watching the whole commotion and now made up his mind about the pet carriers. Like a furtive shadow, he retreated to his hiding place on top of the bookcase in the storage room. In the meantime, we carried on with the blogger's tip and acted as if nothing had happened. We cooked our supper, opened a bottle of wine, and pretended to be enjoying TV; all this was done amid horrific and pitiful cries for help emanating from the pet carrier.

After half an hour of this trauma, our nerves were completely shot. As we started to snap at each other, it was time to end this poorly thought-out experiment and let the cat out of the box. Like the day before, he shot out like a rocket and disappeared for the night. We abandoned the idea of getting the cats to like the pet carriers and decided to worry about getting them inside a bit closer to our departure. Unfortunately, this problem would not go away unless we cancelled the move or decided to leave the cats behind. This meant that the nights leading to our departure, I spent many restless hours pondering different types of Sophie's Choice scenarios in my mind.

'What if we have to leave for the airport and one of the cats runs away?' I worried. 'What if the door to a pet carrier accidentally opens at the airport and one of the cats runs away and hides? Do we still take our flight to Spain or stay and search Dubai airport for a fugitive cat?' The number of scenarios where I had to decide whether to leave one of the cats behind or miss the flight were endless. Thus, in the days leading to our departure, the two cats were not allowed to leave our bedroom under any circumstances. The night of our departure was smooth and trouble-free. Our friend picked us in the car that we had sold him the month before. The cats, confused by being moved around in the middle of the night, got into the pet carriers without too much of a fight. And we set off on our new adventure.

We arrived at Dubai airport looking like a Victorian family who was off on a spa holiday for the summer. In addition to the two giant pet carriers, we carried a large rectangular wooden box that contained a bass guitar. There were two enormous suitcases, weighing over thirty-five kilos, and hand luggage, which was only 'hand' by name. To move everything across the terminal, we needed an oversized airport trolley and a skilful porter to help us manoeuvre it through the crowds. We spent an inordinately long time at the check-in counter and then wandered off to the excess luggage counter and paid a small fortune to have our baggage and the pets transported with us.

It was with great relief to see all our suitably tagged suitcases disappear on the conveyor belt. We took the cats to the dedicated pet check-in station and left them there with the professional ground crew. I looked inside each cat box to wave them goodbye, but they were both sulking quietly in the far corners of their respective boxes and not interested in me at all. I wasn't worried. The crew acted as though they had done this many times, and so we walked away. Now that our luggage and cats were taken care of, we were free and unencumbered for the next nine hours until we were to be reunited with all our earthly possessions in Madrid. I felt a weight lift off my shoulders. We wandered off to the business lounge with a sense of freedom and upcoming adventure.

It's a strange feeling to have a glass of Sauvignon Blanc for breakfast. When you drink it in the evening, it tastes delicious and refreshing. As a morning beverage, it is somewhat dull and sour. Despite my love of wine and feeling relieved that the first step on our journey went so smoothly, I could not force myself to drink a whole glass of chilled white wine for breakfast. This was disappointing because it was the first time in days that I could finally relax.

Personally, I find few things as exciting as sitting in an airport lounge, drinking free wine, eating a lot of French cheese, and watching people coming and going. In the past, I have been known to leave for the airport well in advance of my departure to enjoy the buzz of the business lounge — but this was usually in the evening or at night. But this time, things did not seem right to me. I couldn't force myself to drink my favourite wine in the morning, which made the buffet food taste foul, and the morning crowd did not have the same level of energy as the evening travellers. Since I was not going to follow my usual lounge routine, it was time for a new one.

After a quick cappuccino and a Danish, I approached the spirits' table. You may wonder why there would be a spirits' table next to a breakfast buffet, but that's the charm of an airport lounge — time and space are suspended here. All logic and the philistine principles that tie us down in our everyday life are thrown out of the window. You might think that I was the only one browsing the spirits, but you would be incorrect. I had to wait in a queue to have my chance to properly consider the collection. The more seasoned spirit drinkers quickly identified their brand, presumably from the colour of the label and the font type. But when my turn came, I needed time to think. I started to browse the bottles with appealing labels and tried to read what they were. After a minute of picking and choosing, I started to sense impatient eyes rolling behind my back. So I grabbed the only two bottles that I could easily recognize — Martini Bianco and Jack Daniels — and poured two generous glasses for Robert and me. With drinks in hand, we sat in plush leather chairs and whiled away the time, unaware of the hard times that were to come.

Waiting for our flight, I wasn't anxious or worried anymore. It was not the first time in my life that I was leaving 'home' or moving to another country. I left my mum's house in Gdansk, Poland, when I was eighteen to study at Warsaw University, three hundred and fifty kilometres away. It was June 1997 when I received the letter of acceptance to study in Warsaw. I told my mum that I'd be back in September and went hitchhiking in France and Italy with two girlfriends.

Five years later, I started getting depressed by my capital city's grey streets and applied to study in the Netherlands. On my last day in my home country, I sold my old TV to my roommate, threw away anything that I could not carry, and left with a backpack and some carrier bags. A few years later, Robert and I left Sweden in a similar fashion. We gave away our furniture, TV, pot plants to friends and colleagues from work; we shipped books and clothes to Dubai and left Sweden, never to come back. On the day of my departure from Sweden, a close friend, Cristina, told me that she had felt as if a family member had passed away, and she had inherited their earthly belongings. Out of a sudden, her normally empty student lodgings were full of cupboards, chairs, and plants.

Perhaps it's the ones that we leave behind who suffer the most. But

I didn't think about them. It's selfish, but I didn't think of my friends. Theresa spending weekends alone by the pool in Al Ain with a rapidly warming Mojito in hand. Julie going to an empty staff kitchen every day at noon to eat lunch by herself. Claudia calling out random ideas across the thin cubicle wall, which we used to share. When I find myself at a crossroads, I don't reminisce about the past or feel nostalgic. I look forward to the adventure. If I had looked back, I would have never left my hometown, Gdansk, in 1997.

EIGHT
WHERE IS THE TAP?

When we finally arrived at our new home, after more than eighteen hours of travelling, we thought it best not to let the cats out of their carriers outside the house. I was worried that they might seize the opportunity and disappear into the adjacent fields in an effort to shake off being closed up in their transport boxes. Before we opened their boxes, we ensured that all the windows and doors were closed to prevent any escape. As it's in a cat's nature, once the boxes were open, they refused to get out but insisted on hiding in the far corner. We left them there and let them explore the new home at their leisure while we unpacked some of our things and opened a bottle of wine to recover from the journey.

While I sat pondering the enormity of what we had done — this was, after all, our new home and our life savings were sunk into it — on close inspection, there was not that much to show for it. It was a stone cottage in the middle of nowhere. I didn't know what to expect from this new life but found myself at peace with this new environment. It wasn't a home yet, but I had great plans for this place and our future here. As I was musing, I noticed the cats sneaking upstairs. When they caught my eye, they ran like hell upstairs and decided to make the second floor their new dominion. I went to the stairs to look at what they were up to and saw them both sitting at the top landing and looking down at me with disappointment for the betrayal I had shown them.

'You won't fool us again, getting us into those boxes,' they seemed to say. They both gave me the stink eye and ran away to look for places to hide. I thought it best to let them be and recover from the ordeal. This is the reward one gets for months of researching how to transport your pet cats in the most comfortable and least stressful way.

The cats had to stay inside for the next few days because I was still worried that they might disappear into the bushes. During the year that we were away, the grass and the weeds once again had grown high and thick. Unless you didn't mind encountering snakes, lizards, and thistles and getting your legs cut on razor-sharp grass, most of the grounds around the house were inaccessible. In the summer, the weeds around our house dry out and turn into instruments of torture. One type is very sharp and cuts your skin, leaving bleeding welts on your shins. The other type has millions of tiny paper-thin thistles that attach themselves to your socks and trousers and stay hidden forever until they make their presence felt at the most unexpected moment. They are so inconspicuous that throughout July and August, I kept on finding them in my wardrobe, in the sock drawer, and on the sofa — soon, I surrendered and got used to the constant sensation of being stung by something. As we were still new to this type of countryside, we had no idea how to keep the weeds down to a manageable height.

While we avoided going near the grass, I was sure that once the cats wandered outside the house and into the grass, we would never see them again until we cut the grass down again. The year before, it took Robert several weeks to cut the grass down with a petrol strimmer and clear approximately five thousand square metres of our land. The memory of the heavy labour he performed in forty degrees heat was still surprisingly fresh in his mind, and he was in no rush to take the strimmer out of the garage. Our nearest neighbours live too far from us to be bothered by the terrible state of our land, but I could see their beautiful, neatly trimmed field that borders ours, and I knew that we were letting the side down. I hoped that, since we were newcomers, they might forgive us our untrimmed land that year. In tacit agreement, we chose to ignore the fact that ninety percent of our property was inaccessible and focused on making plans for the future. It has been my experience that if I ignore something for a very long time, it either fixes itself or I decide that it is, in fact, an asset and not a problem. There is also a third option: someone who can no longer stand my uselessness comes along and helps me.

As it happened, one evening, we were sitting on the patio and enjoying the long summer evening with good wine and delicious tapas when a woman walked up our driveway. She introduced herself as Antonia, José's wife, and pointed to her house on the hill behind our house. We nodded and introduced ourselves, and she handed us a note. The note was written in English and it read:

My name is Pepe. I'm your neighbour. I cut your grass with a tractor for 30 euros.

It was evident that she was not the tractor-driving Pepe, and seeing a slightly puzzled look on my face, Antonia explained that Pepe was her son. Pepe obviously used Google to translate to get the message across and then sent his mum to deliver it. She thus appeared as a godsend. We were not entirely sure how a tractor could cut the grass, but since we wanted it gone and there was now someone at our door wanting to do it, we took a chance. We agreed that Pepe would bring his tractor around the next day in the afternoon or *por las tardes*.

'What time is he coming?' Robert asked me as we waved Antonia goodbye.

'*Por las tardes,*' I looked at him. 'Did you not hear her?'

'But what time is that?'

'After siesta.' I shook my head, signalling that this was common knowledge.

'But when does he finish his siesta?' My English husband was not happy with this imprecise time arrangement.

'After four or five,' I guessed.

The next day we awaited said tractor with great anticipation. At around four-thirty, we heard the tractor descending from the hill behind our house. The trip down the hill to our place took Pepe almost twenty minutes, but then once he aimed the tractor at our overgrown field, we could not believe our eyes. The tractor had a special attachment fitted to it, and as it moved, it literally pulverised the grass with large steel rotating hammers. Where once was thick and heavy bush, there was just a cloud of dust left behind. The pulveriser, as the name suggested, not only cut the grass but annihilated it. We were both mesmerised by this wonder of technology and started to congratulate ourselves on a job well done (although Pepe was actually doing the work). It would have taken Robert weeks of hard labour to do what now would be done in less than an hour. After a few more minutes of watching this engineering marvel, we went back to our regular chores. A few minutes later, I saw Pepe in the doorway to the kitchen. He looked hot and bothered and was saying something about *agua.* I took a cold bottle of water from the fridge and offered him a drink, but he shook his head frantically and summoned me to follow him. He was trying to explain something and kept repeating the word *agua* in every sentence. Because I was accustomed to hearing simplified teacher-Spanish via audiobooks and not a natural language, I struggled to grasp anything but a few individual words.

We passed the pool and went down to the field; there, right behind a small hill where the pool was located, was a geyser of water coming from the ground and shooting two metres high in the air. The view took me by surprise, and I could not make sense of it for a good minute. The things that I saw in front of me were not adding up to a coherent world view. 'Have we just discovered a hidden stream?' I wondered. Pepe ran to the new water feature and put his hand on the ground. This reduced the power of the water jet and made it possible for me to come closer and inspect it. As I looked down, I saw a broken pipe; the end of this pipe was completely severed, and the pieces had probably been pulverised since they were nowhere to be seen. Pepe's hand stopped the water from gushing up into the air, but it simply redirected the flow; now, the water was streaming at a rapid pace down into the weed-infested field. While I was trying to comprehend the situation, Pepe kept telling me to turn off the water supply. By now, Robert had heard the commotion and came by to see what the fuss was about. He and Pepe started to put stones around and on top of the pipe to stop the water from gushing out while I went away in search of the main water tap. I had absolutely no idea where to look for it. The problem with buying a house built many years previously by someone else and then remodelled by at least two different generations is that it usually takes several years to learn where all the pipes and taps in the house are. Some of our taps no longer controlled water because they were disconnected; some have to remain closed because they would flood an adjoining bedroom; others have remained hidden.

We had already run the gauntlet with the taps when we first came to the house the year before. As a precaution, the people who were looking after the house during our absence had closed all the taps — even those that did not seem to have any purpose. As soon as we dropped our suitcases in our newly bought house, I decided to wash my hands after the journey. To my dismay, there was no water in any of the taps in the house. I called Robert and informed him of this, and he went out to search for the mains tap. The first place he looked was a white box by the pool that contained five different taps. This now required marital collaboration on our side — while Robert turned different taps on and off, I stood by the kitchen sink where the tap was already open and waited for the water to start flowing. On the first sight of water, I was to shout to Robert to let him know that there was water in the house. I stood there for good five minutes when I saw Robert in the doorway with an exasperated look asking me why I was not saying anything.

'Because there is no water coming from this tap,' I replied indignantly. The tension was now starting to build up, and we were both silently accusing each other of doing something wrong. It was time to inspect each other's jobs.

'You stay here, and I will turn the taps,' I said and left the kitchen. 'Shout if there is water,' I reminded my husband, implying that the error was at his end of the stick. I knelt down in front of the tap box and quickly realized that I had no idea what I was looking at. I went back to the house.

'How do you know whether the tap is on or off?' I asked. My dear husband sighed, silently implying that he was right and went with me to the box.

'When the lever is parallel to the pipe, it's open.' He demonstrated.

'Obviously,' I thought. 'Why couldn't I figure it out?'

'Obviously,' I said, rolling my eyes, forgetting that it was I who had asked him for the explanation just a few minutes ago.

'OK then. Go and watch the tap.'

As soon as he was inside the house, I started to turn the levers on and off. The whole procedure reminded me of trying to play the pipe organ. If you have ever been to an old Catholic cathedral, you might have noticed a giant pipe organ with hundreds of pipes of different sizes. If you go up the steps to the balcony in the back of the church, you can usually inspect the instrument that controls all the pipes. I have often wondered about the person who controls all these pipes from behind a little wooden console with hundreds of buttons and levers. The thing is that it takes years of training and a skilled musician — aka a technician — to operate a church organ. If an amateur like you or me sat behind the organ console, we would not be able to get a single whistle out of any of the pipes. If you don't know what you are doing, you might sit there for hours moving levers and pushing buttons, and not a single peep will come out from the mighty pipes.

As I sat on the concrete outside the tap box, I was quickly running out of possible combinations. I first tried switching all the levers on and off one by one. I gave each tap a minute or two, thinking that the water might need some time to travel through the pipes. But all we were getting on the other end was just cold air and dust. I then thought that I should turn all the levers on at once — that would surely force some water up the pipes. But no luck; not even a dry cough came out of the pipes. Running out of ideas, I thought that maybe some pipes being open prevented other pipes from running water.

I was clearly losing my mind at this stage but was unwilling to admit defeat, so I started to turn the levers on in twos and threes; there were only five taps in total, but no configuration seemed to entice water to come out. By now, my hands were filthy from playing with dirty and rusty levers. Yet, there was not a drop of water to be found in the pipes. We were both upset and blaming each other for the lack of water. While there are many things in life that one can do without, water is not one of them. We sat on the stairs outside the swimming pool and looked bleakly into the future.

'I think you need to call Andy and ask him where the water tap is,' I said.

'You call him,' Robert answered.

'But I don't like to speak English on the phone,' I replied; it's always good to have the foreigner card in hand to use in such a situation.

'What?' Robert was not buying the poor foreigner act. 'He likes you more.'

We both knew that Andy had the answer to our water mystery, but the truth was that neither of us wanted to call him because we knew that it would make us look stupid. We had already asked him a gazillion favours and called with millions of silly questions, like where our post-box was, how to pay the electricity bills, where to buy a sim card, how to connect the internet, what is this, what is that, etc. I was sure he was getting sick and tired of babysitting two city idiots who thought they could live in the middle of nowhere in a foreign country.

'Maybe there is no water in the well,' my genius husband announced.

It was an option worth investigating before we announced to the whole expat community that we were clueless.

Invigorated by this new, albeit depressing, alternative, we marched down the hill to inspect the well. Our well house is a metre and a half high, and in order to get inside, I have to bend in half and walk through a tiny wooden door designed for the Borrowers. As soon as you walk in, you have to jump down — still bent in half — over the metal cover situated over the well. Since Robert, being almost two metres tall, refused to get inside the tiny house, he stood outside the well house and directed my investigation from there. First, I lifted the well door to look inside. To our relief, the well had plenty of water. As I was about to close the lid, Robert peeked inside the well house and started to shout, which made me pause.

'There is a rat inside,' he announced from a safe distance. As I'm not very observant by nature, I had to squint my eyes and look carefully. And yes, indeed! A poor drowned rat was floating on the water's surface. A thought occurred to me of brushing my teeth with dead rat juice, but there was no time to dwell on it. We needed to get it out of our water supply, or we'd have to sell the house.

I looked down in dismay at the slimy iron ladder attached to the wet stone walls of the well, and my future seemed bleak once again. I decided to put that thought aside for the time being. While I was staring down the abyss, Robert appeared at the well house door with the swimming pool net that we use to scoop the leaves and dead insects from the pool. My awe for his brilliant idea had no limits — especially since it saved me from having to go down the well. Robert fished the poor rat out and catapulted his dead body into the field, wishing him better luck in the afterlife.

While misfortune often comes in numbers, quick resolutions often follow one another too. As we congratulated ourselves on solving the rat dilemma, Robert looked at the water pump in the well and realized that it had been switched off all that time. With one push of the red button, the water started flowing from the well and up to the house. We ran up the hill to the house to be welcomed by the sound of water gushing from all the taps. We switched off the taps that did not seem to have any purpose and settled on a system that seemed to work. In all the excitement, we never bothered to learn which tap in the white tap box served what purpose.

This recklessness came to haunt me now that I desperately needed to find a tap to switch off the water gushing out from the pool onto the fields. Hoping for the best, I switched off all the taps and ran down to where Robert and Pepe were trying to suppress the water flow. Already, from a distance, I could see that the water was still flowing out at an unrestrained rate. I retreated and went to inspect the pump room under the swimming pool. I hoped to find a secret tap inside there. The pump room had been designed by the same mind who created the well house, and in order to get there, you have to bend yourself in half and, crouched over, half crawl down some tiny steps. Banging your head on the metal door frame was customary. In a hurry, I not only hit my head hard on the door frame but then walked straight into a giant spiderweb.

Since there was no time to curse or get angry, I proceeded to look for taps. I closed all the swimming pool pump taps and a few other random taps located inside the room. I was confident that now the water leak was contained and went out into the daylight to give Robert and Pepe the good news. To my dismay, the water was still pouring down the pipe. Assuming that I had not closed the taps properly, Robert now went away on a mad search for taps. After a few minutes, he came back to tell us that we had already lost two squares from the pool. This meant that the water level in the pool dropped by two mosaic tiles, which is about five centimetres. If it continued at this pace, we would not have a pool to swim in for the rest of the summer. Because of the heavy drought in southern Spain, it would have been impossible to fill in the pool during the summer.

The situation was really becoming unacceptable. To make matters worse, Pepe could not comprehend why there was no tap in the pool pump room to stop the water from flowing, and so he and I went together around and inspected all the taps once again while another thousand litres of water ran into the field. As we passed the pool, on our way back to the unwanted geyser, Pepe suggested that we cover the two drains at the bottom of the pool with plastic to stop more water from gushing out of the pool. This was just the type of task that I needed in a time of distress.

While Robert and Pepe went off to look at the broken pipe and hope for a simple solution to occur to them, I went inside and grabbed my snorkelling fins and a mask and two giant shopping bags.

Equipped with these, I commenced my underwater battle. The bottom drains are over two metres deep, and so with my height, I needed a good kick to dive to touch the bottom. While this was achievable on its own, it turned out that plastic shopping bags don't like to stay underwater. Each time I was near the hole, the bag would puff up like a giant jellyfish and float away from me, or cover my face like an alien creature intent on suffocating me, or worse.

After several attempts, I went out and fetched a broom and a big stone. I planned to use the broom to hold the slippery alien bag down while placing the stone over it. Trying to defy gravity and hydro-dynamics is not an easy task. While the bag fought its way upwards over and over again, the stone turned out to be just as uncooperative under water. It was heavy and difficult to manage. As I was 'dancing' in the water with my broom and a stone, with my fancy snorkelling mask and fins still on, I saw a figure at the edge of the pool. I stuck my head out of the water and took my mask off to greet the stranger, who asked me where Pepe was. As I found out later, the visitor was Pepe's brother-in-law, Jaime, who had been called upon to help.

After some more struggle, I realized that I could simply put the stone inside a bag and place it over the drain hole. As soon as I covered both drains, I changed into dry clothes and went to see the progress being made at the end of the broken pipe. My underwater adventure did not seem to slow the flow of water from the severed pipe, and the men gathered around it did not believe that I had covered the drains properly, but there was no time for discussion. By now, the water had dropped lower than eight tiles, and my dreams of spending the rest of the summer by the pool were draining away as each watery minute passed us by. As we found out over the years, Jaime is a bit of a MacGyver and the go-to person if you need anything fixed. That was the reason why Pepe had called him for an emergency consultation. In typical Andalusian fashion, Jaime commenced by laying out the problem that was staring us all in the face.

'The pool drainage pipe is broken,' he told us. Robert and I nodded while Pepe kept trying to slow the flow down.

'It's broken. You will lose all the water,' Jaime told us.

Following the rules of Andalusian discourse, he then reiterated the same utterance a few more times while nodding his head and looking stern.

My personal theory is that this technique of conversational delay and creating suspense when dealing with a problem gives any self-respecting macho man some time to think of a solution. While their mouth is busy restating the obvious in a slow and sombre tone, their minds are racing to quickly find a solution and surprise all the spectators with their smarts. And, like a magician, after several minutes of repetitious monologue, Jaime pulled the rabbit out of the hat. He looked around and saw a piece of olive branch on the ground. He picked it up, pulled a small knife from his pocket, shaved it into a conical shape, and rammed this improvised plug into the broken pipe. The water flow immediately slowed down to a small leak, and we all felt relieved.

Being a lifelong perfectionist, Jaime was not happy with this job. He told Robert to keep the stick inside while he went away. He must have gone to his work-shed, which was a little over five hundred metres away in his wife's uncle's house because he came back with a long piece of black rubber and another stick — this one a bit thicker and bit sturdier looking than the one he had found on the ground — and a hammer. He checked the diameter of the new stick against the broken pipe, shaved off a few millimetres, wrapped it in the black rubber, and replaced the provisional stick with his new one. He then hammered it in so that it was well and truly firmly wedged up the pipe. Jaime explained to us several times that we should wait until winter to repair the pipe because then we will be able to drain the pool and refill it again.

'You know there is no water now because it's summer. So, no rain, no water. In winter it rains, so you have water. You can fix your pool in the winter when you have water,' he spoke to us as if we were little children. We didn't mind but just nodded gratefully and invited him for a cold beer, which he refused as he had to run off to another job.

The provisional stick that Jaime installed to stop our pool water from completely draining remained there — like a loaded gun ready to explode at any time — for another two years. We only got round to replacing the end of the broken pipe with a proper tap when we had our plumber visit us two years later to put in new taps in the guest accommodation. Luckily, we did not have to drain the pool; two plastic bags were placed over the bottom drains in the pool (properly, this time) while Paco, the plumber, cut off the damaged end of the pipe and glued a new piece to it, with a tap at the end. It took him about ten minutes to fix the pipe, and we could only wonder why it took us two years to get it done.

NINE

THE ROOF

O ur real misfortunes started in mid-October. One night, we
woke up to the distinct sound of a waterfall. At first, we
thought that a water pipe had burst somewhere in the
house, but we were wrong. The torrent was falling from the skies,
down the staircase, and into the living room, flooding everything we
owned. The reason why there was a torrent of water flowing inside the
house was that we had completely removed the roof of the house.

Our initial plans were to start the renovations in early August of
2014 and to have a new roof over our heads before the winter. We
spent our first winter in Spain with no roof to the house because we
could not find a builder until late September. When we permanently

moved to Andalusia at the end of July 2014, we were very keen to start house renovations. Yet, no one in our area was even remotely interested in working for us at that time of year. It had now been two years since our initial house-hunting trip. After we had bought the house in 2012, we worked for another two years in the Gulf and saved every single penny. Now, with the cash in hand and the renovation plans approved by Montefrio's architect, we could not wait to start.

We spent the first two weeks of our new life in Spain trying to contact our architect, who vanished into thin air and did not answer our emails or phone calls. He reappeared after the summer holidays, at the end of August. As an excuse for not answering his phone or writing any emails, he showed us a bandaged index finger that was supposedly broken during a car accident. Apparently, he tried to get in touch with us, but he had to spend days in hospital. The only injury, thank God, was the broken finger.

Not wanting to get involved in this first grader's excuse, we wished him a speedy recovery and asked him to find us a builder who would be able to undertake our project within a set budget. The main aspect of the renovation was the complete removal of the decaying roof. We then wanted to increase the height of the walls on the second floor so that anyone of average northern European stature might be able to walk around upstairs freely, without having to curtsy every other step like a Victorian parlour maid. Raising the walls had been Robert's first objective even before we moved to the house.

When he first saw the low-hanging wooden beams in the three tiny bedrooms upstairs, he immediately crossed the house off the list of possible buys. It has to be said that the majority of our neighbours are of a certain physique, specific to Andalusia. They are mostly short and stout. The tallest men in our neighbourhood reach the height of one hundred and seventy centimetres which is about 5'5 feet. Women are, in general, petite but surprisingly brawny. We often observed, in amazement, our seventy-year-old neighbour Mercedes running up and down the olive hills and rocky terrain like a spry mountain gazelle. She would come by to say hello, and as we were talking, she would remember that she had a gift for us in her cottage down the hill. Before we could protest and insist that we get it ourselves, she would be halfway down the steep hill, her slippers leaving a cloud of dust behind her. By the time the dust settled, she would be running up with fresh chicken eggs in a plastic bucket. It's been observed that Spaniards have the longest life expectancy in Europe. I can see why.

Needless to say, considering their average height, low ceilings do not pose an inconvenience for them. In most cases, the wooden beams are well over their heads. We asked our architect to find us a builder, preferably several, and get some quotes for the project. Whilst we waited, we started to worry that we might not be able to replace the roof before the winter. Hoping to speed things up, we decided to search for builders on our own.

Not knowing how to proceed, we went to *Little Britain*. There, we found a whole plethora of name cards and flyers for different English-speaking builders. Our Spanish had improved slightly since the previous year; we could now greet people in confidence and answer questions about our names and who we were. However, we were still ignorant of the crucial building-site vocabulary and the expressions related to wants and needs. Even though we pretended to be unbiased, we hoped to find a cheap builder who spoke fluent English. With a handbag full of flyers and name cards, we went home and started emailing and messaging different builders and asking them to give us a *presupuesto*, or a quote, for our project. While we waited for the first visitors to come and discuss the project, I did some online reading on how to choose a builder. There were numerous websites and blogs that advised newbie property owners what to look for in a prospective builder. The gist of all my reading was that we should not hire a builder who smelled of booze, arrived late, and didn't speak Spanish. This seemed common sense, and I was starting to wonder how out-of-date these tips were. Surely no one in his right mind would come to meet a potential client reeking of alcohol. It wasn't the 1980s anymore. How little did I know!

The first duo of English builders showed up two hours late. They got out of their clunker, followed by a miasma of cheap, stale wine. The staleness of the odour emanated from their clothes and their skin pores. They hadn't just had a quick glass of wine with their lunch. These two smelled as if they had fallen asleep in a mediaeval tavern next to a leaky oak barrel. As soon as I smelled them, I knew that we were not going to hire them. Not because I discriminate against alcoholics; I find their company amusing at times. But I would not hire these two because I discriminate against idiots who think that they can show up smelling like a brewery and ask for my hard-earned money. You don't need to be a corporate tycoon to grasp this basic business principle. If you want my money, you should at least shower before the first meeting. This simple rule had not been embraced by these men.

Unfortunately, we were too polite to say anything straight away, and as a consequence, we spent two hours in these goons' company pretending that they were still in the running. We first took out the elaborate architect's plans and showed them to the two stooges. We walked around and explained to them what we wanted to be done. They did not seem to have any questions. They nodded and scratched their heads but did not ask about any specific details. I suspected that the wine buzz was starting to wear off, and they were in the hazy dominion that occupies one's mind between being tipsy and a looming hangover. The walking was also starting to get to them.

They had arrived during the hottest part of the day, and it was now about thirty-five degrees Celsius. Walking in the direct sun and climbing up and down the stairs was not helping their disposition. And then Robert suggested that we all go up onto the roof and inspect it closely. We brought over the ladder, and we all went up. I watched the two men's complexion growing a darker and darker shade of red and their eyes glazing over as Robert went on talking about the roof tiles and what he wanted the roof to look like. To get them out of their misery, I suggested a cup of tea. I hoped that they would use it as an excuse to decline and explain that they must rush home for some reason. But not these two idiots; they would not grab the lifeline. Yes, of course, they'd love a cup of hot tea, they said. I did admire for a second the English perseverance of drinking scorching beverages in hot climates but decided not to make a generalisation based on my current sample group.

Once their tea was ready, we sat in the shade of the patio staring at the two cups of steaming liquid. The thought that this was going to take a very long time flashed through my mind. The men seemed visibly relaxed now. They appeared relieved that the walking part of their visit was over. I expected that now that they had seen the scope of the project, they might bombard us with questions and ideas. But silence fell upon the table.

'Is this Earl Grey?' one of the men asked me.

I confirmed and he nodded pensively.

'I haven't had it before, but it tastes all right.'

'Yes, it's quite nice.' I grabbed the conversational straw. 'I don't usually drink tea, but Earl Grey is quite nice. Sorry that I don't have English Breakfast.'

'That's all right,' he said, absolving me.

This ended the topic for me, but he appeared to have more to say about it.

'I drink a lot of tea. But for lunch, I drink coffee. I like instant coffee, not one of these brewed coffees. It tastes the same, but it's a lot of work; that's all I say.'

His mate did not have much to add to this, and even though I fundamentally disagreed, I did not want to seem contrary, so I refrained from any further comments. We sat in silence and let the topic die on its own. Wishing to go back to the business part of this tête-à-tête, Robert asked them when they would be able to email us the quote.

'I don't do email,' said the other man.

'What do you mean?' My husband — who, if allowed, would do everything by email — could not compute such a statement.

'I don't do email,' the man reiterated, clearly assuming that Robert was hard of hearing.

Seeing our confusion, his mate decided to elucidate.

'We don't do computers. It's just a lot of mumbo jumbo.'

We remained speechless while millions of questions assailed our minds about these men's business model.

'OK. So, will you call us?' I tried to help them move the topic along.

'Yeah. We will discuss the quote, and we can meet at El Paso.'

This sounded like their usual mode of communicating with

clients. It was a step up from sending us a smoke signal, but it made me wonder how they survived in this dog-eat-dog economy. El Paso is a bar next to *Little Britain*, and it sounded like their company's headquarters. There was not a chance in the world that we would ever meet with them at El Paso to discuss our project, but we nodded and agreed and assured them and feigned interest; we did everything we could to get them back on the road. Satisfied with our response, they finished their tea and got up. As we approached their car, the shorter man cursed under his lip. He ran to the car and opened the door. The smell of rotting flesh hit us all in the face and left us motionless; the stench formed an impenetrable wall now separating us from the car.

'I forgot to open the windows,' the man explained.

'Clearly,' I thought, but it did not explain what the dead corpse was doing in his work van in the first place. Seeing alarm in our eyes, the man gestured us to come closer and see the stinky cargo. The car's whole back was filled with crates of pig bones, mostly trotters and long bones.

'It's for me dogs,' he explained.

If you only ever buy dainty pork chops at your local butcher, you may not be familiar with the size of a whole pig's leg bone or trotters. They're huge. I imagined this man's home with the hounds of Baskerville guarding the gate. I could see him getting out of the car and tossing the giant bones at the beasts, their monster jaws crushing the bones into powder and salivating for more. I'd decided it was wise to inquire where he lived so that we could avoid that part of Andalusia forever.

'Not far from here. You know the Richards in La Fuenta. They're me neighbours. Mine's the second house on the right.'

There's a certain type of mind that assumes that their private points of reference are well-known to the world. As it were, we had no clue who the Richards might be. We expected that they might own massive dogs too and vowed never to go to La Fuenta — wherever that was. As we waved our visitors goodbye, I felt exhausted. The whole absurd encounter did not curb my enthusiasm for this new life, but I was taken by a sudden craving for a serrano tapa paired with a glass of

Crianza. We locked the gate, opened a bottle of wine, and sat on the patio, going over the events of the day in detail.

As unfortunate as it sounded, we had to repeat the same scenario several more times. Not all the builders were drunk and inept. Some were just cowboys with no real credentials or experience. Even though we wanted to start as soon as possible, the professional builders were all busy with current projects. The good professional builders were either engaged for the next six months and/or too expensive. Eventually, we settled on a mediocre builder who assured us that he could do the job within our budget. Only when our budget started to shrink and the work was not finished did we find out that he was numerically challenged. As it turned out, he could not calculate how many bags of cement he needed from one day to the next; never mind calculating how many bags he would need to renovate an old stone cottage and put on a new roof. He pulled his estimate from the top of his empty head, and we accepted it because that was what we could afford.

All the hours of watching *Grand Designs* had been for nothing. From the start, we had repeated the same mistake that almost all greenhorn homeowners-cum-developers make: we underestimated our budget by fifty percent. At this stage, we were still oblivious to this mistake and were sustained by our vision of our future home. If you ask me what I felt at that time, I can't describe any specific feelings of angst or worry. We were far too busy to stop and think about our new life.

Even though we were not gainfully employed at the time, every day was filled with a new challenge of settling in a new country, conquering language barriers, solving new problems, and learning how things are done. We had a weekly plan. This week we will look for a builder. Next week we will register our residency in Spain. Then we need to find a company to get the satellite internet connected. Go to the post office and find out where our post can be delivered. Find the location of Montefrio's Town Hall and register as a *padron*. Call the shipping company and find out where our container is. Try to locate the lost architect. Register as self-employed. Get a tax number. Buy a working fridge and figure out how to get it delivered to a house on a hill in the middle of nowhere. Get a phone number. Get Spanish debit and credit cards. If you are well-settled in a place, most of these things take a couple of hours at the most. But when you're a stranger in a new country, it takes days to figure out how to do them and then a day or two to get them done. But we didn't mind. It was our new life, and not once did we look back.

Going through a parade of builders and cowboys was now a regular event in our lives. And since this circus show titillated our appetite to start the project, we decided to put matters into our own hands. One day, we went up onto the roof to survey the extent of the job and dream of the future. As I climbed up, I felt one of the tiles move. I bent down and started to jiggle it. Sure enough, it disconnected from its neighbours and was now loose in my hand. I looked at it in disbelief. Intrigued by how easy it was to remove a roof tile, Robert jiggled its neighbour. Again, the tile detached with surprising ease. Encouraged by how seemingly straightforward it was to strip off roof tiles, we thought it might save us a lot of money if we removed all the tiles ourselves.

We went down to the house, put on our work gloves, sunscreen, and straw hats, and went back to work on the roof. The job was eerily satisfying and not difficult. The most effort went into preserving the tiles. They were old baked clay tiles, and we had an idea — taken from an episode of *Grand Designs* — to reclaim these. I thought that we would carefully store the precious tiles until the time when we could clean them of moss and black mould and reuse them on our new roof.

This idea significantly slowed down our work. We now had to create small piles of tiles on the roof structure and then take them down the ladder and place them in a secure spot behind the oak tree in the corner; that's where we stored all our building trash since the tree hid it from our view. We could only carry five or six tiles at a time; otherwise, they would break. We divided up the task at hand, and so one of us would take off the tiles and arrange them into neat piles by the edge of the roof while the other would go up and down the ladder and carry the tiles to the oak tree. Because taking off the tiles was easy and required little effort, we took turns with these jobs.

Soon enough, the first challenge presented itself. We had started to remove the tiles from the lowest part of the roof — barely two metres from the ground. Now, as we moved up, we had worked on the ridge of the roof and near the steep side, which was four metres off the ground. Sudden vertigo hit us both in turns, and doubt crept into my mind about what we were doing. This was a job for teenagers, not a middle-aged couple.

When I was a child, I was fearless of heights. Walking on a wooden plank across a ravine seemed like a nice way to spend one's time. Bending over the twentieth-floor balcony to chat with the neighbours' kids was just another Sunday afternoon in my aunt's flat — I was a child in the eighties, after all. Climbing any tall building or scaffolding within sight was a common pastime then. On school trips, we would entertain ourselves by balancing on the edge of any balustrade that we could see, hoping that others would notice how brave we were. The teachers didn't care much and would be conspicuous by their absence on most school trips. They were probably at a bar drinking hot tea with vodka and hoping that the museum's curators would take care of the rowdy kids.

Since those days, I presumed myself to be a fearless Alpinist — even if only in my imagination. But now, standing on the ridge of our roof, I started to feel woozy and was gripped by a strange feeling of wanting to get away from this precarious position but not being able to let go of the tiles I was holding on to in order to save my life. I wanted to go back to the lower section, but my feet became as heavy as lead. I couldn't lift them.

I decided to get hold of myself and stop staring down at the precipitous drop, and refocused on the roof tiles that I was clutching. A thought came over me that what we were doing was extremely careless. We didn't have ropes or hard hats, which seemed like the minimal safety equipment for this type of job. I did put on plenty of sunblock, so if I fell and lay unconscious for hours, I would not get sunburnt. I wondered how many days it would take someone to find our dead bodies if we fell off the roof in some freak accident. Our neighbours might stop by one day; they regularly brought us fresh fruit and vegetables. But they'd just made a delivery of watermelons and tomatoes that morning, so I would not expect them to be back for a few days. Our families would not be bothered if we were incommunicado for a couple of weeks. Even if we were out of contact for a month, they might think we were busy with the house renovations and would not want to bother us. We were not avid Facebook posters, and so people would not miss our intermittent posts. The future appeared gloomy.

With our happy-go-lucky attitude regarding health and safety, I realized that we needed to make some friends in this country so people would feel our absence in case of a senseless self-inflicted accident. With this thought fresh in my mind, I started to climb down the roof's ridge when my foot went straight through the straw and *yeso* clay of which the roof's substructure was composed and right through the ceiling of a second-floor bedroom. It was a scary moment, but since I'd already looked death in the face once that day, I calmly pulled my foot back up and investigated the somewhat flimsy layers that the ceiling was made of. It appeared that the space between the wooden beams was filled with anything that the yesteryear builders could find on the farm. Most of it was straw mixed with clay mud. This was reinforced by small stones and bits of odd plastic, and rotting pieces of wood.

Intrigued, Robert got a claw hammer and started to peel away the *yeso* clay and straw. Suddenly I started to notice a change in our ambience. The number of wasps around us seemed to have multiplied, indicated by the angry buzzing that now surrounded us. Some wasps decided to take a rest from their aggressive buzzing on a neat stack of roof tiles next to Robert's hand. Instinctively, he started hitting them with the hammer. We looked at the precious artisanal tiles that were now smashed to bits and did not see a single dead wasp. Even though there were no casualties, the unprovoked attack angered the mob. They were now landing on our arms and legs and making a real nuisance of themselves.

I realized that against all odds, we had to remain calm. Running down the roof like lunatics would only end in one of us either falling down to the ground or right through the ceiling to the bedroom below.

'Just stay calm,' I told Robert. I didn't have to repeat myself. We both started to descent the roof with the speed of an amateur bomb disposal unit.

'We need to get to the pool,' Robert informed me in a stern voice with his eyes steady on the roof. I knew exactly what he was talking about. Anyone who watched enough cartoons in the eighties would know that jumping into a body of water was the best way to escape a cloud of enraged wasps. So, I followed obediently. We crawled down the unsafe roof and slid down the ladder. As soon as I had my feet on the ground, I ran straight for the pool. We spent the rest of the day submerged in water with our straw hats bobbing up and down, taking shelter from the vicious insects.

The next day, we devised a plan of attack. We put on long pants and long-sleeved shirts, thereby ensuring that every part of our bodies, excluding our eyes, of course, was covered. With a couple of tins of insect spray in hand, we approached the enemy line. The roof was eerily quiet, and so we went back up to yesterday's battlefield and inspected the damage closely. We could now see that there was a well-established wasp nest between the straw and mud that constituted our ceiling. We decided to strike at the heart of the enemy and sprayed the hell out of it until the tins were empty.

As the drugged and paralyzed wasps started emerging from their nest, we had just enough time to get back down and drive off in the car. We spent a lovely day sauntering the streets of Alcalá's old town and pointing out to each other features of the various houses that we liked or disliked, taking photos of anything we fancied and wished to emulate in our own house. Not discouraged by the initial setbacks that we had experienced, we spent the following week taking off the roof tiles and removing the straw and mud ceiling. Our work accelerated when we created a hole over the old garage, and instead of carrying everything down the ladder, we now zealously threw any debris down into the garage. Initially, we only threw away tiles that were broken or damaged. But once we noticed how much easier it was to throw them away instead of carrying small stacks down the ladder and to the oak tree, our assessment of what constituted a good tile became much more stringent than before. Now, even a hairline fracture would deem the tile unusable, and any poor reject tile would land on top of the other discarded tiles on the floor of the old garage.

Fuelled by this efficiency, we finished taking the roof off before our builders could start work. It took us almost two weeks of hard and dangerous labour, but we really felt that we had accomplished a giant step in the project. Strangely, once they arrived on site to start the project, our builders did not shower us with compliments at our great progress. It was only when I saw them demolish the whole animal house (which we had deemed a ruin) in half a day that I realized what amateurs we had been. Now I just sat and watched as work was being done with great pace and proficiency while Robert helped the builders mix cement, carry an endless supply of bricks, and operate the wheelbarrow.

When you renovate a house, you have a number of options regarding where to live while the project is ongoing. You can live in a caravan on-site, you can rent an apartment nearby and live there, or you can choose the worst option and live in the very house that is being renovated.

Since we never put much thought into this part of the house restoration, we assumed it would not be a big inconvenience for us or the project if we restricted ourselves to living in two rooms on the first floor. We used one as a bedroom and the other as a living room with a small kitchen. The only problem was that the staircase to the second floor was in the living room. Each time a worker wanted to get to the second floor, he had to march between our dining table and the kitchen, leaving a trail of mud, wet concrete, and powdery dust. It also meant that no matter what happened the day before, each morning, we had to get up really early to use the bathroom, shower, and eat breakfast in some comfort before the workers swarmed the house.

Living among the rubble with significant parts of the old house now demolished meant that we spent the late autumn being cold and dirty. The several months that it took to put the house's main structural parts back together were probably the most bitterly cold and miserable in our lives, both physically and emotionally. It was in mid-October that we experienced our first torrential rains in Spain. The first one took us by surprise. After nine years of living in the desert, I forgot that it rains in Europe in the autumn, even in sunny Spain.

That first rainy night, we spent most of it in wet pyjamas shoving rainwater from one place to another. Because there was no roof on the house at all, the rainwater was collecting on the floor of the second floor. Once it reached a certain depth, it started to run down the staircase and into our living room, cascading like a spring waterfall. We scooped up water in buckets and dumped them out of the house. The task closely resembled the manic speed and desperation of people trying to get the water out of a sinking boat. It was a futile endeavour. As I stood on the staircase trying to control the waterfall, I looked up at the black sky and the torment above. 'What are we doing?' I wondered for a second, but really, there was no time to moan and complain.

After an hour of scooping up the water streaming down the staircase onto the sweeping pan and into a plastic bucket, we were desperate for a break. As was inevitable, we started to argue and question each other's technique of catching water. Harsh words were exchanged — not the first or last time that terrible autumn. I got angry and kept sweeping water in silence with heavy rain still falling on my back. That's when Robert dropped the mop and left the house into the cold, stormy night.

I didn't even feel like asking any questions and expected that he was outside, Job-like, venting his anger. But then he reappeared carrying a bag of cement. He dropped it at the top of the staircase and went down to get another. With several cement bags strategically laid on the edge of the old doorway and the stairs, we managed to create a temporary water barrier. It stopped the furious waterfall down the stairs and gave us a few minutes of respite.

Pleased with the new dam, we decided to go back to bed and turn a blind eye to the torrent on the second floor. Things always look better in the daylight, so I hoped to approach the rain problem early in the morning. We changed our soaked clothes and slipped under numerous blankets. As I was blissfully falling asleep, I felt that there was water on my forehead. I didn't want to stick my arms out from underneath the warmth of the blankets, and so I just wiped my head on my pillow. 'It must be sweat,' I convinced myself.

After several more drops fell on my face, I knew that it wasn't sweat. I hoped that Robert would get up and deal with the problem on his own, so I waited several more minutes. I suspect that he was thinking the same thing because we got up simultaneously and were equally aware of the water falling on our heads. We moved the bed so that our pillows were no longer directly under the falling drops of water.

Closer inspection revealed that the ceiling over our heads had several points where water was dripping at regular intervals. This was easily fixed with big plastic water bottles cut into half to serve as makeshift buckets.

But then I saw that water was streaming down the walls in the living room and the kitchen. This type of leak is impossible to catch with a bucket and requires constant mopping and changing of towels. As Robert mopped, I went upstairs to have a look at the source of this leak. Our dam was still holding. In fact, it was holding so well that the whole of the second floor was now under several centimetres of water. Since there was no other place for the water to flow, it flooded into the downstairs rooms by running down along the walls and through various cracks and crannies.

To limit the effects of the flooding, we had to attack the water on two fronts. One person stood on the second floor in the pouring rain, scooping bucket after bucket of water off the floor and then throwing the water out of the window into the garden. The other person did damage control in the living room and mopped up the streams of water that were now pouring down the walls and the ceiling. Since one of these tasks was obviously more emotionally exhausting, we took turns. We worked like that until five in the morning when the rain ceased for a few hours. When our builders came on-site at eight, they were confronted by the mere shadow of the people they had left the day before.

We didn't have to tell the story in great detail. Our humble abode was saturated with the evidence of the events of the previous night. Plastic buckets dotted the living room, bedroom, and kitchen.

Numerous mops, towels, blankets, and newspapers were lying all over the floor. When the builders went upstairs, they saw the pièce de résistance — our homemade dam!

I could see that they were not too impressed by how we had used the cement bags, but they did not dare argue with us, seeing the wretched state that we were in. They spent the first part of that day putting a plastic cover over the second floor to protect us from the future rains that were predicted to fall that month.

With the tarpaulin over our heads, I felt more positive again. While the makeshift roof did not stop the flooding completely, it reduced the amount of rainwater collected on the second floor. This, combined with some strategic placing of the buckets around the house, allowed us some sleep on the nights when it rained. There were several more nights that autumn when we had to get up in the middle of the night and move our bed around to avoid water dripping on our heads. There were other nights when we took turns getting up to empty the buckets before they overflowed, but that was nothing compared to the first night of torrential rain. From then on, I consulted the weather forecast religiously, and before the stormy nights, I would mentally prepare for the nightmare to come. There was not much time to feel sorry for ourselves. We just ploughed on because there was no other option. The thought of selling up or giving up never occurred to me. That would have been a total failure and I would have never accepted such an outcome of our adventure.

For added stress, that autumn, I got a contract to write content for a new English language learning app. Every morning, as soon as the workers arrived, I would sit by a makeshift table in a cramped, dirty bedroom and work on my laptop until they left around 6 pm. I never told my boss in the UK that I was in the middle of a massive house reform as I didn't want to worry him. We needed the money, and with Robert busy non-stop on site helping with the work and supervising, someone had to earn some money. I had several skype team meetings on my tablet with my colleagues in the UK while the builders above me were knocking down walls or laying steel for the new roof.

'Is everything OK in your house?' my editor Jenny asked once during a skype call after hearing a particularly loud bang that shook the whole house.

'Yes, it's just a small renovation thing,' I would lie because I knew deep down that she would be concerned if I'd told her the truth; it was a nice and caring team of colleagues. Fortunately, I met my deadlines and worked on the project until the summer of the following year. It would have been sensible to rent a place to write quietly, but we were both overwhelmed with all the logistics that the renovation entailed and never got around to looking into that option.

On many rainy days, I would sit by my laptop writing and get up every thirty minutes to mop the floor and empty the buckets, and go back to writing as if it was a normal thing to do. Thank God that women are multitaskers! As soon as I got used to living among water buckets and the mud that was regularly tramped in by the workers, I was forced to face another trial — the severe cold. Before we bought the house in Spain, we had options of either buying a house in the UK or building one in Poland. We decided to disregard our home countries because after so many years of living in the sun in the Emirates, we could not face going back to the grey and cold that our respective homelands offered.

Living in the sun adds colour and flavour to your life. It makes food taste better, and it allows ordinary people to glow. The sun saturates bright colours and simultaneously hides ugliness in deep shadows. There are few things in life that a deep-blue sky and the view of a white cottage on an olive hill can't fix. While life in Andalusia can be sunny most of the year, it can also get cold and rainy and incredibly miserable. That's when the rain and the greyness dull your emotions and perhaps dampen your love for the region.

After a month of rain and cold, I forgot that most of the year, I could run around in a T-shirt, even in the month of October. I began to feel that the cold and rain were the natural status quo and that it was the sun that was the anomaly. I found out that autumn that the name of our nearest village, Montefrio, was not — as I had hoped when we purchased the house — arbitrary. The 'beware of ice' road signs posted on the roads near our house suddenly made a lot of sense. It even became a running joke when talking about the weather.

'*Hace frio hoy,*' a worker would say in the morning, billowing condensation from his mouth.

'*Si, es Monte Frio.*' Robert would grin at his own wit in a foreign language.

That winter, 'Cold Mountain' felt like the coldest place on earth. Everyone we met admitted that it was a particularly chilly November for Andalusia. The low temperatures were exacerbated by the lack of a roof and several gaping holes in our house. There was one huge hole on one side of our house where the animal house used to be. Then the staircase to the second floor did not have any doors, so the wind outside swept across our living room and up to the second floor practically unimpeded.

Because we had no space at the house to unpack our possessions which we had shipped from Al Ain, most of our belongings were in a storage facility in Granada. This meant that all we had to wear were clothes that we brought in the summer in our suitcases. They were adequate for Jumairah beach or a night out in Dubai but offered no real protection from the freezing cold that we now found ourselves living in. We bought a few sweaters, woolly hats, boots, and jackets at the hardware shop. This formed our limited but effective wardrobe. We now looked like the builders who were on-site with us and not lost tourists. The only difference was that the builders were able to go to a clean and warm home at the end of each day and change their clothes, while we sat on a dirty sofa, cold and miserable in the same work clothes until it was time to go to bed.

That winter, if anyone peeked into our living room after seven p.m., they might have mistaken us for homeless people who were squatting inside a building site. Most days, after the workers went home, it would take us another hour to wrap things up, start a fire in the fireplace, tidy the kitchen floor, and start preparing supper. If rain was forecast, we had to make sure that all the building materials, especially the cement bags, were safe and secure from the rain. We would then open a cheap bottle of Tempranillo and watch *Grand Designs* on YouTube.

Why, after a day on the building site, we chose to watch that wretched show again, I would need a degree in psychiatry to explain. I suspect it was the uplifting denouement of each episode that gave us hope to live another day. It was also reassuring to watch others in similar circumstances: it gave us comfort to see others suffer like we were suffering.

Thus, we spent our evenings watching different sets of unfortunate couples discussing their grand designs and where they went wrong. We, of course, were experts by now and could speak with confidence about building a house. This evening entertainment allowed us to forget the woolly hats and the winter jackets that we were wearing while watching online videos on our laptop. The poor cats, born and bred in the hot desert, cuddled together on the armchair by the fireplace and spent their evenings staring at the fire as if it was a mythical god or a long-lost friend. In the morning, I would often see them looking mystified at the dying coals inside the fireplace and searching for the source of the fire from the night before. While the evenings were cold and chilly, with a gentle breeze blowing across the dining room table where we sat, the nights were a never-ending nightmare.

TEN

THE SPANISH BED

W hile our belongings and some of the furniture we shipped to Spain were in Granada's storage space, we slept on the old bed that we had inherited with the house. In Spain, it's called *cama de matrimonio* — to ensure, I believe, that any adulterous activity that may occur in it would be classified as a mortal sin in front of any Catholic jury. Quite misleadingly, this 'bed of marriage' is often translated as a 'double bed,' purely because *matrimony* usually consists of two people. This interpretation could not be further from the truth. For anyone taller than a hundred and sixty centimetres or five feet, a *cama de matrimonio* would be better described as a large single bed.

The size of the Spanish double bed is also one of the biggest complaints among tourists visiting Andalusia when they are duped into believing that what they are sleeping on is what the rest of the world calls a double bed. No, it isn't! It's a 'bed of matrimony' in that it will test any couple's love and commitment. Your night on a Spanish bed of torture usually starts quite ordinarily. The bed is on the petite side as far as beds are concerned, but you can fit in it. As long as you both lie recumbent like a pair of corpses on display in an open coffin funeral ceremony, you will both be fine. The suffering starts when you fall asleep, and your limbs start moving to avoid the early onset of rigor mortis. As soon as you turn onto your side, your dear spouse wakes up.

'Stop moving!' your loved one shouts.

Since you cannot remember whether you just turned onto your side or you were pushed there, you let it go and decide to sleep on that side for the rest of the night. At that moment, it feels a much more comfortable position than the petrified mummy position that you assumed for the first two hours of the night. You pull your woolly hat that fell off back on and slip your hands under the pillow to prevent frostbite — don't forget you still have no roof over your head — and think of all the nice, clean places that you had slept in during the first thirty-six years of your life.

No sooner do you drift away than you get hit on the back with your husband's elbow and smacked on the head with his beloved iPad. You can either take a stance and argue your case or smack him back and pretend to be asleep. As you choose the latter, you are now fully awake, though you are both pretending to be asleep. It takes your husband several minutes to stare at the evil machine and try to figure out what happened. Now it's your turn to retaliate for the previous outburst.

'Switch off that damn iPad,' you snarl. 'How am I supposed to sleep with the light shining right in my face?'

This is an obvious exaggeration because your face is turned away from the light, but it's a great subterfuge that allows you to stop feigning sleep. This also seems like a good time for a trip to the bathroom, which entails rearranging all the blankets and pillows. Now you are both ready to sleep again.

The charade of kicking, smacking, and complaining continues in this exact order throughout the night. Until, at around four a.m., you're finally too exhausted to kick back and shout; you hope for a few hours of respite. That's when the cats wake up and start jumping up and down on your legs and meowing into your face. Because the fire in the living room has gone out, the two rascals decide to relocate and sleep on your blanket on top of your legs. Now with two humans, an iPad, and the two cats, there is absolutely no room to manoeuvre in this bed. And so, you resign yourself to spend the rest of the night posed like an Egyptian mummy with two heavy felines at your legs like some divine guards.

During that winter, we didn't get much sleep. Our nocturnal activity would have been better described as deep meditation interrupted by screaming and shouting. The inability to move for many hours at night and the chilly temperatures meant that we both developed rheumatism in our hands and fingers. Many mornings I would wake up and not be able to close my hand into a fist. It took another year and a very hot summer for our hands to recover their normal motor skills. We didn't want to buy a new bed or a new mattress because we had an excellent king-size bed and mattress in storage in Granada. We just had to wait a few months until the house was sealed before bringing our belongings to the new home.

In addition to temporary rheumatism, I also developed a slight PTSD when it came to the weather. Even a year after the reform was complete, I would shudder and get a panic attack each time I heard a raindrop on the roof. In those wretched days, we constantly checked the weather forecast. On bad days, we checked it every hour, hoping for some good news. We used one website that was ninety-eight percent accurate in their hourly forecast. On particularly dreadful days, we would search other weather websites and choose to look at the erroneous forecast just to cheer ourselves up.

'Look — Weather Underground says that it's going to be twenty-eight millimetres of rain and thirty-five-km-an-hour wind,' I would inform my dear husband.

'Is this correct?' he would ask, questioning the pessimistic website.

'I'm not sure,' I would say, encouraging this madness. 'Because HERE it says mostly sunny and light rain.' I would show him another weather site.

'I hope it's sunny today because the guys are getting sick,' Robert would say, concerned about our workers.

'I'm sure it will be OK. It says light rain. It can't be much.'

This conversation would continue in this fashion for a while. At the same time, outside the window, the rain would be falling down horizontally, and the wind would be pirouetting the empty cement bags from the construction site outside our doors.

Rain and wind were the regular topics of conversation now. We just could not figure out how homes were built in colder climates like Poland or England. First, we had been promised to have the roof over our heads in the middle of November. This gave us hope and made our lives worth living again. But with the rain and cold, the workers' enthusiasm for the project started to disappear. The middle of November came and went, and we were still mopping the floors and carrying buckets around the house.

By the end of November, I stopped asking when the roof would be ready and resigned myself to the lifestyle of a homeless person in Irkutsk. Stories of severe hardship started to appear on my reading list. I read the autobiography of a Jewish girl who survived the war by hiding in Lviv's city sewage system with her family. While the story made me realize how good I had it, I could easily empathize with the excerpts detailing how her shelter got flooded with water and how her family fought against the damp and the mould.

A month after our first flooding, black mould started to appear on the walls in our bedroom. We ignored it at first, hoping that it would go away on its own. But it didn't. While we neglected it, it secretly grew in strength and spread. Until one day, I woke up and saw that the whole ceiling over our heads and most of the walls were now quite black. It was definitely time to do something about it.

I went directly to the internet and searched 'black mould'. The opinions on how harmful it was to humans seemed to be divided. Many American contractors on YouTube would wear masks and breathing apparatus to have it removed. This was alarming since we had slept in the mould-covered bedroom for over a month. They showed some of the worst cases of black mould infestation, and they were nowhere near what we had managed to cultivate.

The European vloggers were less panicked about black mould. They agreed that all you needed was a chlorine solution and a sponge. Since we could not decide whom to believe, we asked some of the English people around us. It turned out that black mould is a very common problem in Andalusia. The English seemed to agree that most homes have it. Apparently, washing off the mould with chlorine and repainting your house is a common wintertime activity. One English builder suggested that we use a magic spray that gets rid of the mould.

'I buy it in Gibraltar 'cause they don't have it here.' He told us the secret. 'It's great stuff. You just spray it, and the mould is gone.'

'Hmm.' We looked at him, amazed.

'I think I still have some left at home. I'll get you a tin.'

He never got us a tin. I suspect that his wife told him not to give away this precious concoction that could only be bought in Gibraltar. Once I realized that we were never going to get the magic mould killer, we set aside a weekend to clean the walls with water, chlorine, and a sponge.

I used the powdered chlorine that we had in vast supply for the swimming pool and mixed it generously with water to make a strong potion. I got out the rubber gloves and a sponge and started to wipe the walls. Like magic, the black stuff was removed from the walls. The only trick with removing black mould from your bedroom walls, we learned, was that you have to change the dirty water quite regularly; otherwise, you end up smearing the mould back onto the wall.

We took turns and worked incessantly for several hours. The worst part of the job was removing the mould from the ceiling. As I applied the sponge to the ceiling, my face would be sprayed with tiny particles of super-strong chorine water and mould. For protection, we donned sunglasses and woolly hats and worked in that fashion for another few hours. When we were done, I got off the ladder and looked around.

The room was transformed. From the nasty coalminer's break

room that it had become through our negligence, it was now a respectable accommodation with the walls in the shade of light granite. The room suddenly felt luxurious and posh to us, even though it smelled like a public swimming pool. By now, I had lost any ability to smell, and my eyes were starting to water. I opened the window, despite the pouring rain outside, and went to wash the chlorine and mould crust from my skin.

By eight o'clock, we were all washed and cleaned and well pleased with the day's work. We opened a bottle of wine and started to make supper. As we were discussing which of the episodes of *Grand Designs* to watch that evening, darkness like I had not seen before fell upon us. We sat in the pitch black for a minute or two, not comprehending what had just happened.

I soon realized that the electricity had gone out. It was not the first time in our lives we had experienced a power cut, but here in the Andalusian countryside, with no light pollution and with the heavy clouds covering the moon, the effect was quite scary. The expression 'pitch black' suddenly made sense. It wasn't dark or shady. It was so black that we could not see each other's silhouettes.

I searched the kitchen countertops for my phone and turned it on to help me find the way to the fuse box. Inside, as I expected, the main fuse switch was off. I pulled it up, but it immediately fell down with a resolute click. I tried it a few more times, but it was determined to stay down. I went back and sat on the armchair. We didn't have any candles to light the room, so we relied on the illumination in the phones and the embers in the fireplace. I added a few logs to the fire and opened the vent to light the place. What really hit us hard was that there was nothing for us to do without electricity. Emptiness like I had never felt before fell upon me. There was no internet, no YouTube, no videos to watch. How were we supposed to fill in the hours until it was time to go to bed? I didn't have an e-book reader back then. I could read a book by phone light, but the battery would last only an hour or so.

Not knowing what else to do, we ate our supper by the phone light and went to bed at nine p.m. Lying in bed, I wondered about times past, before people had electricity. I thought of people getting up in complete darkness and getting dressed by candlelight—what a dark, horrible existence. In the morning, we could sleep in. Since there was no electricity, our water pump would not work, so there was no way for us to use the bathroom. I got dressed but then collapsed back onto the bed.

When the workers came in, I found it impossible to get out of bed. I remembered one of the women in *Grand Designs* saying that she could not get out of bed for several weeks because she was too depressed to face the project. Was it my time to resign myself to bed? I wondered. Sadness and dark thoughts came over me, and my limbs refused to move. It must have been late November, and I was too tired and exhausted to even cry. As I lay there, I was immobilised by the wretchedness of my new life; I looked at the layers of dust on every surface, my raggedy clothes and personal belongings crammed in suitcases, and the horrible giant wardrobe that stared me in the face.

We inherited the hideous wardrobe from the previous owners, which was their pride and glory. The faux mahogany, three-door monstrosity with mirrors inside the doors stared me in the face as I lay on my bed. It belonged to horror movies, not a sunny cottage. I suddenly remembered *The Yellow Wallpaper* — a story about a woman's mental breakdown. Locked in her room, the woman peals away the wallpaper to free another female figure hidden behind it. I took another look at the dark menacing wardrobe and understood the story. I had become the madwoman; I wanted to take an axe and smash this hideous creature that was mocking me all the time. 'I hate this new life,' I thought. I missed my beautiful villa in the desert where the electricity never gave in, where Marvie polished the furniture every week and changed my bedsheets, where hot water never ran out and where no strange men were creating a mess in my house every day.

I could hear Robert and the builders in the living room discussing the electricity problem. Without electricity, there was very little for them to do. They figured that the rain must have soaked the cables and that we would have to wait until they were dry again to start work. The idea that I was going to pay all these men a day's wage with them doing nothing was all I needed to get out of bed and get them to work.

As I got out of the bedroom, I saw two of them setting up a system to heat the exposed electric cables with a portable gas blow-torch. I'm not an electrician, but I had a strong conviction that electrical wiring and open flames should not meet. After an hour of chaos and lack of direction, we managed to give everyone a task and waited while the senior builder rewired the fuse box. After his changes to the fuse box's wiring, we only had light in the living room. Now, each time it rained, not only did I worry about the flooding, but I also waited for the electricity to switch off. But now, we were ready for this calamity and copied a bunch of movies to our laptop to watch while the darkness invaded our primitive dwelling.

We lived through November with the promise of a roof. We were going to have it finished the first week of December, but then a disaster stuck that set us back another week. As the workers were finalizing the roof and getting it ready to pour the supporting concrete, a hundred and fifty-kilometre-an-hour hurricane swept across our valley. It had started in Malaga and destroyed a petrol station and several buildings. As it continued its vicious journey through inland Andalusia, it swept away barns, small outbuildings, gardening sheds, and anything else that was not tied down or anchored with concrete.

At that stage, our roof consisted of slabs of polystyrene that were tied down to a steel mesh with thin wires. The night before the hurricane, the workers had just finished the last internal supporting wall on the roof. That night, the hurricane wreaked havoc outside our house. It destroyed our neighbour's water collection system and had strewn the corrugated iron sheets that usually lie around any self-respecting working farm across the wheat fields. It shook the olives off the branches and broke the limbs of many an oak tree.

Used to living with extreme weather, with wind hollering over our heads and rain pounding on our exposed walls with all its strength, we did not give much thought to what was going on outside that night. And that's perhaps for the best, for we might have been decapitated by one of the flying metal sheets or trapped in our own steel mesh. In the best-case scenario, we would have been knocked down by one of the polystyrene blocks dancing across the fields outside our house.

Oblivious to the night's mayhem, we woke up to witness the aftermath of the hurricane. At first, I thought that it had snowed the night before. The field was dotted with what appeared to be snowdrifts. On closer inspection, we found out that these were the polystyrene blocks that had been covering our roof the night before. We got dressed and started to collect them from the field. Walking back to the house with the piles of polystyrene, I saw that the internal supporting wall that was supposed to support parts of the new roof had been demolished. That was the final straw. I stopped dreaming of having a roof over my head ever again and resigned myself to this new cave-like lifestyle. But, miraculously, the builders, although sympathetically deflated by the setback, continued as ever, and two weeks later, we were ready to pour the concrete on the roof.

The morning when the concrete mixer truck showed up in our driveway is a morning that I may never forget. I was armed with a camera and filmed every boring detail. Like a proud father attending the birth of his baby, I wanted to be part of the moment but had no clue how I could contribute. Filming every mundane aspect of it gave me some sense of importance and made me look like I was doing something. But the job was really done by a crane operator who filled a giant funnel with concrete and then lifted it over our heads and dropped it onto the roof. The mass was then spread out by the builders.

I filmed this exact same sequence around ten times when I realized that my movie needed another angle. So, I went around behind the house and filmed it from there for half an hour. In need of new content for my film, I decided to include the driver of the concrete mixer, who just stood by his truck and pulled a lever when shouted at by the crane operator.

After two hours of filming, I decided that I had covered everything but stayed put with my camera in hand in case there were some new developments. There weren't any. After five hours of steady work and two large concrete mixer trucks emptying their loads, we finally had the roof of our house. We were not completely watertight at that stage, however. We still needed roof tiles, windows, and some doors, but it was a massive leap forward in our journey. It took another two weeks for the workers to tile the roof, and it was ready a week before Christmas.

ELEVEN
MEET THE NEIGHBOURS

F eeling ecstatic about the roof, we decided to organise a big party for all our neighbours and everyone we had met since we moved to Spain. We first went to our devoted website and checked the weather forecast to find a nice and sunny day for the roof party or *fiesta para techa*, as we explained to the invitees. Then, in our enthusiasm, we started to invite everybody that we came across.

First, we invited all the builders and casual labourers who had been working with us since October. We invited people who sold and delivered our building materials, our accountant, the banker, and a few shopkeepers. Most of the people in the latter group struggled to understand what kind of fiesta it was. Since they did not live nearby, they had not seen us go day by day without a roof. They might have thought that our enthusiasm for a roof was a little bit over the top, and most did not come to the party. The different trades and professions made up the scope of our acquaintances. I was not too hopeful about the group dynamics that might evolve, considering that most of these people did not know one another. We sat down and made a list of all the people we knew were not related to our house renovation adventure.

There were three. The truth was that between renovating the cottage, working on the language app, living in a cold and damp house, and having only dirty work clothes to wear, we had not made any friends *per se*. On most days, we were too exhausted to go out to any bar to seek friends; and more importantly, we did not have the time to sit in a bar looking for friends. When the workers were not around, we were busy making orders for windows and doors, buying fireplaces, ordering tiles and appliances, and planning the next steps of the build. If we ever went out, it was to the hardware store, the carpenter supplies, or the tile shop.

'We really have no friends,' I stated the obvious.

'What about Mercedes, José, and Rafa? They must come.' Robert insisted.

These were some of our neighbours. We knew most of them now. We live in a valley where the houses are spread along the road that goes on for several kilometres. Most houses are a few hundred metres apart from one another, which means that the neighbours don't bother one another but at the same time manage to maintain a sense of community.

The first neighbours we met were Mercedes and her husband, Juan Carlos, whose house was just opposite ours. It was during our first summer in the house, a year before we moved to Andalusia to do the reform. We heard that they were an elderly couple who lived in Montefrio and only visited their campo house a few times a week. They kept some chickens, three goats, some cats, and two dogs — as we guessed by the noises coming from the house. Before we met them in person, we were treated to a flamenco recital coming from their property every evening from ten o'clock until around midnight.

The first night that we heard the very loud music and the horrendous singing, we thought that our neighbour, Juan Carlos, had gotten drunk and lay in his garden singing at the top of his lungs. We didn't dare go down to his house and ask him to keep it down as the tone of the singing voice was rather decisive and ready to fight. And so, we sat on our patio at night, smoking, drinking, and listening to him slaughter chickens with his singing.

I felt deeply disappointed. We had bought a house in a secluded spot in the middle of nowhere to get away from this type of unprovoked manic noise-making that we often endured when living in apartment blocks or housing compounds. What was supposed to be a tranquil and serene existence was now being disturbed by a mad flamenco soloist.

It has to be said that my judgement of the singing might have been biased since I have never acquired a taste for flamenco. The type of gipsy flamenco that we get around Montefrio often reminds me of the kind of screaming produced by a drunk person while walking on hot coals and glass. It's never one long, continuous cry but rather a series of random shrieks and squeals uttered at different time intervals and with differing force. The guitarist and the vocalist are never in sync either. They both seem to be performing different pieces. As music, I find flamenco nerve-racking.

Listening to a private flamenco concert every night for a week made me understand why some music critics say that it expresses the poor man's angst. The torment was evident in every note. As we listened to the drunk wailing the second night, a storm was brewing inside our heads. Something had to be done about this. Were we to be hostage to this mad singer forever? If a house was an ordinary consumer product, I would have gone straight back to the shop and demanded my money back. But, unlike with smaller purchases in life, a house is something you can't give back.

Another issue was that neither of us had the faintest idea of how to approach this subject in Spanish. This type of situation required some lexical hedging and the use of full sentences. We also were loath to meet our neighbour for the first time under these circumstances. This would not bode well for our future relationship. The mysterious thing was that we could not hear a single peep coming from that house throughout the day except for the goats, chickens, cats, and dogs. We could not detect any human shapes working in the garden or sitting on the veranda. Yet, every night at exactly the same time, the singing would start and go on for a couple of hours.

It was on the third night that we made a breakthrough in our mystery. First, we started to wonder about the exact sequence of the musical numbers. Surely a drunk maniac would not remember exactly what he had performed the night before and in what order. As we listened closely, we started to think that the music was recorded and turned on and off automatically. This suspicion was confirmed on the fourth night when the damned CD kept skipping its track and played the first twenty seconds of a song over and over for two hours until the equipment shut itself off. Listening to what we thought was an intoxicated farmer, letting go of his life's worries and fears in a musical piece was one thing. There was a dash of old charm and romance in it. But listening to a broken flamenco CD for two hours was on par with psychological tortures invented by the CIA.

. We were now so disenchanted with the place that neither of us dared to discuss the noise issue. In line with some misguided interpretation of linguistic relativity, I hoped that not talking about the problem may make it disappear from our lives. The next day we worked for several hours carrying stuff to the skip. When we sat down to lunch, we noticed a car parked in the neighbour's driveway. This was a new development. It was time to act and meet the neighbours.

We grabbed a bottle of wine and a box of chocolate-coated dates — we had brought several boxes with us from Al Ain to give as gifts to people we met — and we ran down the hill to Mercedes and Juan Carlos's house. On the way, I managed to rehearse a couple of sentences in my head to introduce us to these people.

As we approached their house, I saw old Juan Carlos standing by his pile of firewood with a small axe. He was chopping wood sticks into smaller pieces while smoking cheap Andalusian tobacco. I worked hard with the first person singular and plural forms of the verb *be* and explained who we were, what our names were, and that we were both teachers. The conversation was stagnant, but it covered the first two units of my Spanish coursebook, and I felt obliged to give this man all our personal details. We were, after all, *extranjeros* who had just moved across the road.

Juan Carlos grunted and repeated what I told him. He then looked at us and said something that sounded like *propietario*. I guessed that he was asking whether we were the new owners of the house on the hill and confirmed his deduction with multiple exclamations consisting of the word *si*. As I handed him the wine and the dates, his wrinkled face lit up. He inspected the bottle — it was a cheap Crianza, but it was all we had at hand when we ran out of the house. He seemed pleased with the vintage and called his wife. A petite lady with short dark hair came out of the house.

As soon as she saw us, she started to talk incessantly. There was a slight whine to her pitch, and we were not sure whether it meant anything. Juan Carlos showed her the wine bottle and the dates and repeated everything I told him about us. She kept on interrupting her husband's account with squeals of excitement and clasping her hands in front of her chest in joy as if she had just heard that they had won the lottery. She nodded and waved her arms while listening and then started telling us something. The only two words that we could distinguish were Gabi and *tia*. We remembered that *tia* means *aunt* and puzzled the rest together. Mercedes was Young Gabi's aunt. Her father had built our house, and she and her brother, Old Gabi, were born and raised there.

This was very interesting, but since I had no more Spanish left in me, I was not able to ask her any more questions. And so I listened to her, picking up random words and filling up the gaps with my own conjecture. We learned that her husband, Juan Carlos, had been in *guardia civil* for over twenty years. This was valuable information, and we were glad we did not call the police to report the disturbance with the broken CD player.

Mercedes talked *at* us for several more minutes. It was all very pleasant, even though I had no idea what she was talking about. Then Juan Carlos said that he had to prepare a barbecue — we understood that from the word *barbacoa* and the sticks that lay scattered around him — and so we said *adios* and *hasta luego* and went back to our house. We didn't hear the crazy flamenco CD ever again, and they never mentioned it. I suspect it may have been an old policeman's cunning way to keep thieves at bay by pretending that someone was occupying the house when, in fact, they were away.

Another neighbour who we met that first summer was Rafa. As we sat on the patio one summer evening, we noticed a short, sturdy figure jumping up and down around a large pile of hay bales in the small wheat field adjacent to our land. As it was already August, the wheat had been collected and the hay bales had been left in the field until a tractor would come and collect them in September. As we watched the man dance around the hay bales, we assumed that he had some vested interest in the hay and the field. Soon, we saw raindrops start dropping onto the ground and realized that the old man was trying to cover his hay bales with a huge piece of plastic. Since the bales were stacked in a neat pile that was over two metres high, he was going to be fighting the merciless plastic cover and the wind that was now picking up for a long time.

Not wanting to watch him get wet and his hay get ruined, Robert went out to the field and helped him cover the bales and tie the plastic around the stack. He came back after a few minutes and told me that the old man was called Rafa and lived in the next house down the road.

The next day Rafa came by with a cardboard box filled with the biggest and ripest tomatoes and peppers I had ever seen. It was the nicest welcome gift that we could hope for, and throughout that summer, we received a steady supply of tomatoes, cucumbers, peppers, onions, courgettes, and watermelons. They were of the highest quality and tasted the way real fruit and vegetables should taste. The fruit and vegetables that our neighbours eat are grown on small vegetable patches scattered among the olive groves and are cultivated with great love and patience from March to late November. It is not exactly organic food since a good amount of pesticide and fertilizer is used to grow it. But what makes the food grown on Andalusian soil taste so special and unique is that these plants have a chance to fully mature in the scorching sun.

And the plants take full advantage of this situation. Delicious watermelons rest peacefully in the shade of the olive trees and get bigger and bigger until they're the size of cannonballs. The tomatoes are the size of handballs and deep crimson when you cut into them. They taste sweet and sour at the same time and are so juicy that sometimes all you wish for on a hot summer afternoon is a sliced tomato with some salt and pepper. The red peppers are sweet too, and the onions are flavourful and savoury. Once, we made a whole pot of French onion soup from a single giant onion.

This quality of produce is generally not to be found in European supermarkets, where tomatoes and seedless watermelons taste like water. The peppers taste like juicy cardboard, and the courgettes remind you of sponges. In Andalusia, a simple tomato and onion salad tastes like heaven — it is sweet and sour and slightly tangy. The homegrown food is so good that I've seen our friends' kids eat raw baby garlic heads from our garden as if it was candy. I've had parents warn me apologetically, as I set food on the table, that their child won't like the lettuce, only to see the same child polish off the plate and ask for seconds. And that was not due to my marvellous cooking skills — they're average. Such juvenile appreciation of the food is a function of the food quality that we can grow here.

And so, we were very grateful for all the wonderful produce that we received, and we looked forward to times when we would be able to grow our own fruits and vegetables. That summer, Robert also developed an intense interest in Rafa and everything that our neighbour did. He would go over to Rafa's house and spend hours watching the old man go about his day, which usually involved: cutting steel rods into supports of some kind, cutting wood, digging holes, making ditches, moving things around, and all sorts of things that retired farmers liked to busy themselves with.

What they discussed was a mystery to me because Robert could not say much past *Soy Robert*. And I assumed that he had covered that topic at the first encounter. For the next couple of weeks, every sentence from my husband's mouth started with *Rafa*.

'Rafa has an angle grinder. He cut this piece for me.'

'Rafa has a nice garden. It's like paradise.'

'Rafa said that it's going to rain.'

'Rafa helped me dig the soil away from the fence. He lent me his *pico*.'

'Rafa can dig really fast — he's so strong.'

At some stage, Robert's reports on Rafa started to remind me of a child giving daily school updates to his mum. While Rafa seemed to be a supernatural being to Robert with his powerful work ethic, he became invaluable to us the next year when we came back to settle for good. Since there is not much going on in our valley, Rafa decided to view our construction project as someone else might view their favourite sitcom. As soon as there was some significant activity — like a digger knocking something down or a loaded concrete truck laying a new foundation — Rafa would appear and watch the activities for hours at a time. He just stood there, his rotund silhouette facing the action. He did not lift a finger on site — and we were grateful that he didn't, because of his age — but he seemed to enjoy watching young men work like donkeys.

Sometimes, standing in the open air and watching good work being done is just as fulfilling as doing it yourself. Usually, after a couple of hours of taking it all in, Rafa would go home and start his own projects. At some point in late October, we realized that our well was drying out. Ironically, while we were getting flooded on a regular basis, the well was on its last legs. The amount of water used every day for the construction was far too much for our little well to supply, and the water level was frighteningly low. Now daily, I would go down to the well, open the lid, and stare down into the darkness at the exposed planks that supported the pump at the bottom of the well.

When we came in August, the water had been a few metres over the planks. Now it was well below them. Instead of the clear spring water that once graced the well, I was staring at its muddy dregs. Knowing what the future would bring, Rafa suggested that we buy a trailer and a plastic thousand-litre cube to bring water to the house. A trailer with a water cube on its back is a common sight where we live, and so we were not put off by his suggestion. Rafa told us that we could bring water from our municipal tap in the village of Montefrio.

TWELVE
BRING THE WATER

R afa seemed adamant that a trailer with a cube was an
essential purchase for our future survival, so one day we
went with him to a trailer manufacturer in Priego and chose
a trailer that he advised us was the best for country roads. We then
went with him to a farmer's centre and purchased the prerequisite one-
thousand-litre cube. As we drove back with this expensive new
purchase, I had my doubts about how necessary it was. Little did I
know that the following summer, our well would dry up completely
and that we would rely on this trailer and the little cube to bring water
to the house for more than seven months of the year. In hindsight, it
was one of the best purchases of our lives.

How farmers previously survived for centuries in Andalusia without these two essentials has been a puzzle to me. While I can maybe fathom getting used to life without the internet, I don't think I would ever get used to life without running water. Imagine spending precious hours every day walking to some hidden *fuente* in the mountains to bring some water home in small buckets — just enough to drink and to cook with.

But back then, the water worries were not yet part of my daily life, and I wondered whether we hadn't gotten carried away by indulging in this expensive purchase. We arrived at home and dropped Rafa off at his house. The workers had already gone, so we decided to go to Montefrio to get water for the cement mixer for the next day.

The municipal tap in Montefrio is located in a picturesque spot behind the main square and next to stunning rock formations that border the village. Because of its proximity to natural springs, the area is lush with pink oleander, red marvels-of-Peru, and deep green ivy. There are giant palm trees and silhouettes of several old mansions. It's also a favourite spot of the local drunks, who gather in close distance from the tap to watch farmers and campo dwellers like us come and collect water for their daily chores.

The drunks usually stand in a small group and share a one-litre bottle of Cruz Campo beer. They shout, scream, and giggle like little girls with nothing else to do to occupy their hours. I imagine their wives at home getting a few hours' respite from the raging madness that seems to seep from their very being. Ironing and cleaning, trying to keep a semblance of a normal life until the drunken idiot gets back home and shatters the little peace that his wife and kids may enjoy. Soon we would have to collect water from the tap in Montefrio a few times a week, and we could easily recognise the familiar faces of this ensemble. However, since it was our first time at the pump, we stood by the tap as the cube slowly filled and did not know where to look.

We could hear them jeering as we figured things out with the pipe running from the tap and the cube on the trailer, but we chose to discuss the conkers that were scattered across the pavement instead. After fifteen minutes, the cube was full, and we set off home. As we drove home, Robert noticed that something was wrong. He got out and, on closer inspection, realized that the cube had shifted on the trailer when it was still empty, and it was now off centre. It was too far forward on the trailer, towards the car, and putting a great force on the hook and the back chassis. We could not drive like this home. The chances were that the one-ton cargo would cause damage to the car on the way up the mountain to our house.

We drove a little bit away from the water pump until we saw a suitable spot with some olive trees by the road and a deep ditch. We stopped and opened the tap to get rid of the water. The water flooded the trees and the side of the road. Because the exit tap was small, it was taking longer than we expected. All we could do was wait and watch the water run. As we stood there throwing water into someone's field, our contractor drove past and waved at us with a somewhat confused look on his face. Then we saw the delivery truck from the brickyard that usually delivered our building materials. He also gave us a friendly hoot. A few more people that we knew went past us before the wretched cube was empty.

I wondered about what stories they would tell that evening. How would they explain why the two foreigners were flooding the side of the road? I never found out because more cube worries were to come that evening that overshadowed this business. Once the cube was empty, we went back to the water pump, obviously now giving our local drunks something to think about too. Were they having a group session of *déjà vu* that they each refused to admit to? Any normal person would not have been able to explain how we were able to drive away to the campo — presumably to our house — and be back fifteen minutes later, ready to load another ton of water.

This time, we paid closer attention to the filling process and made sure that the cube was well centred on the trailer for the trip home. We filled it like experts — it was, after all, the second time in our lives that we were doing it — and off we went. We felt like we were moving forward with this new activity. Our enthusiasm was short-lived, though, just outside Montefrio when, going uphill, Robert noticed water gushing out from the top of the cube. I looked at the back

127

window and saw that, indeed, water was gushing out from the top of the cube in huge waves. This was happening because we forgot to screw the plastic cover back to the cube's top. We must have left it on the wall next to the pump. Since the road between Montefrio and our house is narrow and twisty, there was no space where we could turn back with the trailer — we also were loath to have to go back to the damned pump for the third time that evening. We decided that we would look for the cover another day.

'They must sell spare ones in a *ferretería*, for sure.' We convinced ourselves that losing the cover for a cube was a common occurrence in the countryside, and hence any hardware shop would have ample supplies of these. But, no, they don't, and we never got the cover back. We drove home, throwing water left and right, back and forth. We were maybe two kilometres from home when a police car from the *guardia civil* drove behind us and started flashing their lights at us. Since we were driving up a very steep hill at the time, Robert did not dare stop in case we would not be able to start again. The *guardia* did not seem bothered about how steep the road was. They drove next to us and rolled down their windows.

We expected them to stop us for causing a hazard on the road, and I had some basic Spanish with excuses and apologies running through my head. But the policeman did not seem interested in stopping us. He shouted something across to us, and when Robert shouted back that he did not understand, the policeman gestured to the water flowing out of the cube and used sign language to indicate that we may be in need of a cover for the top of the cube.

We thanked him through the rolled-down window only to see their car speed up and pass us. Relieved that it was the end of our troubles for that night, we drove up our driveway and parked the trailer next to the cement mixer and the pile of building sand. We felt quite pleased with our afternoon's work and could not wait to see the workers' faces the next day when they would see a ton of water strategically positioned next to the cement mixer.

But with the car still attached to the trailer, the whole tableau did not look as neat as I hoped for, so I suggested that we unhook the trailer from the car and move the car out of the builders' way. Unhooking a trailer with a ton of water, minus what we spilt on the way from Montefrio, is not an easy task and should not be attempted by light-hearted folks. It should also not be attempted by two city goons who have just moved to the campo.

Nothing in our whole experience of country living made us look as stupid as what was about to happen. And had we just paused for a minute and considered the basic physics of the operation, we might have avoided the near-death experience that followed.

While Robert started to unhook the steel safety wire that connects the trailer to the car, I started to roll down the third wheel at the front of the trailer. Once the trailer wheel touched the ground, some strength and persistence needed to be applied to remove the trailer from the car hook. It was heavy work that involved a lot of jiggling and shaking.

All of a sudden, the trailer arm unhooked itself from the car, but instead of stopping above the hook, it flew in the air right in front of our noses. Time slowed down, and we watched in astonishment our brand-new trailer do a backward somersault in front of us like a surreal elephant. It eventually landed on its back door and remained in that position with the vicious trailer arm triumphantly facing the skies. The cube was still attached to it because we had secured it with tie-downs. What happened was that the ton of water in the cube was still balancing inside it after the twisty journey up and down steep hills when we decided to unhook. The gentle motion of water inside the cube must have unbalanced the trailer and made it flip over backwards.

As I looked in shock at the brand new trailer, now smashed and dented on its back, it occurred to me that I had nearly lost my face, or part of it, from the flying arm of the trailer. I remembered a National Geographic program about a man in Siberia whose face was half eaten by a bear. To show the wonders of modern medicine, the producers flew him to Germany or Austria to reconstruct his face.

Thinking of this poor man with the bear teeth clearly imprinted on his skull made me see a glint of hope in the near-miss situation. By now, it was getting dark and cold, and we both fell silent. There was no point in assessing the damage because it would only upset us further. We also could not lift the trailer back on its wheels until all the water from the cube had drained out, down the driveway, uselessly. And so, we went inside to spend another cold and sombre evening in our half-broken house.

THIRTEEN
MEETING OF THE LIGHT

The first autumn, when we started renovating the house, our dear neighbour Rafa took us under his wing. Like a mother duck preparing her young ones for departure, he made sure that we learned some of the ways of the campo. He never commented on the trailer fiasco, even though he could clearly see its embarrassing silhouette planted at the top of our driveway. I wonder whether his pity on us had been sparked by seeing what we had done to the spanking-new trailer. Or perhaps it was seeing us live without the roof over our heads that made him want to help us.

On one November day, he appeared with flower bulbs wrapped in a newspaper. These were saffron bulbs that he had dug up from his own garden. Not trusting that I would do right by them, he took a *pico*, or a small pickaxe, from his car, and we walked around the land for him to find the best spots where we could plant the saffron bulbs. When he was satisfied with a spot, he would dig a small hole and I would plant the magic bulb. Saffron is a pretty little flower that one might confuse with a crocus. If planted in the right spot, it does not need much attention. It multiplies easily and does not require any care throughout the year. It's one of these plants that thrives when left alone. And every year, you forget about your saffron bulbs until November, when their dainty purple flowers start popping up around the land.

The difference between a crocus flower and a saffron flower is that the crocus is a beacon of spring and summer. In Andalusia, saffron flowers indicate that winter is near. They appear in plentiful abundance, but only for a short time. You also need to find the best time to harvest them just before the heavy rains and winds arrive since they will destroy the precious spice. The saffron spice comes from the orange strands that you pull from each flower. The easiest way to harvest saffron is to remove all the flowers from their stems *en masse* and place the delicate strands in a clear and dry container. A few weeks after I planted my bulbs for the next year, Rafa brought me a basket of saffron flowers ready to dissect. I spread the beautiful consignment on the patio table, prepared a small plate for the spice, and started plucking the thin strands from the flowers.

I felt sorry for the pretty flowers that were being discarded and placed them carefully to the side. I put some water in a shallow bowl and hoped to keep the flower heads fresh for a few more days so that we could continue to enjoy them. Saffron plucking is a thankless task. While you go through the flowers, you realize that the amount of debris is significantly larger than the gain. While the pile of discarded flowers was getting higher and higher, the amount of saffron on my little plate was barely noticeable.

I had to be careful not to touch the sides of the precious strands since most of the saffron dust would be transferred to my hand. As it began to get windy that afternoon, I moved my work inside to the living room to protect the specks of dust from being blown away.

When I was done, I had a mountain of flower heads and a few millimetres of saffron in a small glass jar. I placed the jar in the kitchen cupboard and had to be careful not to throw it away by mistake.

Since collecting it took so much mindless work, I was reluctant to use it in any old dish. As a result, I would often forget that we had it. A couple of times that winter, I would spot what I thought was an empty glass jar on the shelf and stare at it, wondering why I had put an empty jar in the spice cupboard. Only then would I remember the orange film at the bottom of the jar.

Tired of falling for the same trick every week, I eventually threw the precious spice into a paella dish. The experience was somewhat disappointing. I expected an outburst of flavour like I had never tasted before, but the result was mediocre at best. The next year, I let the attractive saffron flowers that Rafa helped me plant live and enjoy the sunshine until the last autumn day. I did not think that a micro dash of a somewhat underwhelming spice warranted another saffron flower massacre.

One day in early December, Rafa brought us a piece of paper that read: *Estimados vecinos hay reunión de luz miércoles 17.00*. He clearly did not trust our listening skills in Spanish and decided that putting this important information on paper would give us time to translate and comprehend the message. He was, of course, quite correct in his assessment. Robert took the note and read aloud the only part that was clear to him:

'*Miércoles cinco.*' He stated these two words as if they explained everything.

He then passed the note to me, but I could also only understand *Wednesday at five*. *Reunión* was obviously a false friend because we'd only been in Spain for a few months, and there was no one here to reunite us with. But we both nodded and pretended to understand.

Rafa took it that we agreed to show up and left us with the note. As soon as we saw the back of his car, we activated the internet and went straight to our old friend Google Translate. We found out that the first two words showed appreciation of us as neighbours. We suspected that it was a regular salutation. Once we got *esteemed neighbours*, the rest still did not make sense, however. According to

Google, there was 'a meeting of the light on Wednesday at 5 p.m.' Since this did not make any sense to us, we then checked the meaning of the individual words and all possible semantic fields related to these words, but we kept ending with 'a gathering of light'. I left the translation for a couple of days to approach it with an unbiased mind.

In the meantime, we looked for clues in our neighbours' behaviour. One clue came early on one December morning. We were still in deep sleep (as the workers only showed up at eight am) when we heard a horrible screaming outside. The screaming might not have been that loud, but let's not forget that we had no roof and several gaping holes in our house; hence, it was not the most soundproof of dwellings. As we sat up in the bed, perplexed, the terrifying squeal erupted again.

'They're killing a pig,' Robert announced as if it was something that happened every day.

While I tried to go about my morning, ignoring the horrifying wake-up call that I had been subject to, Robert got dressed and went up to José's house to see the event. José' house is on top of the hill behind ours — it was his son, Pepe, who pulverised our grass the year before. He's also the cousin of Mercedes and Old Gabi and also grew up in the valley.

Robert came back a few hours later and told me that the family had killed two pigs. While the men drank brandy and sweet anis, the women of the house worked around giant cauldrons with boiling hot water. The whole event took place in their open courtyard, and the meat was being processed with speed and proficiency. The blood was collected for the local speciality called *morcilla*, or blood sausage, with fried onion. Every part of the animals was being utilized.

The women would spend another few weeks preparing sausages and preserving meat for the whole year. Since José regularly gifts us with a few packets of his homemade *salchichón* and *morcilla* for Christmas, I can attest to their superior quality. As we later found out from a shopkeeper in Montefrio, the *matanza*, or pig slaughter, takes place in the late fall every year. On the way to the shop that afternoon, we saw a pig's carcass hanging on a patio of one of the houses by the road. Now, we thought, the clues about the mystical *reunión de luz* were falling into place.

Armed with this new information, we went over Rafa's note again and agreed that *reunión de luz* must be some kind of a post-pig-killing party. I imagined the chummy farmers gathered by a giant bonfire while women prepared pork chops to be slow-roasted over an open fire; people eating and drinking in an evening celebration of the horrible slaughter committed earlier in the week. All this in my mind was happening at twilight as part of some long-forgotten pagan ritual — hence: *reunión de luz*, 'meeting of the light'. Now we got really excited, especially for the large haunches of pork that I imagined would be cooked over an open fire. I'd only ever seen it done on cooking shows, and I thought of this mode of cooking as some kind of a fairy tale. To contribute to the festivities, I made a huge bowl of potato salad. I thought that it would complement succulent pulled pork quite well. On Wednesday afternoon, we packed the giant bowl of cold potato salad and a six-pack of one-litre bottles of San Miguel beer and drove in the direction of Rafa's house. When we parked outside his house, we noticed that his car was not there. Since we assumed that the party would take place in his house, we were somewhat confused. We expected to see at least some guests and some party preparations. But as we looked through the car window, we noted the patio was empty and the doors and windows were shut.

We must have been parked outside his house for some time because his wife, Loli, came out after a few minutes. She figured that we were looking for the party's location and directed us to a house further down the valley. We asked her why she was not going, and she said that she had to look after Rafa's dying father.

It made sense, so we waved goodbye and moved off in the direction of the party. As we came close to the house Loli sent us to, we saw many cars parked outside. This looked more like a party scene. We parked next to the other cars and looked through the windshield at the gathered crowd. We knew some of the neighbours — Rafa, José, and Jaime were all there, but there were also many new faces. As my Spanish was still a bit wobbly, I took deep breaths and left the car, bracing myself for the avalanche of quick and loud talk. The scene in front of us still did not look right. Yes, there were about ten people. But there was no food, no drinks, no rustic tables set out on the driveway — and definitely, no party atmosphere. As we were still new to this country and only lived here permanently for four months, most of which were spent renovating our house and not socializing — I kept an open mind. Perhaps this was a Spanish party. I had no idea. But we did decide to leave the potato salad and the beers in the car for the time being.

'Let's see what's going on here first,' I suggested.

Robert agreed. We got out of the car and waved at Rafa and José, who were listening to the other men talking all at once. The men stood in one circle and were talking about something quite fervently. There were only two women present, and they were not included in the circle of men. They were in the background, collecting saffron flowers. A thought flashed through my mind that they were collecting the saffron to season the succulent pig that was still on my mind.

'Go and talk to them,' said Robert, who was always eager to send me out to talk to complete strangers.

As I'm not too crazy about talking to people, even on the best of occasions, the prospect of talking to two total strangers in a language that I wasn't fluent in was not very appealing. But since I was on their property (I assumed one of them was the owner of the house that I was standing in front of), I decided to make some effort and be polite. I also hoped they may be roasting that pig later on, so it was best to be in their good graces.

Having a witty and engaging conversation in a foreign language is a skill that takes years to develop. I still don't possess it in Spanish, so my usual trick is to point to things around me, name them, and use simple adjectives to describe them. As Spaniards are generally eager to talk, I usually get a good response, and an innocent bystander might think that my interlocutor and I are having a meaningful chat. Unfortunately, most of the time, I'm engaging in a discussion about the woodiness of a wooden chair and the strength of a strong concrete slab.

This time was no different. As soon as I saw the saffron flowers, I had my topic laid out for me. After I introduced myself to the ladies, I got straight to the point.

'*Azafrán*,' I stated, pointing at the flowers.

They confirmed in loud and cheerful Spanish and went on talking about the flowers for a bit. Worried that they may ask me questions I wouldn't understand, I took the conversation into my own hands and added, '*Muy bonito.*'

The ladies were overjoyed. They cheered and saluted my judgement and confirmed my exquisite assessment of this particular species of flora. On this good note, I decided to end the conversation and pointed to the group of men, suggesting that I had to go talk to them now. The women nodded and went back to picking the flower heads. Since I had absolutely no intention of taking part in whatever the men were talking about, I stood on the fringe of their group and pretended to be listening. I nodded occasionally and looked at the grass.

'What are they talking about?' I heard Robert whisper behind me.

'I have no idea.' I smiled and pretended that I was interpreting for my husband.

'I think the party is in La Viñuela,' Robert said, his hopes still up. 'They have a car with a table over there. I think they're ready to go to roast the pig.'

As I looked in the direction Robert pointed, there was indeed a pickup with a big folded table tied to the back.

'Maybe we will indeed go to another place for this party,' I thought to myself. 'Maybe this is just a meeting point before we go there.'

I imagined the twilight party among the olive groves. It sounded enchanting. While I'd hoped to lie low, our talking got the crowd's attention.

Now Rafa was retelling me everything that the men had discussed so far. While he talked in his thick Andalusian accent, he kept pointing over the hills in the direction of a hamlet called La Viñuela and repeating the word *luz*.

'I think you're right,' I told Robert. 'I think the party is going to be in La Viñuela, but they are waiting for the sun to go down.' I loosely interpreted the two words that I understood.

But things were not adding up completely. A few other words that

I managed to gather from Rafa's rapid flow of campo Spanish had something to do with *line* and *voltage*. As others joined in explaining the electricity problem to us, it became clear that the meeting was about *electricity*.

While *luz* means 'light', it's also commonly used to refer to electricity. The several houses in our valley are connected by very old (and very thin) electric cables. The poles are made of wood, and in strong winds, the antique cables are often ripped away from the glass isolators at the top of the poles, leaving us all without electricity for hours. In addition, the cables that we have can only carry a low voltage. Consequently, when I turn on a modern water kettle, all the lightbulbs in the house dim and flicker. When we want to start the air pressure pump, we need to switch off all the house's electronic devices. It's also virtually impossible to run a swimming pool pump and a water pump at the same time. One of them always switches itself off.

Needless to say, we don't have a microwave oven or a toaster, as these modern luxuries would definitely suck all the electricity from the whole valley. As my neighbour Maria told me, there are times when she can't even start her washing machine. This made me feel very bad because our house is the first in the valley, and so it felt like she was accusing me of hogging the electricity. The problem of weak voltage and archaic electricity poles was why all our neighbours had gathered for the *reunion de luz*. Since neither Robert nor I had any idea of what could be done to fix it, we were happy to leave this issue with our esteemed neighbours.

As I listened to my neighbours exchange complaints about the electricity supply, I nodded in agreement and interjected with a sombre *Claro!* now and again. Since we were all in agreement that something had to be done about the poor electricity supply, the members of the assembly started to peter out. No one indicated that they were going to a pig-roasting party. And so, Robert and I went back to the car and drove back home, where we ate copious amounts of potato salad and drank cold beer that was nicely chilled in the car.

Even though my imaginary pig roasting party was a fiasco, I felt content that evening. I was happy that we left the food and drink in the car as it spared us some embarrassment. But more important was the feeling you get when you know that you are part of a community. There is no word in English or Polish that describes it. It's somewhere between the German word *heimlig* and the English word *safe*. It's a feeling of peace and tranquillity because you know you can rely on the people around you. They are hardy people, hard-working and down-to-earth. They welcomed us without any prejudice and accepted our broken Spanish and lack of farming experience. They were willing to help us solve problems and eager too. I felt that I was part of something that I hadn't been since I left my hometown almost twenty years earlier. I was home.

FOURTEEN
A SPANISH PARTY

The *reunión de luz* was great because we met most of the neighbours from our valley. The two women who were picking saffron were Encarnación, or Encarna, and her best friend, Rocio. Rocio, which means *dew*, is an Andalusian name that has been testing my Spanish pronunciation for years. The owner of the house outside of which the meeting took place was Rocio's husband, Paco. There was also Juan — commonly referred to as 'Don Queso' because he owns a famous cheese factory in Montefrio — and a few other olive farmers. Most of these farmers own land in our valley but don't live here permanently. For our roof party, we invited all the neighbours that we had met at the *reunión de luz*, our builders with their families, and two expats who we befriended since we had moved to Spain in August.

I felt it would be a good idea for the neighbours to have a nose around our house. After all, we were the only *extranjeros* in the valley, so they deserved to get to know us. I consulted the weather website and chose a sunny day. Since we were not in a position to entertain inside the house — only the tiny living room/kitchen and an adjacent bedroom were habitable — the party had to take place outside. In Andalusia, even in December, the blue skies and the strong sun allows us to party outside. I decided on a day a few days before Christmas because I thought everyone would be in a festive mood.

A couple of days before the party, we realized that, in our enthusiasm, we had invited over thirty people.

'Usually, only half will show up,' I reassured Robert, who was nervously counting how many chickens he would have to barbecue and how many pork ribs we would need to buy.

'If there are twenty people, we'll be lucky,' I said, driving home my point.

On the morning of the party, we woke up with a ton of things to do before the guests' arrival at two — the usual lunchtime in Andalusia. While a barbecue is always a good idea for a big party — because it takes away a lot of pressure off the hostess, who can designate the cooking to her husband — there were still lots of things to prepare. In addition to salads and potato dishes, I decided to make a huge pot of bean stew, something resembling a goulash but with Spanish sausages and sweet pepper. As beans are a staple in Andalusia, I thought it would win people over, especially if the weather turned cold. I set up the bean stew as soon as I got up and then realized that we had overlooked one thing in our planning: cleaning the few rooms we lived in.

As I turned away from the stove and looked at the tiny living room and the patio where our dear neighbours were supposed to gather, I saw what a stranger would see clearly: total squalor. It is often impossible to see your own filth, but it's never difficult to spot other people's dirt.

In our case, the guests would not have to look hard. Busy

managing the construction site during the day, working from the bedroom for the app company, and defending ourselves from cold and rain at night, we had really let things go. There were spiderwebs the size of small curtains hanging all around the ceiling. The windows were caked in mud and concrete from all the work done outside and the weeks of heavy rain. The water leaks that we suffered throughout the autumn had left brown marks all over the walls. The patio outside the living room was covered in a mixture of concrete and mud. There was a layer of fine cement dust on all the surfaces inside and outside the house.

I looked around and could not believe that I missed how squalid our living conditions had become. There was not a single place where you could serve food or relax in a civilized manner. Once I set the stew on the stove, I started to clean the place like a mad person. We decided that the bedroom would not be accessible to the guests and shoved anything that was not pleasing to the eye in there. Now that the living room was free of clutter, we started working on the spiderwebs. Between vacuuming and dusting, I peeled the potatoes for the salad and marinated the meat for the barbecue. The problem of trying to clean a place that is located in the middle of a construction site is that each time you move, you just shift the existing dust and dirt around. You clean one area, but as soon as you turn around, it gets covered in the dust that has just fallen from your clothes.

By now, it was noon, and we were nowhere near ready. There were still salads to prepare, and because I had been preoccupied with the cleaning, the stew turned slightly sour and was not pleasant to taste. The only thing that I thought might rescue it was more wine, so I poured a generous amount of white wine into an already boozy stew and let it sit on low heat for a little longer. I hoped that it would fix itself with time.

While I was working inside, Robert prepared some makeshift tables from the yellow boards used a couple of weeks earlier as shuttering for the concrete ring beam we made to support the roof of the house. Since these shuttering-board tables were too wobbly to sit at, we decided to serve the food buffet-style on the boards and have the guests put their plates on their lap or walk around with their food. We definitely did not have enough chairs for everyone, so people would have to mingle. This was not how I imagined the party would be. But by now, it was half-past one, and I expected the guests to show up soon. There was no more time to clean the windows or the floors. I took a shower, and while I was still getting dressed, some early guests arrived.

A Spanish party in Andalusia, or at least in the Montefrio area, has stages that are clearly delineated by the different types of food and booze served. It doesn't matter whether you all sit at one long table or mingle around with plates of food — guests will always know what stage of the proceedings they are in by the type of drinks served and the food offered. As you arrive, you are always offered a glass of cold beer. It is usually served from one-litre bottles, and it is usually *Cruz Campo, San Miguel,* or, in aspirational circles, *Alhambra* or perhaps something foreign, like *Stella.*

You can also tell the middle-class-wannabes from honest farmers by the receptacle from which the beer is served. The hardworking down-to-earth farmers choose one-litre bottles, whereas social climbers choose small tins. The price difference is minimal, but the social gesture is significant. If you come from other parts of Europe and would like to start your party with a glass of wine — tough luck. A bottle of red wine is set on the table, but it's clearly reserved for later on, for the meal. As an exception, if you are in the host's good graces, they may serve you some red wine with orange Fanta.

Before I came to Spain, I had heard stories of South Africans drinking red wine mixed with Coke. I did not think much about it and treated it as if it were some sort of urban legend, repeated from one person to another until there isn't even a grain of truth left in it. But here I was, at my own house, thinking that I misheard Encarna when she asked me for red wine and Fanta. Since the beers were available to guests to take freely from a cooler box on the patio, I had to go to the kitchen to prepare this special order.

On my way to the kitchen, I repeated what I heard in Spanish in my head and was confident that I must have heard 'red wine *and* a Fanta' and not 'red wine *with* Fanta.' I made the executive decision and filled one glass with red wine and another with sparkly lemon-flavoured soda, as I didn't have any Fanta.

I presented Mercedes with the two glasses and saw a smidgen of confusion on her face. She asked me what the sparking soda was for. I explained that since I did not have any Fanta, I could offer her this lemon soda. This, as it turned out, is not an approved additive to red wine. Orange Fanta, yes, but lemon soda, no. Even people who mix wine with other beverages draw a line somewhere.

Thinking on my feet, I suggested adding some Cola to the wine, and the alternative seemed to please her. Since no one else had any special orders, we proceeded to the next stage of the party, which is cold meats, cheeses, and olives. This stage of a party can last as long as you wish. People drink their cold beers and snack on homegrown olives, delicious goat and sheep cheeses, thinly sliced *salchichón*, *chorizo*, *jamón serrano* and *lomo* — a dry-cured pork tenderloin. The meats and cheeses are interspersed with small pieces of white baguette soaked in our local olive oil. This stage of a party usually gives the hosts time to relax for a few minutes, talk to the guests, and prepare the main courses — or, in our case, grill the meat.

But at this party, there was no time for us to stop. The guests kept on coming with their families and children, showering us with gifts of homemade sausages, cakes, Andalusian doughnuts, and bottles of Rioja. Except for our banker and accountant (who live some distance away in town), everyone else who was invited showed up, dressed in their best clothes and curious to see what we were doing with the old *cortijo*. Unlike many English parties that I have attended in my lifetime, where long intervals of complete silence are common, not a single second of silence fell over the gathering. The virtue of having Spanish guests at your party is that they talk pretty much non-stop. They don't shy from talking to strangers; they don't create secret groups which no one dares approach; they laugh and have a good time and make your party buzz all the time.

Unfortunately, while everyone else seemed to have a great time, we did not have much time to relax or chat with the guests. Within ten minutes of serving the bread and meats, I noticed that all the bread was gone from the plates. I could not believe my eyes! We had bought eight baguettes for the party and thought that that would be plenty. I did not expect everyone to eat loads of bread. From my experience of throwing parties for Europeans and North Americans, most of the bread served at a party is usually thrown away at the end, as we are all so carb-conscious. My Andalusian neighbours did not seem to be aware of that fad.

As I looked around, people were holding huge pieces of baguette in their hands. I evidently had sliced the bread far too thick for it to go around, and after the first helping, there was nothing left in the breadbasket. I saw José and Rafa searching the serving tables for bread. The word *pan* started to shimmer like a gentle wave around the crowd. Those who were lucky enough to get a piece were chowing down on it at an alarming rate.

I had suspected that the local Spanish people love bread by observing the Formula One bread delivery van race past our house every morning to deliver bread to the most remote parts of Montefrio municipality. Still, I did not realize how much they love it and how much of it they are willing to eat before their main course. The fittest who got to the bread first were now waving baguettes in front of the slow — the children and the elderly. For a split second, I saw the ugly face of humanity and tried to avoid an uprising. Soon the parents would refuse to share their half-eaten baguettes with their kids, and the wives would turn their backs on their husbands.

'We need more bread,' I whispered to Robert, who was by the grill chatting to our builders.

'What? There's lots of bread.' He looked in the direction where the bread used to be and could not believe his eyes.

'It's gone.' I informed him. Since Robert did not seem to have a solution at hand, I rushed back to the kitchen and searched frantically for more bread. I found a few more baguettes in the freezer. 'It will take half an hour for it to thaw.' I thought. 'I can't keep them waiting for the bread that long.'

In a moment of inspiration, I put the frozen bread on top of the fireplace and went out to the patio to assure the restless crowd that more bread was coming soon. In a couple of minutes, the smell of 'freshly baked bread' went through the crowd. Only a few guests who were lingering in the kitchen knew that it was, in fact, frozen bread that had been revived to resemble a freshly-baked version of itself.

This time I did not take any chances. I sliced the bread as thinly as I could and set a platter of it onto the serving table. It was gone before the plate hit the table, so I rushed back to revive some more of the frozen bread. I served a few more rounds of thinly sliced bread until there was no more, but by then, everyone seemed to be content with the amount of bread, olive oil, and meat that they had eaten, and we could proceed to the next stage. The next stage of a Spanish farmhouse party is usually marked by the opening of the red wine. Respectable homes tend to serve *rioja* with the main course. If you prefer white wine to reds, you would be well-advised to bring your own white wine, as they are not very popular around Montefrio — and that may be for a good reason. For years I have preferred white wines to red. Sauvignon Blanc and Shiraz are my favourites —both are light, crisp, and refreshing but still full of flavour. When we first arrived in Spain, I bought a few local white wines, as Sauvignon Blanc and Shiraz were not to be found around Montefrio. Well, this may be an embellishment since I had not spent any time searching local *bodegas* — I'm not that kind of wine fanatic — I had only looked in local supermarkets.

You first notice something is off with an Andalusian white when you pour it into a glass. You don't need to be Gordan Ramsey's sommelier to note that the colour is slightly unusual. Instead of a crispy crystal-like translucence, the white grapes that grow in Al-Andalus give the wine a deep yellow tint, something resembling the colour of the urine of a dehydrated runner. The taste, on the other hand, is that of a paint stripper mixed with vinegar. It's a foul drink which taste can only be hidden in fatty pork stews and chorizo-infused paella dishes. Other than that, you can serve it to your enemies or visitors from abroad who should have known better than to demand white wine.

As the guests switched to red wine, we served the bean stew and the barbecued meats. I also reheated some store-bought tortillas, which in Spain refers to a variety of potato omelettes. Tortillas are a local staple, and in addition to beans and bread, complement most meals.

After several hours on the stove and some additional time to rest, the stew was a knockout. Both Rocio and Encarna were sitting on our small patio sofa, eating the stew while smacking their lips and telling me how rich it was. Or so I thought.

Only a year later did I learn that *rico* means 'delicious'. I spent a whole year convinced that the Spanish were obsessed with how many calories and how fatty the food was. Whenever I witnessed any gathering with food, I would hear them say '*Es muy rico*,' which I translated in my head as 'It's very rich' or 'It's very fatty.' In the meantime, I searched a few times for a Spanish equivalent of 'It's delicious,' but Google Translate did not seem to get it right; it suggested '*Es delicioso*' — an expression that I have never heard used at a table. A few times at parties, I would say 'Es delicioso,' but it seemed to fall on deaf ears — no one reciprocated, and they seemed to insist that the food was 'rich'.

While our guests were eating, I took the opportunity to practice my Spanish. First, by popular demand, I listed the ingredients of the bean stew. This was a topic I was fluent in, for I'd had ample experience reading food names in the supermarket. As the wine flowed, I was getting better and better at my Spanish and chatted with most of the guests. This was not difficult because I repeated the same limited number of expressions to each person I talked to. I explained where we used to live and that we used to teach at university. I told my neighbours Antonia and her daughter Maria that I was a writer for Cambridge University Press and I was writing an app to help people learn English. Maria, who is my age, seemed very impressed. She looked at her mum, pointed at me and said:

'Es una persona muy importante.'

I was happy to be able to tell them a little more about myself. I didn't want my new neighbours to think that we were some sort of riff-raff. I was very pleased with Maria's words, even if they were somewhat exaggerated. Maria looked down at the pram that she kept rocking and introduced me to her newborn baby girl, Lucia, sleeping peacefully in the middle of the uproar.

By then, we were joined by some other women, Encarna, Rocio and Inma – *Inma*, I found out later, is short for *Inmaculada*, which is short for the full name: *María de la Inmaculada Concepción*. They were all listening attentively to my broken Spanish. Rocio told me how sorry she felt whenever she drove by to see us living in a house with no roof. I assured her that it was not a problem. Soon we were going to finish the rest of the reform. I told them that we were planning to rent out two rural apartments for tourists. This idea generated a lot of *ohs!* and *ahs!* and I took the ladies around the house to show them what the plans were for each unit and what we had done so far. I showed Inma, the wife of our chief *albañil*, the great work her husband has been doing for months. She seemed very proud.

I'm not sure that they understood my plan for the holiday rentals as the walls were still just raw red brick and no windows or doors had been installed, but they pretended to be impressed. An Andalusian farmer may find it difficult to understand why tourists would want to spend their holidays in the middle of nowhere. They themselves go on holidays to the seaside in Almeria or visit a big city like Madrid or Valencia. While I was entertaining the ladies, I noticed that Robert had also become fluent in Spanish. He was talking incessantly with everyone and reminiscing some of the building adventures with our builders and retelling them to our male neighbours. Rural Andalusia is sometimes quite formal, and it's common at parties for the women to form a group of their own whilst all the men congregate in a likewise fashion.

As the main course was winding down, one of our labourers — a red-haired gipsy from town — was handed a guitar and started playing flamenco. As with my previous flamenco experience, his guitar skills were rough-and-ready. He compensated any misgivings with woeful singing, and soon everyone was enchanted by this somewhat romantic spectacle. The singing provided a good soundtrack to coffee and dessert.

Our neighbours must have had a good intuition that we would screw up dessert and brought lots of creamy cakes, roulades, and deep-fried doughnuts covered in sugar. At first, I thought that we would be left with all that cake, but I underestimated how much hardworking people of Andalusia love sugar. Only when I moved to the countryside and got to know people who make a living with the sheer power of their muscle and physical strength did I realize the importance of sugar for a working man.

Running up and down steep mountain slopes while picking olives for four to five months a year — often in freezing cold and rain — requires a different type of fuel than what's needed to sit in front of a laptop for hours. I have often seen workers and farmers drop four or five spoons of sugar into a coffee cup large enough to hold about two sips of coffee. Then they would add a dash of hot milk into the sugary liquid, drink it, and go back to work. This mixture of warmth, high calories, and a dash of protein would keep them going for another two hours.

As I was stuck in the kitchen brewing endless cups of coffee and having Robert distribute shots of brandy and whiskey, Encarna and Rocio were cutting up the cakes and serving them to the sugar-crazy crowd. By now, everyone was high on their drug of choice — be it beer, wine, spirits, coffee, or sugar. As the sun was going down and the guests started to disperse, I thought that I could not have asked for better neighbours. It was the days like this when we basked in the glorious December sun, ate delicious food, drank good wine, and enjoyed the company of unpretentious people that made all our sacrifices, our sweat and tears, seem worthwhile.

FIFTEEN
OLIVES, OLIVES EVERYWHERE

First-time visitors to Andalusia are often, quite rightfully so, amazed by the number of olive trees that grow on the hills and mountains in this vast region. When driving through the spectacular landscapes surrounding Cordoba, Granada, and Jaén, we often marvel at the olive farmers' resourcefulness as they use every last metre of their land to plant olive trees. You see olive trees hanging off rocks, on top of rugged mountains, in all manner of nook and cranny, and at the bottom of pits; if there is an unused bit of soil, it is merely waiting for an olive tree to be planted to fill in the gap. From a bird's-eye view, the landscape where we live looks like a dotted fabric that stretches across southern Spain — the dots are symmetrical and neatly lined up. While a satellite image accurately portrays the enormity of the olive production, it has to be experienced in person to be fully appreciated. Whenever we take our visitors from the airport in Malaga to our place, one of the first questions is, 'Do they grow both green and black olives?'

Hearing this question makes any expats living in Andalusia smirk in response to the ignorance of 'the foreigners'. It's also a signal for a short lecture about olives and an opportunity to show how much of local culture and lifestyle we have absorbed. Because, surely, it's obvious that there are no distinct black and green olive trees. All olives become black with time. This information causes awe and gasps among the guests sitting in the backseat, and as they look at the trees with renewed admiration and tell you how they always preferred black olives to green and so on, you feel free to continue with the lecture.

'There are many different varieties of olives,' I'd hear myself explaining to visitors from abroad.

'Most Spanish people know them all and can distinguish them by sight. They can also tell you which types of olives were used when they taste an olive oil sample,' I frequently found myself exaggerating, but it felt good to embellish the achievements of the people we live with. The fact is that there are over a hundred different varieties of olives, and the Spanish farmers we know like to pretend they can tell the difference. Still, it is more likely that they can distinguish but a dozen of local varieties. Some may even tell which olives were used in the production of a given bottle of olive oil, but these are typically professional tasters who take part in olive oil competitions.

As we drive home with our guests and share olive-related stories and 'wisdom' with them, our passengers come to the conclusion that they won't have to buy any olives during their stay — they will just pluck them off of the trees and plunge them directly into their martini glasses. What a life!

When we first came to Spain, before we bought our house, we asked the landlord of the cottage that we were renting whether we could taste the delicious-looking olives that grew on his patio. Being a good host, he told us not to eat them because they don't taste nice. These were his exact words, and I suspect that due to his poor language skills, he used the understatement of the century because we didn't listen to his advice, and as soon as he left, we plucked a couple of fresh olives from the tree.

To say that olives picked fresh from the tree 'don't taste nice' is a lie; they taste like eating hell or kissing a poisonous snake. The immediate sensation that you feel as you bite into the hard, green skin is that of mouth paralysis. This taste could be the mixture of different parasite poisons sprayed on all the trees generously each spring, but it gets worse as you get to the olive flesh. By then, you are spitting like a rabid dog and running with foam in your mouth in all directions; you wish someone would just cut your head off to stop the bitter poison from getting into your throat.

The word often used to describe the taste of fresh olives is *bitter*. I can assure you that it's the wrong word. *Bitter* describes a flavour that, while not as pleasant as sweet or salty, has its place on the human palate. A beer can be slightly bitter, but I will order it again; coffee is supposed to be bitter, and I drink it every day. Even a sour grapefruit has not put me off forever. But once you taste a fresh olive, you will never try it again. It may be, in fact, that we need a new word to describe that taste. Just like the Japanese have *umami*, Spanish should have a word that describes the paralyzing toxic vileness that is the taste of fresh olive. As it stands, words fail me, and so I recommend you try it yourself.

It was in November — in the middle of the reform — when Rafa taught me how to prepare olives for human consumption. He did it then and not later in the winter season because the olives for home-curing are picked first — when they have just ripened and have not become too watery from the rains or too wrinkly from the sun.

As it was common for his little home economics lessons, he appeared one afternoon on the driveway — without any warning — with a container of fresh olives to teach me the ways of the Andalusian farmwife. Until then, I was convinced that the only method that transformed the vile green fruit into a delectable snack was some sort of complicated chemical reaction that should only be attempted in state-of-the-art factories. I resigned myself to eating tinned olives and never considered that there was a way to get the bitter poisonous taste out of our own olives.

Little did I know that soon — that's a relative term in case of curing olives — I would be eating my own homemade olives. Curing olives was not the only thing that Rafa taught me that autumn. He took it upon himself to make me into a proper Andalusian farmwife and taught me that the woody fruit that grows by the gate to our driveway was, in fact, delicious quince that can be made into a delightful fruit jam called *dulce de membrillo*. He instructed me how to plant and harvest saffron and showed me where it grows wild in the forest. He came around in December and demanded that I plant our garlic right then and there, and, while I was planting the garlic under his watchful eye, he showed me how to look after the wild asparagus that I was not aware grew in our garden. He showed me how to make delicious roasted almonds from our own harvest. Once, he even suggested that I collect the *bellotas*, the acorns, from our Iberian oak tree and eat them in the winter, but that's where I drew the line.

He often brought samples of these Andalusian country staples made by his wife, Loli, and I started to believe that it was Loli who was teaching me the ways of an Andalusian farmwife from behind the scenes. Whoever had the idea, I can only be grateful. Without their guidance, we would be sitting on a beautiful farm with no clue about which plants could be used for what purpose.

So, when one day Rafa arrived with a huge container of freshly picked olives, I was ready for my next lesson. Olives harvested at the beginning of the season are truly lovely — they are plump but not too soft and often half green and half purple. In addition to the huge container filled with fresh olives, Rafa was holding what appeared to be a small empty brown beer bottle. I assumed that he had picked this piece of rubbish on his way to us and wanted me to throw it in the bin, but no — this was the tool that we were going to use to prep the olives.

He sat on an old stump under the oak tree and pulled over another wooden stump to use as a worktable. He took one olive out of the container, placed it firmly on the wood, and gave it a good crack with the bottom of the beer bottle. He repeated the process for five minutes or so, clearly enjoying himself, and then gave me the beer bottle to try.

As it turned out, the smashing of the olives had to be just so. On my first attempt, all that was left of the fruit was a sliver of mushed pulp, which was clearly not the way to prepare edible olives. I scraped the mashed flesh off the bottom of the beer bottle and threw it away while my instructor grunted something under his breath. I tried a few more times, but I was left with an oily green mash each time I hit the olive. Rafa took the beer bottle and demonstrated the art of the gentle crack. The trick was, he explained, to have the skin of the fruit open up a little bit so as to allow the future salt baths to penetrate and rinse the bitterness out of the flesh away. Given this explanation, I approached the fruit with a more careful attitude.

Once Rafa was satisfied with my progress, he left me with the giant container to process the olives on my own. He kindly loaned me the beer bottle, which, as I now understand, must have been a precious kitchen utensil. I promised to return it as soon as I was done gently whacking the fruit. Once he drove off, I realized that I had forgotten his complicated instructions on what to do next. I decided to take a break and find out online what exactly I was getting myself into.

Google suggested that I was to put it all in water, completely submerged, and keep it that way for the first two or three weeks while changing the water every day. After that, I was to prepare a salty brine of three-quarter cup of salt for every four litres of water and keep the olives in this brine for a week or so. After the medium salty brine process came the strong brine of one and a half cups of salt for every four litres. Vinegar and garlic could be added to this final brine. This was the final resting place of the olives for several months. The online instructions matched somewhat what I understood from Rafa's directives. According to the internet and my neighbour, the olives were ready when they no longer tasted bitter. I wrote it all down and went back to work on the olives.

As I marched off to finish smashing the olives with the beer bottle, little did I know that it would be six months before I would taste them. As I was about to learn, the whole process is tedious and time-consuming and may challenge the best of temperaments.

I set up my station on the patio and started smashing the olives — it was a good thing that my mentor was not watching me because many pieces of fruit ended up as mush in the nearby flowerbed. Soon the table, my clothes, my hands, and my face were covered in the oily residue that was being ejected each time I hit the olives. As the process took me several hours, the juice that was covering the table was oxidizing and looking darker and browner by the second. The smashed olives in a bowl in no way reminded me of the olives from a jar in a shop. Instead of having uniform shapes and clear incisions, mine looked like First World War combatants after a particularly fierce battle. Their wounds were uneven and erratic — some were gasping for life while others received mere flesh wounds.

When I finished the job, I put the olives in four very large Tupperware containers and rinsed the brown sludge off them. Once the water was running clean again, I set the four huge containers aside, put the lids on, and placed them in the dark room behind the kitchen. The room was being used as storage for building tools but would one day become a modern, open-plan kitchen. At least that was the plan then.

The problem with placing things in a dark room in a remote part of your abode is that you tend to forget that they exist. Instead of rinsing them every day as instructed by Rafa and the internet, it was three days later that some inane comment triggered my memory, and I dropped what I was doing and ran to the dark storage room to check on my olives. The water had become dark and unpleasant to smell, so to counter the days of neglect, I gave the olives an extra-thorough rinse and set them aside. As soon as I left the dark room, I would once again forget about the curing olives.

And so it went. Instead of receiving daily baths, my olives were subject to bi-weekly showers at best. Despite the nuisance of the process, I had, by now, invested so much time and energy into curing this batch of olives that I was loath to stop the experiment altogether. After three weeks, I had to face some hard truths. The irregular baths had caused some casualties. While two containers seemed clear and on their way to becoming good olives, the other two were completely spoiled. The thick stinky froth that started to form on the surface of the water each time I took them out for a bath was a clear sign of my neglect. These two batches would never end on a tiny tapas plate as a talking point of a party.

I threw the vile froth and the oily sludge into the field and washed the two containers thoroughly. By now, it was time to stop the daily rinse and prepare a strong salty brine for the olives to sit in for months on end. This type of curing seemed right up my alley as it did not require daily attention — in fact, it was highly recommended that you forget about the curing olives and check them in a few months when you stumble upon them by mistake, which is exactly what I did.

The next time I looked at the olives was in late January. They seemed happy, but I dared not taste them yet. I changed their salty bath and set them aside for a few more months of curing. It was in late April that, when searching for a hammer or a screwdriver, I spotted the two forgotten containers. The water was clear and the olives looked happy. I rinsed them and tasted one — they were still bitter, but this was an acceptable level of bitterness, one that could complement a cold beer or a slice of *lomo*. I changed the water and placed them in more presentable jars, and set them in my fridge. To my surprise, people ate them at parties and barbecues, and no one ever got sick. Some asked me for a recipe, so I regurgitated the instructions from the internet — but the truth is that the complex procedure of forgetful neglect and then fastidious attention through which I put my olives would be impossible to replicate.

The homemade olives were a big hit and gained me some notoriety in the expat community. Two years later, at parties at my house, people would eat delicious store-bought olives and ask me if these were mine. I wish. The process of making the olives was so utterly tedious and exhausting that I took a break from it for the next two years. Instead, we started to make our own olive oil, which, while it is much more complicated a process, only required a day's attention on our part.

SIXTEEN
HIT IT HARDER

The first autumn in our house, we were too busy fighting floods, checking weather forecasts, and motivating the builders to put on the new roof to even notice when the olive harvest had started. Our olive trees had been abandoned for the previous two years, and, because of that, the amount of fruit on them was minimal. The hurricane that swept across Andalusia the first November when we lived in the house did not help with the yield either. It stripped our trees of the few olives that we had. As a result, we didn't bother to even discuss picking olives that year. We resigned ourselves to watching handfuls of them get old and fall to the ground on their own.

It was then to our surprise when our neighbour José suggested that he and his son Pepe show us how to pick them. It was already late February, and they must have been almost done with their trees. But the nature of an Andalusian farmer is not to waste anything. José must have hated looking at our abandoned trees with their wrinkly dry olives hanging on by a thread.

The two men appeared one day armed with the olive tree shaker, giant black nets, and plenty of sacks to put the olives in. Following José and Pepe, we inspected all our trees. Of the thirty trees on our property, only five had produced a meagre harvest that José felt worth collecting. We helped lay the black nets under the first tree. Pepe then turned on the shaker, grabbed a thick branch of the tree with the extended arm of the shaker, and shook the living daylights out of the olive tree while we were showered with falling olives. When he finished, we rolled up the net's ends and transferred about ten kilograms' worth of olives into a sack. I thought back to the dozens of sacks that I saw at the back of José's 4 x 4 and guessed that he might have an optimistic nature. The way we were going, we would be lucky to fill the one sack that Robert was holding now in his hand like a treasure.

The four of us moved from tree to tree, and half an hour later, we finished our sad harvest with just three sacks of olives. While we felt deflated, José kept up his optimistic mood and entertained us with stories of the snows on the Sierra Nevada mountains that we all stared at in the distance. Even though our harvest was miserable, a week later, Pepe showed up at our gate and handed us six litres of olive oil — one five-litre bottle and one one-litre. I didn't think much of it until the next day at lunch, Robert decided that he would have olive oil on his bread instead of butter. He was sitting with our builder, Dani, and wanting to impress him with his agricultural prowess, he must have told him that he picked his olives and now can enjoy his own olive oil.

Dani must have challenged his ego because my butter-loving husband decided to abandon all that is English and ask for olive oil. I brought the one-litre bottle from the storage room, handed it to him, and left the patio; as soon as I was out of sight, I heard Robert and Dani squeaking like teenage girls in a makeup shop.

Apparently, according to my husband's 'unbiased opinion,' it was the most delicious olive oil he had ever tasted. I chose not to mention the fact that he had never before deliberately put oil on a plate and dipped bread in it with the intention of eating it. He sat there smacking his lips and pouring more oil on his plate while Dani, not wanting to appear diffident, copied his manner. The two of them kept dipping the bread in the olive oil and tasting it as if it was some kind of olive oil eating competition. These two 'connoisseurs' in their construction clothes and with sledgehammers and concrete buckets scattered around the lunch table seemed oddly misplaced.

In the excitement of the moment, Robert announced that he could eat this olive oil and bread for the rest of his life and not need anything else. I looked sceptical and made a note to remind him of this commitment the next time he tried to convince me that a Flintstone-sized beef steak from the butcher's is good for one's health. Our olive oil turned out to be delicious despite our ignorance and neglect. Because of this positive experience, we vowed to look after our trees, and that spring, we pruned them and gave them nutrition and even watered them — we still had some water on the property at that time. The following year, we were ready for our own first harvest. And so, let me fast-forward for a second to tell you how *not* to pick olives.

At the start of the next olive picking season in late November 2015, we inspected the trees and noticed that our care and attention had not gone to waste. After the spring and a summer of tender care, we now had at least twenty trees to harvest. At first, we decided to buy the motorised tree shaker, similar to the one that Pepe had used on our trees the year before. However, once we found out the price of a new machine, we decided to pick our olives using the traditional method, which involves hitting the branches with a long stick and collecting the fruit from the nets laid under the trees.

Full of ambition and feeling a bit smug that we would follow in the footsteps of the Andalusian farmers, we went to the local *ferretería* or a hardware shop. Because of the extensive renovations that had now lasted for over a year, we were welcome customers in the shop. The owner, Carlos, and his wife, Mercedes, seemed honestly bemused when they heard of our intention of picking the olives with a traditional stick. But being good shopkeepers, they dutifully provided us with two giant nets and one very long stick.

In the past, olive farmers used simple wooden sticks. Since then, the olive-picking stick technology has advanced; the modern olive-picking enthusiast can choose from a vast array of sticks made from various modern materials. We selected a very technologically up-to-date stick made of lightweight fibreglass, packed our nets into the car, and went back home. The next morning, we ate a hearty breakfast since we'd need all the energy to get us through the hard, physical labour that we were about to launch into and set out as soon as the temperature outside was warm enough to work.

I thought that we might start arguing as soon as we began to lay out the nets, which turned out to be far too big for our needs, but that did not happen. It must have been the years of camping and setting up tents on various campsites that had taught us not to make any comments or give any instructions while working with a giant piece of fabric, such as a tent cover or a tarpaulin. The olive-picking nets seemed to require similar restraint, and we proceeded to lay them in respectful silence and without bickering. Then Robert picked up the long stick and started to strike the branches. I expected a torrent of olives to fall down, but not a single piece of fruit was persuaded to fall from the tree. The farmers that we have seen working on the hills made it look effortless — they would gently strike a branch, and each tap would be followed by an avalanche of olives. This was not happening now. The olives seemed super-glued to the branches, and no matter how much strength and energy Robert exerted, they did not want to let go.

Annoyed, he started to fight the tree as if it was some medieval demon. He hit the branches in all directions, a kind of madness in his eyes. It was clearly not how I had seen farmers do it, so I started to correct his method.

'Don't hit the big branch; hit the small branches. Shake it a bit. Don't hit it so hard. Hit it harder. Hit it softer but more frequently. Don't hit it so fast.'

'Shut up.' I heard in response. 'You try it.' I was handed the stick.

Despite my best efforts, no olives fell down. The process was now getting very frustrating. With the giant nets set up and the fancy stick in hand, we were starting to look like fools. While fighting with the tree, I constantly looked over our shoulders, checking the road and hoping that none of our neighbours was driving past. Should they see this pathetic display, I knew they were sure to drive up and intervene. Our pride could not take that. We did the best we could in this situation and started to argue with each other.

After a few sharp but hurtful comments, a quick period of separation was in order. I went back to the house to sulk and contemplate all the previous situations in which Robert acted like a fool while he, in my absence, decided to make a martyr of himself and continued 'olive picking' alone. A couple of hours later, we reunited for lunch, and we both chose not to talk about the olives. In the afternoon, Robert did not go out again to pick the olives, which made me believe that he had done all the trees in my absence.

Since I did not want to discuss the touchy subject, it was only the next day that I found out that he only did two trees.

'All by myself,' he emphasized several times and with accusation in his tone. 'I always have to do everything around this house by myself.'

Not wanting to listen to this tale of martyrdom for the next decade, I decided to bite my tongue and offer assistance. We laid the net under another tree and started the 'picking' once more. I was surprised that Robert did not object to my taking the olive-picking stick and striking the branches in the technique that I was convinced would yield better results than the day before. It didn't, but being a good husband, Robert chose not to point that out. As I was desperately trying to persuade the tree to let go of the fruit, he seemed to have developed a brand-new technique unknown to any Andalusian farmer and having its roots in Swedish blueberry picking.

More than a decade before, when we lived in Sweden, out of boredom that would befall anyone on a cold, wet summer day in Sweden, we decided that we fancied picking some blueberries and making jam. The idea gave us an excuse to drive to a hardware shop and buy a lot of jars for our preserves, some pectin, and two blueberry pickers. The tool used to pick the berries is of a somewhat genius design. It combines a rake and a sack in one. As you comb the berry bushes with the rake, the fruit falls directly into a small sack at the back of the tool.

Since finding blueberries in a Swedish pine forest is the easiest thing in the world, we spent a happy week making jam for the winter and pretending that there were no shops where one could purchase a rarity such as blueberry jam. But it was our own production, and we did enjoy eating jam for months to come. We also chose to suppress the knowledge that making your own jam is not a particularly cheap exercise if you consider the cost of buying the picking tools, jars, pectin, sugar, and time needed to clean forest berries.

With our past blueberry-picking experience in mind, I could see that Robert had adopted the same technique for picking olives. Instead of shaking the tree, he used his fingers as a rake and combed each branch from the base down while the fruit fell onto the net laid at the bottom. I hated to admit it, but his method was yielding more crop than the stick, so I abandoned the wretched stick and started to comb the fruit of the branches. The method itself was very soothing and had a therapeutic quality to it; standing in the middle of an olive tree and gently combing each branch may one day be proven to cure anxiety and stress.

While the process was much more relaxing than the relentless hitting with a stick, it was slow and tedious and not very thorough. It took us almost an hour to do one tree, and we still had about seventeen to do. At this pace, it would take us two more days to finish harvesting our small plot.

It was around noon when our neighbour Mercedes saw our labour and decided to join in. She didn't seem one bit dismayed by the slow process and followed suit in hand-picking the fruit. She told us this used to be her job when she was a child. When picking olives with her parents and her baby brother, known to us as Old Gabi, her task was to pick every last piece of fruit from the tree and collect whatever fell on the ground next to the tree where the nets failed to cover the ground completely. Our mad method must have transported her to her childhood because while we suggested moving to the next tree, she was adamant that we must not move until *every single piece of fruit* was plucked from the branches and picked up from the ground.

The idea that one must not waste anything — even when the time and effort needed to do so is more valuable than the thing itself — is deeply ingrained in the Andalusian farmer and speaks to the hard past that generations who live here have experienced. I can easily imagine winters past when, after a particularly dry spring and summer, all they would have to eat was a handful of almonds or acorns. Out of respect for this cautious and anti-consumerist attitude to life, we humoured Mercedes and picked every last piece of fruit from the tree and from the ground.

Despite being only one hundred and fifty centimetres in height and having the build of a ten-year-old boy, Mercedes can be surprisingly strong-willed. She inspected our previous work and was not one bit satisfied with our poor attention to detail. She was especially critical of how we had left the odd fruit on the branches and on the ground. Like a little female Napoleon, she commanded that we go back and do it right this time. So, without a word of complaint, we did.

Andalusian farmers have a natural propensity to gather and inspect each other's work. On seeing us working with Mercedes, her brother Gabi came around to see what we were up to. While Mercedes's nature is to always jump in and help, her younger brother likes to advise from afar. He picked up the olive stick that we now abandoned and leaned on it. With the usual *andaluz* whine in this voice, he had a lot to say about how hard it is to pick olives and how he and his parents and his sister, Mercedes, used to work all day when he was a child. All that talk about work did not seem to whet his appetite for any. He chose to supervise rather than lead by example.

While we bent down like little children picking up fruit from the ground, he went on with the lecture on the art of using a stick to shake the fruit of the tree. The talk was far too nuanced for us to understand or take note of, but we nodded our heads and agreed with everything he was saying.

While three people gathered in a field are a sure sign that something interesting is going on, four is simply an invitation for others to join. And so, while Robert, Mercedes, and I were busy searching for every last bit of a fruit that might have gone astray and

Gabi giving us a history lecture, we were joined by Pepe and José, who were working on their olives on the hill opposite. While Mercedes and her bother Gabi are retired and only come to the *campo* on the weekends, their cousin, José, is a full-time farmer.

José, not able to comprehend what we were all doing, scratched his head and smiled jovially while Pepe, who is always more down-to-earth and matter-of-fact, asked us directly why we didn't ask him to lend us his shaker. It must have been the price of the machine that put us off asking anyone to lend us one. We thought it unfair to take advantage of such an expensive investment. But Pepe and José were unwavering; they felt it ridiculous that we were trying to collect all the olives using a stick — we didn't dare mention our handpicking method. We finished for the day, and the next morning Robert went up to José's to borrow their shaker.

As it was our third day of picking the olives, we were growing very skilled at setting the nets. We set up the machine the way Pepe had taught Robert the year before, and we started to work. Once the shaker's long arm grabbed hold of a branch, Robert shook the living daylights out of the poor tree. A torrent of olives fell on our shoulders and heads, and we rejoiced. That was the way to pick olives; it was quick and almost effortless (at least for the person who was watching the other operate the machine) and much more thorough than stick and hands.

After the previous two days of struggling to whack a single olive off a branch, we were in awe each time a shower of olives fell down onto the nets that were placed beneath the trees. With the shaker in hand, we finished our harvest in a few hours and were done by lunchtime. Before lunch, Robert took the shaker and several sacks of olives to José's house; they, in turn, took our olives to their mill in Brácana.

A week later, Robert went to the mill to collect our olive oil; that year, we collected more than twenty-five litres of delicious extra virgin olive oil that we enjoyed until the next season. In our third year of olive picking, in 2016, we were smarter and waited for my family to come and visit us for Christmas before we suggested picking olives as a new Christmas tradition.

SEVENTEEN
DO IT YOURSELF

One of the recurring themes that we observed during hours of relentless viewing of *Grand Designs* was that, when the budget ran low, the couples chose to finish building their house themselves. The idea that, at some stage, we would take over work from our builders had always been on our minds. It became a reality when in December — two months after we had started — our main contractor, an Englishman from Montefrio, admitted that he had miscalculated his initial estimate. His quote, which was clearly pulled out from thin air, included finishing the reform: that is, rendering all the walls, plastering, putting in new electrics and the necessary plumbing. However, by December, he had already spent his estimated budget, and we were far from being finished.

From late September until early December 2014, the English contractor and the Spanish workers he had hired to work on the project knocked down the animal house and the garage. Then, they rebuilt these two, previously structurally unsound, sections of the house with thick insulating bricks. They built up all the structural walls on the second floor to the same height and put a steel-reinforced ring beam around the top of the whole house. Finally, the house was graced with a new concrete roof. This was just the first part of the reform, and it had taken all the money that we had saved to pay for the whole project. The new brick walls were not rendered or plastered, and there was no sign of electrics or new plumbing. We were lucky that I still had a steady income from writing content for the new app, which paid the incoming bills, but it also meant that we had to rethink our spending and make cuts where possible. We agreed that the workers would finish tiling the roof, as this job seemed to be over our heads, and that we would take over from there.

As soon as the roof was finished, the Spanish workers left to pick olives. Even the unskilled labourers from Montefrio were eager to stop working on the construction and go work in the fields since they didn't want to lose their precious contacts with the farmers who, by December, needed them urgently. In preparation to take over the reform, Robert and I spent the evenings watching a series of YouTube tutorials on rendering, plastering, and tiling.

We knew that the first big job would be to render the house with concrete and then cover it with the white mixture called *capa fina*, the final cover. The main obstacle that we came across was that the tutorials on rendering and plastering that were in English taught the English or British style of rendering, which involves a very smooth finish and requires the use of materials that are not commonly available in Spain. We thus chose to take the gist of the tutorials but filled in the gaps by asking advice from one of our Spanish builders, Dani. During the renovation process, Robert had become Dani's apprentice or wingman and would sing praises about his skills whenever he could. After a day's work, he would often call me outside to show me a newly built wall and point out how straight it was.

'Look.' He was in awe of Dani's precision. 'We could put a laser here and check. Look, it's straight to a millimetre.'

We did put the laser to his work a few times, mostly to allow Robert to prove his point, and Dani's work did pass scrutiny. He was a perfectionist and would often spend a lot of time measuring things and calculating the angles to ensure that our new walls stood straight for a long time. Unfortunately, by late December, like the rest of the workers, Dani was keen to finish renovating our house because he had to attend to his own olive harvest.

In the last week of his employment, Robert spent several hours being tutored on how to render the brick walls, and on Dani's last day, we were confident that we could now take over the reform. Upon his departure, Dani mentioned that he would be available again to work on our house at the end of April when he was done with his olives.

'April?' I thought. 'Give me a break. We will be finished by then.'

But I kept my thoughts to myself and told him that we would surely contact him again in the spring if we needed help bringing the project to an end. After an evening of watching YouTube tutorials, we felt ready to take on the task of rendering walls and went off to Montefrio to buy some building materials to start with the project.

At the builders' yard, we discussed the matter of wall rendering once again with the shop owner, Ángel. Ángel is one of the few small business owners in Montefrio who can speak English, and he prides himself on his language skills. According to his own testimony, he used to be rubbish at school in all subjects but English. 'I loved English' were his exact words when I asked him about his language skills. Being able to communicate in English with the growing number of English expats who moved to Montefrio in the mid-2000s and wished to reform ruined cottages did not hurt his business. As the owner of one of the biggest builder's yards in Montefrio, Ángel knew almost all the expats in the village and the surrounding area. He was also familiar with most expat renovation projects. When he heard of our DIY intentions, he didn't try to dissuade us. On the contrary, he went into a long lecture on how to render a house the Spanish way.

'You know, Robert.' He rightfully assumed that Robert would be doing most of the rendering and so addressed his speech to him. 'You need to make a snowball with concrete. Like this.'

He showed us with his hands how one would make a snowball and looked at us to confirm we understood the first step.

'Then you throw it on the wall. Very hard, so it sticks.'

He mimed throwing the invisible snowball against the wall and waited until we nodded our heads as a sign of understanding.

'So, you make a snowball, throw it on the wall, and then spread it quickly, like this.'

He mimed spreading the concrete mixture onto the wall.

'But push hard; it's not easy. Do you understand?'

We nodded our heads, as the instructions seemed simple enough.

'You may need glue. It helps,' Ángel added.

'What kind of glue?' I asked.

'You spray it on the wall before you put the concrete. It will help the concrete stick to the wall. Makes it easy.'

We looked at each other, silently congratulating ourselves for asking Ángel's opinion. None of the video tutorials mentioned a glue that helps the render stick.

'You put the glue in the air pressure spray can and spray the wall twenty minutes before you render,' Ángel instructed as he set five expensive bottles of this glue on the counter.

He then loaded a giant bag of sand and several cement bags onto our trailer, and off we went back to the house to start on the project. It was now my job to be the unskilled labourer, and Robert started to teach me how to make concrete suitable for rendering the house. He started to throw spades full of sand into the cement mixer and an occasional spadeful of cement. He then added water now and again. I asked him to explain what he was doing.

'Just put in some sand and then some cement. Add some water. You can see how much you need,' Robert explained while adding more sand and a little bit more cement to the mixer.

As whatever he was doing lacked any discernible pattern, I asked him for the recipe. Any good baker — and as a child, I did my share of baking my own cakes — knows that a good mixture is all about keeping the right proportions. I demanded to know the recipe. Robert seemed to give in and told me to add a spade of cement for every four spades of sand. As we looked into the cement mixer, we both started to wonder what consistency was needed to use the mixture as rendering. I could see a clear hesitation enter his head as he wandered off to the house. He came back a few minutes later with his iPad.

'What do you need that for?' I asked.

'I need to check something.'

When unsure of their work, men have a strong tendency to remain vague; having seen this approach before, I did not insist on an explanation but let him Google his doubts. He looked at the screen on the iPad and compared whatever was there with the content of the cement mixer.

'Yeah, I think it's good,' he said.

I shrugged as it all looked quite the same to me. Well-aware of our DIY limitations, we decided to start rendering at the back of the house and experiment on those walls first as they would not be visible to the passing public or visitors. As we were about to pour the fresh concrete into the buckets to transport behind the house, we realized that we had forgotten to put the glue on the walls. I took one of the bottles from the garage and read the instructions. After the initial application of the glue, we were supposed to wait for about twenty minutes before applying the rendering. We left the concrete mixing and went off to spray the walls with the glue. The spray gun was already handy in the garage, as it had been used previously during the renovation. I volunteered to spray the walls, as the task did not seem to require much brawn.

The thing that a novice builder like me learns incredibly quickly on the job is the importance of health and safety. On a construction site, even a tiny accident is usually a lesson one never forgets, like the time when Robert came into the house pulling off his clothes and shouting as he ran to the shower. What happened was, he had been using a hammer to remove the old rendering from the walls, and a minute piece of stone fell into his eye. When he found that he could not remove the sharp flake of stone, he ran to the shower to wash the thing out. After almost losing an eye, he grew religiously attached to his safety goggles.

Unfortunately, health and safety lessons can only be taught first-hand, so I started to spray the walls with industrial-strength glue when a tiny droplet splashed off the wall and fell into my right eye. Just like my husband a couple of months earlier, I dropped everything and ran for the shower. Most modern household chemicals have instructions on the back telling you what to do should the given product splash into your eyes. Like most of the world's population, I ignored that part of the label and wondered what kind of dimwit would take this poison and squirt it into his or her eye.

Were it not for the fact that the warning and the first-aid instructions were usually heavily illustrated, I would not have known what to do with the glue that had fallen into my eye. Not to mention the fact that having glue in your eye can severely impede reading. But thanks to the amazing foresight of the label designers, as I stood in the shower with glue in my eye, I had a clear recollection of all the first-aid illustrations that I have ever seen. They all seemed to agree that one should force open one's lids and pour cold running water directly onto the eye. This seemed straightforward, if not for the simple fact that, under times of duress, one's eyes have a mind of their own and refuse to stay open when you try to pour running water into them.

Each time cold water touched my eye, it would automatically shut. With the situation getting hopeless, I decided that a very long shower might be just as effective, and hopefully, some water would get into my eye and dilute the glue. After about ten minutes in the shower, I was still unable to assess whether my eye was fine or not; the water itself had irritated the eye, and my vision was now blurred. I decided to get out and look for some eye drops.

Once I got dressed again and put eye drops in my right eye, I went out again to see what Robert had been up to in my absence. Because the whole drama in the shower had taken so much time, we were now running against the clock to put the rendering on. We went back to the cement mixer and saw that we had left it on all that time; we could not decide whether it was good or bad to mix the concrete for that long. We reasoned that the more you mixed it, the stronger the material you'd get at the end, so we poured the mixture into large plastic buckets and carried them to the back of the house to start the rendering. Since I did not feel confident with the task, I let Robert start. I reckoned that I would observe him for a few minutes and pick up the skill by watching him through my blurred eyes.

He started with the snowballing technique that Ángel so vividly illustrated to us. He made a concrete snowball and lobbed it against the wall. I expected that with the glue and the mixture being now extra strong, the concrete would simply stick to the brick and stay there. But no, against all our hopes and expectations, the concrete ball merely splatted against the wall and then fell to the ground, leaving only a wet stain on the brick. He tried a few more times, but each time the mixture just disintegrated and crumbled. It was time to abandon this traditional Spanish method of applying render and try the English techniques that we saw in the video tutorials online.

I brought two trowels, and we started by taking concrete from the bucket and spreading it like icing on the cake across the brick surface of the new wall. Icing a cake is usually much more difficult than it looks and, in amateurish hands, can turn a beautiful gateau into an unappetizing mess. 'Icing' a brick wall with concrete had the additional constraint of fighting gravity. As soon as I thought that I had skilfully covered a metre of the surface, the fresh layer of render would start to peel off. At times, the peeled-off layers resembled cake fondant; while unwilling to stick to the wall, the whole section was holding together and simply required that it be pinned down with both hands until it set. Other times, the whole batch of concrete would not stick at all; it would crumble and fall and refuse to attach itself to anything but my hands.

That's when I thought that a fusion of the Spanish snowball method and the traditional English rendering technique might solve the problem. I made a snowball, but instead of throwing it against the brick wall, I squeezed it into the bricks and then smoothed the surface with a trowel. The method seemed to work, and I hoped that Robert wouldn't notice my 'improvement,' as he could be a bit pedantic when it came to so-called craftsmanship. Since the rendering turned out to be much more complicated than we had ever envisioned, we worked in silence and did not scrutinize each other's patch.

After several hours of heavy work, we stepped aside and saw that we had barely finished one small wall behind the house. Because it was our first attempt at the task, we avoided tricky bits, like corners or windows, and rendered most of the flat areas around the windows. We considered making more concrete and continuing with the job, but that would require a few more hours of work, and we were both feeling sick and tired. I decided to clean the tools and resume work the following day.

A couple of hours later, after cleaning up and eating supper, I went outside to inspect our work. After looking at brick walls for so many months, I had forgotten the look of a clear and smooth concrete wall. Seeing the rendered wall was indeed a happy sight and a glimpse of the end. With a renewed spirit of hope, I inspected the rest of the house and calculated how many days it would take us to render the outside of the house. As I walked around, I noticed that there were many corners, and I was not sure how we would handle those. I also noticed that parts of the house were four metres off the ground and would require some serious scaffolding.

I went back inside and conveyed my concerns to Robert; we agreed to leave these difficult sections till the end and not to worry about them now. The next day, we inspected the render that we had applied so far; strangely, it had not set overnight. It was still wet and gooey, and parts of it fell off.

'It must be the cold,' I offered by way of explanation.

'Perhaps,' Robert said in agreement.

Since it was below zero at night and the back of the house receives very little sunlight, we decided to give the render a few more hours to set. In the meantime, we made a new batch of concrete and started rendering the side of the house. The problem with that side was that it had a terrace and high ceilings, and soon we were balancing on a wobbly homemade scaffolding in order to render the area under the roof. Because of Robert's fear of heights, it was I who was to go up there and render the top of the wall.

Climbing the old and somewhat damaged scaffolding was not a

problem; it was looking down at the narrow terrace and the abyss beyond it that started my legs to simultaneously shake and turn into lead. In an instant, my feet and the scaffolding platform became glued together, and I was unable to take another step. The rattling and the movement of the old scaffolding did not improve the situation.

Not wanting to give up so quickly, I sat down and started to render as high as I could reach from a sitting position. When I was done, there was still a metre-wide strip of exposed brick right below the roof. More familiar now with the old scaffolding, I stood up to finish the job. But as soon as I stood up, the shaking came back and once again, I was unable to take a step to the side. Looking at the spectacular views of the olive hills stretching beyond our roof, I had to admit defeat and went down the scaffolding with a solid promise to myself never to go up it again. Since there was no other way, Robert had to summon his courage and get up the scaffolding to finish the render. While he managed to keep his cool better than I did, we did come across another obstacle. The undulation of the lower surface of the roof tiles required some very tricky rendering where the tiles rested on the wall.

Even though Robert did his best, the final finish was far from pretty. I recalled how nice and even the roof finish was on all the other houses in the area, so I assumed that there must be a special technique that we were unaware of. By now, it was late in the afternoon, so we went to inspect yesterday's render, and to our dismay, it was just as wet as we had left it.

'Oh, look, this part is dry,' I shouted in excitement upon discovering a small section that indeed was dry.

Robert came to inspect it and put his finger to it. He scratched it with his finger, and the surface turned into dust and fell off.

'Why did you do that?' I asked angrily. It is one of Robert's annoying habits to try to break things to show that they are substandard quality — as a result of his 'tests,' things do usually break. This seemed to be the case with our rendering. Surely it was no wonder it was falling off after being scratched so hard, I thought.

'It's not hard. It should stay on,' Robert tried to explain upon seeing my sulking face.

'Well,' I thought to myself. 'We'll never finish if we keep on scratching it off.'

'Let's see what it looks like tomorrow,' I suggested, not wanting him to scratch the rest of the flaky rendering off.

The next day and the day after, we inspected the wall like a pair of students checking the exam board to see their results and hoping against all odds that we had passed. But as the days went on, our disappointment grew bigger and bigger. On the fourth day, we had to admit that our render was not good. Parts of the wall were still somewhat wet, and those parts that had dried were now flaking off on their own. The parts that didn't flake disintegrated under my finger and turned into dust and sand.

'I think we overmixed the cement mix,' Robert said, stating what was now evident.

'Could we have?' I started to question our initial logic. While in my heart, I was convinced that it is impossible to overmix, the internet informed us that, yes indeed, cement can be overmixed, and should this happen, it becomes weak.

Finding this out was extremely heart-breaking, for we now had to remove several days' worth of hard work and start all over again. We spent the next day scraping off the render, which was not difficult at all. Our mixture was flawed and didn't stick strongly to the wall. The patches that did stick looked uneven and out of place. As we summed up our DIY effort, we had to admit that we were at a loss, both financially and spiritually. Tallying up all the hard work put into the wall and our miserable results, we decided to not render for a while and hoped that Dani could come back and help us do it. We obviously couldn't leave the new red brick walls as they were because they were aesthetically out of place in a land of white cottages. Furthermore, they'd get wet in the rain and let moisture inside, and they did not provide much insulation from the cold and heat.

We texted Dani to see if he could come by and render the walls, but since it was only the end of January, he was still very busy picking his olives and told us to call him in April if we still needed his services. Since we didn't know any other Spanish builders, and over the months that Dani had worked for us, we came to trust his judgement and expertise, we decided to postpone the rendering and plastering until a time when he would be available to work for us again. Since there was not much else to say, we decided to spend the next two months doing things that were within our abilities, like cleaning up the front of the house that had become a construction yard, moving our boxes around, and putting in new windows.

EIGHTEEN
WORK, ESPUMA WORK

One might think that after our disastrous attempt at rendering, we would be discouraged from taking on anything as challenging as fitting all the windows to the house, but no. In fact, we were encouraged to do it ourselves by the carpenter in Granada who had made all our windows and doors. When we came by his workshop to pay him for the work, I asked whether we should hire someone to fit the windows. He looked at us as if we had lost our minds.

'No, is easy. Buy some *espuma*, put the window in, and spray. Very easy,' Iván, the carpenter, reassured us in basic English. 'You do it in five minutes.'

By that time, we already knew a lot of construction words in Spanish and knew that *espuma* was a builder's foam. With the carpenter's vote of confidence in our abilities, we drove off to our local hardware store in Puerto Lopez to buy the espuma. Seeing the foam's price, one might think that it was liquid gold, so we limited ourselves to five bottles. We had ten windows to put in, and we calculated half a bottle per window. We put the five bottles into a trolley and started our mindless daydreaming that is usually inspired by the different products that are available at the hardware store.

While you are renovating a house, a hardware store becomes your favourite place to spend time. During the bleak months of our renovation, we would often drive off for a day at BricoDepot or Leroy Merlin. Escaping the cold of a windowless house was part of what drove us there, but the other half was the promise that the project would surely come to completion if we could just find the right tools and materials. Every shelf in every aisle offered an assurance that some part of the project would be over. As I strolled along, I'd see the tile section. Even though I knew that we were nowhere near selecting bathroom tiles, I'd decide to let my mind wander off for half an hour and dream of the beautiful world in which I had a fully functioning, modern bathroom.

'Oh, I like these — these are classy.' I'd point to Robert at some sandstone imitation tiles.

'Yes, they are, but what about these? These look more rustic.' Robert would join the daydreaming session.

'But should we have the same tiles on the floor as on the walls?' I'd say encouraging the madness with questions concerning the finer details.

Since we were not going to buy any tiles at that time, we may as well have discussed them at great length; it didn't cost us any money at all. We would go on like this for a long time until I noticed the paint section.

'Maybe we should paint the walls red,' I'd suggest.

'Yeah, I like this one.' Robert selects a nice deep-burgundy paint.

'What about the blue?' I decided to add more variety to our debate.

'The blue is nice.'

To add further veracity to our insane conversations, I would often take photos of the products that we were discussing at length so that, once we were home again, we could re-examine the photos on the laptop and go over the same pros and cons once more. Even though our local hardware store does not allow for as much mind-wandering as a proper hardware hypermarket because of its smaller size, it does allow you to get carried away and start to daydream of all the jobs that might one day be completed.

'Oh, look — they have the wood stain here,' Robert pointed out.

'Let's have a look. What colours do they have?' I chose to support this mental detour and entertain the idea that one day our pale pine doors would be stained to resemble a wood of a more noble origin, such as oak or cherry. I chose to ignore the fact that said doors would have to be first fitted into what were empty door frames at the time.

'I like this one,' I said and picked up a tin of paint.

'What's *palisandro*?' Robert inquired.

'I don't know — let me see.'

I took out my phone and translated the new word, which turned out to mean *rosewood*. I liked the idea of rosewood; it had a slight nostalgic tinge to it, bringing to my memory some of the beautiful Indian and Arabic furniture that I had seen in Dubai.

'Oh, but I like this one.' Robert picked up another tin. What's *nogal*?'

'It's walnut. Obviously,' I rolled my eyes. I don't know why, but it seemed to me obvious that *nogal* would be *walnut*.

'What's oak in Spanish?' I asked myself, wanting to see a more classic tint. I typed *oak* and repeated the Spanish word: *roble*.

'Here it is.' Robert picked up a tin of wood stain labelled *roble*.

Somehow the oak that I had in mind did not match the colour on the tin. I was not satisfied with the choice.

'They look different than on the tin when applied on the wooden plank,' I proclaimed, drawing on my lifetime experience of buying hair-dying products. 'The colour will change depending on the colour of the wooden planks.'

While I'm not very fussy about the colour that my hair turns out to be in the end, I was adamant that we should test all the wood stains before we buy it in bulk and start applying them to the pine doors and pine ceiling planks that we had awaiting installation in the garage. To be methodical, we selected six different small tins of wood stain, picked our five bottles of espuma, and went to pay for the lot. As luck would have it, while we were at the till, the Englishman who used to look after our property came into the shop to buy some bits and pieces. We exchanged some pleasantries, and it didn't take him a long time to notice our purchase laid on the counter.

'Wow! It looks like you're almost finished. Buying paint?' He seemed impressed and shocked at the same time.

Not wanting to explain that we were about to buy five small tins of wood paint that we didn't really need in order to test what we might one day use to paint the doors and the ceiling that were nowhere near being fitted, I simply smiled and nodded my head.

'Well done.' He was clearly impressed with the speed of our reform. 'Must go. See you.'

We packed our purchases in silence and went home. Thank God we didn't buy bathroom tiles or wall paint because we really had no more space in the garage to keep all the materials that we were buying so far in advance. A few days later, we tested the various wood stains on some wood scraps and decided on *nogal* as the colour for our windows and doors. It's a warm and inviting colour. We then spent a week painting and varnishing all the windows before we could fit them.

Wood is not the modern material of choice in hot and sunny Andalusia. It wears down quickly, changes shape when left in the sun or heavy rain, and can become infested by boring insects. Our neighbours advised us against it and recommended aluminium windows as a much more modern and durable solution. But I could not imagine myself living in a stone cottage with aluminium windows. There are few things in life that I find more aesthetically displeasing than grey aluminium windows on a charming rural cottage. There were fake-wood finishes on aluminium windows, but I wasn't convinced by them. It was my home and I wanted it finished in style. Since we could not use pine for the windows or outside doors because it's very weak and soft, I researched different types of wood used in Spain and learned that *iroco* is a popular hardwood from West Africa and can withstand scorching heat and freezing cold. As it so happened, our carpenter knew all about this type of wood. He made beautiful rustic windows with shutters and doors with Alhambra motives for the whole house. I loved them. All we had to do was paint them and fit them.

The painting took several days. We first had to apply two coats of *fondo*, which is a very toxic transparent liquid designed to prevent insects, fungus, and moisture from destroying the wood. Then, we applied two coats of *nogal* wood stain to protect the windows from the sun and rain. Once the windows were ready to fit, we watched a few YouTube tutorials and went to task. As we both stood in front of an empty window hole in one of the guest bedrooms, I assessed the job at hand. We had a heavy hardwood and double-glazed window in one corner and a few metres away from it a perfect hole to fit it in. Dani had made sure that we could fit the windows into these apertures. Even though the job seemed easy, I was anxious.

'So we just pick the window and put it in the frame?' I asked hesitantly.

'No, we need a spirit level.' Robert went to the garage to get one.

Until we moved to Spain to do the reform, I had never needed a spirit level. Not once in the first thirty-six years of my existence was I ever in a situation where I thought: 'I should use a spirit level to do this job'. Yet, in this new life, a spirit level was as indispensable as a knife and fork. When Robert returned, we set the spirit level, some wooden wedges, and a tin of espuma on the floor by the window.

'We should take the doors and shutters off the frame,' Robert said.

'Aha!' I thought. Yes, taking the heavy glass doors and shutters off was a great idea; it also reduced the risk of the window falling out to the ground on the other side. We did as Robert suggested, and I picked the window frame up.

'Hold it while I check the level.' As I was Robert's only helping hand, I did as I was instructed. I picked it up and placed it inside the designated hole. We made some adjustments as he checked the levels.

'Now, don't move it.' I was told while I was holding the frame suspended a centimetre or so above the bottom edge.

'OK. Hurry.' I was worried my arms would give in soon.

Robert grabbed the espuma, and with the dedicated nozzle, sprayed the foam inside between the wall and the window frame.

'Is that it?' I asked. I could not see how this was going to hold anything, never mind a heavy hardwood window. 'Do it again.'

Robert followed my suggestion and sprayed the espuma two more times. If you know the tale of *The Magic Porridge Pot*, it will be easy for you to imagine what happened next. I might as well have incanted: 'Work, espuma, work' because, on command, it started to grow and grow. The strange spongy and foamy substance was now pouring slowly from every nook and cranny and ballooning into a new entity.

In Grimm's fairy tale, the uncontrolled porridge slowly fills up the house, the house next door and the whole street. Only when the owner of the magic pot, a little girl, comes home and says: 'Stop, little pot' does the porridge cease multiplying itself and saves the village from destruction. How the little girl managed to walk the streets of her village, which were flooded by porridge and then get inside her house to stop the manic pot is not explained. Despite this plot hole, I knew there were no magic words that I could utter to stop the relentless expansion of the *espuma*.

As my job was to hold the frame until the foam set, Robert was left to run around in panic and wipe the exponentially self-multiplying sticky foam from the window frame and the wall. To no avail. The espuma was now running down the wall and covering the wooden frame almost completely. To say that Robert was wiping the foam down is an understatement. You can't wipe down this substance. When wet, it has the consistency of melting chewing gum. It gets stuck on anything it touches and it's impossible to remove. Nevertheless, he tried to control it. A few minutes later, the foam hardened, and I was allowed to let go of the frame. We decided to let it harden for a day before we put in the glass doors and shutters.

Indeed, when inspected the next day, we noted that the espuma had hardened, and we were able to cut the excess off with a carpet knife. We did have to sand the window frame down again and repaint it as the surface was damaged by the foam, but we learned from this. Knowing espuma's strange power to increase its volume by multiple orders of magnitude, we were now more judicial in using it and gave it a few minutes after applying to grow and fill in the holes. In one day, we installed all the windows. Again, we waited a day for the foam to harden before putting in the glass doors and shutters. As we walked around the house the next day, we were both very pleased with our work. It felt like a big step forward to have windows in one's house. I felt that the hardwood windows looked so pretty, and I could only imagine how amazing it would all look once the walls were rendered and plastered. By now, it was early February, and we had just managed to seal the house up before snow and ice came. We spent February inside, Robert translating and editing and me writing material for an app. In March, a plumber and an electrician from Montefrio busied themselves setting up the inner works of a household.

Dani re-joined our efforts in April, and from then, the work resumed its steady pace. The speed and precision with which he applied the cement render and then the *capa fina*, which is a Spanish finishing mortar, made us realize that we would never have had finished it ourselves. Under his careful eye, the walls turned out straight and flat, and the corners were clean and sharp. Each day of his work transformed our house and brought the project one step closer to finishing.

It was only after a few weeks of working as Dani's apprentice that Robert learned how to properly apply the render and *capa fina* and grew in confidence that would be needed later in our renovations. That spring, we also acquired a clear deadline — on the ninth of September 2015, my sister, her husband, and their three children were coming to stay with us for three weeks. At that stage, we were still living in the small bedroom off the living room, and there was no space for company in the old part of the house that we inhabited. We had to finish the guest bedrooms by September.

NINETEEN
THE DEADLINE

F inishing off the bedrooms became a serious logistical nightmare. One of our main obstacles in the race to the finish line was the mountainous number — literally one hundred and fifty-six — of boxes that contained our belongings that were now scattered in different rooms and spaces around the 'project' — the professional way to describe the construction site that we lived in. When we sent the container with our boxes off to sea from the desert of Al Ain, we did not expect to see it in Malaga for another two or three months. As it turned out, our shipping agency was extraordinarily efficient and had our boxes ready for us in Malaga harbour two weeks after we ourselves landed in Spain. This was unfortunate because we now had to pay for the boxes' storage in a warehouse in Granada.

The company charged us about two hundred and fifty euros a month for the privilege of keeping our stuff in an industrial area on the outskirts of Granada. In hindsight, for that money, we could have rented a two-bedroom flat in Alcalá la Real and kept our boxes there; the bonus would have been that we might have been able to use the flat to shelter us from the rain and the wind that we suffered throughout the autumn. If I were able to go back in time, that's exactly what I would have done. But back then, we were too overwhelmed with settling in and doing the reform to think of this easy solution. As it was, we spent the autumn rushing the workers to complete the building of the garage of our house, and as soon as it was ready and it had a metal door installed, we asked the shipping company to bring our boxes to the house.

We seemed to have chosen a very legitimate company. They could not have been more professional, which made us look like two hippies living in a junkyard. They arrived on time on a cold December morning in two spacious vans; we feared that the shipping company might try to bring the whole container to our doorstep, but they must have had a good insight about the Spanish country roads.

As soon as they parked outside the house, we realized our mistake; out of the vans jumped five red-and-blue-clad professional movers who were ready to move our furniture to their proper positions *inside* the house and reassemble it as it had been in Al Ain. They were well-trained and eager to put a household back together. Unfortunately, except for the tiny old section where we slept and cooked our meals, our house was still mostly a brick structure, with no windows on the second floor and no render on any of the new walls. All our possessions were to be stored in boxes in the new garage.

On hearing this, the group's supervisor repeated our request several times in broken English to make sure that he had heard correctly, reversed the truck to the garage, and his men started off-loading our belongings. The five spider-men ran up and down the ramp at the back of the truck, bringing the boxes so fast that I was not able to see all the boxes they carried in. I was watching their work because I hoped to spot and retrieve one very precious piece of equipment that I missed dearly in our house — our old vacuum cleaner.

Not wanting to buy anything that we already had and thus double the number of our earthly possessions, we spent the first five months in our new home with no winter clothes, minimal cooking utensils, and no vacuum cleaner. We did eventually surrender and bought a few jerseys in a hardware store, but a new vacuum cleaner was not deemed to be a necessity. As a result, I cleaned all the construction site dust and dirt with a very old-fashioned broom that I inherited with the house.

The idea of cleaning your house with a broom may seem quaint and nostalgic — it brings to mind a chubby nursery rhyme character eager to rid her house of mice and vermin by sweeping her broom left and right while dancing and singing around the house. As a household tool, it is now so out of use that hipster cafés in big cities use them as decorations to evoke rustic and old-timey associations. They might carefully place an old broom on the wall right next to a hayfork and a spade in order to make us believe that the factory-baked muffins were prepared this morning by a farmer's wife, who might have used the broom to sweep the flour-covered floor just before the baker's van arrived to pick up a tray of freshly-baked goods.

I don't agree with this simulacrum that is generated by greedy corporations. Still, I have to agree that the best place for an old-fashioned house broom is on the wall, but not in a café where it helps create fake nostalgia that sells cakes but as a museum piece. Children should go to such a museum and look at the tools of the past that were used by generations of our grandmothers and their mothers and ponder the number of lives wasted and hours spent on moving dust from one corner of the house to another. It might have been a single evil genius who, in fear that the patriarchal regime might fall and crumble one day, devised a tool that is so pointless in its poor design that it makes Sisyphean labour appear worthwhile. He then convinced us, women, that in order to keep our houses clean — and by doing that, keep things from falling apart — we must use a broom.

As a cleaning utensil, a house broom is a useless piece of

equipment. Unless you wish to get rid of dirt the size of small potatoes, the broom is not your friend. All you do is waltz around your house, moving the dust from one corner to another. The middle of the living room floor starts looking nice and polished, but then you notice that all the debris is now piled up in several small inaccessible corners around the room. Removing tiny piles of dirt from the corners of a room is not the job for a broom at all. You end up flicking most of the particles back into the middle of the room and pounding the rest of the dust into the same corner, remaining there for centuries as testimony to our civilization's failings.

Now that you are done sweeping the floors, you can mop them. The wet mop only accentuates the dirt that is still on the floor in the form of muddy streaks and makes a mockery of your efforts. After five months of using a broom, I was sick and tired of living in dirt and was now desperate to hunt down our vacuum cleaner and snatch it from the busy hands of the movers before they buried it under other boxes.

The problem with seeing your possessions after such a long time was that each box seemed like a secret Christmas gift. The whimsical labels, such as 'tools', 'clothes', and 'kitchen stuff' only whet my appetite, and I just wanted to open all of them and see what might be inside. Unable to resist the temptation, I did remove a few boxes from the human conveyor belt that the movers formed and moved them to our bedroom to open later in the day. It must have been then that the vacuum cleaner was moved from the truck to the garage because when the truck was empty, I still had not identified the box containing my precious vacuum cleaner. The whole process took the movers less than two hours, and when they were done, they asked if they could have their lunch now — it was only ten a.m. — before they went back to Granada.

While they consumed their well-deserved brunch, I went to the bedroom, where I had stashed a few boxes and opened the first one labelled 'clothes and plates'. Back in Al Ain, before we hired a moving company, we did a lot of packing ourselves, and in order to save wrapping paper and bubble wrap, I used our own clothes and towels to protect fragile items. As a result, wine glasses and bed linen were packed together, for example. Similarly, all the kitchen appliances were packed along with items from our wardrobe. As I opened the first box, I could not believe my luck — my old Swedish winter jacket was squashed on the top of the dining set. I put the jacket on. Because of the ongoing construction, the house's doors were permanently open to enable workers to come in and out without any obstruction. This created an ambient temperature in our bedroom and living room of about eight degrees Celsius or about forty-six Fahrenheit.

Pleased with the find, I searched the other boxes. But apart from bone china, a set of towels, and the Indian lanterns that used to decorate our living room — I found nothing else of use to us at that moment in our lives. Disappointed, I waited for the movers to leave and then entered the garage, determined to scavenge and plunder until I found more things that might bring me comfort. I was also still hoping to retrieve the lost vacuum. The mountain of boxes inside was stacked five boxes high. Since I could not check the first four levels, I decided to climb to the top and check the top level. Such is the human desire to find solace in nice things that I did not consider the danger of all the boxes falling on top of me or me falling into a crevice created by the shifting boxes. I moved a few things around and used the edges of the boxes to clamber to the top. I then rummaged and crawled about like a crazy homeless lady who had found a stash of second-hand goods and became delirious with happiness.

And, indeed, I did feel very happy to crawl about on top of my things. I found a pair of winter shoes, some motorbike helmets, an old PC, and so many other things that I had forgotten that we owned. In one of the nooks, I even spotted a glimpse of my long-lost green-and-white vacuum. I dug deep and moved things around, and finally fished the precious box out.

While crawling about on top of box mountain, I spotted our old bed frame and the mattress, which, unlike the Spanish bed of torture, were king-sized and made of memory foam. I reported my find to Robert, and that weekend we folded up the old *cama de matrimonio* that came with the house and reassembled our old bed, which made the bedroom look positively tiny. In our old house in Al Ain, the bed used to take up just a third of the bedroom. Transported to the Andalusian cottage, it looked as if it had drunk a magic potion that made it grow and grow and grow. The only thing that seemed to have stopped our bed from growing more were the walls of the bedroom. We had only a twenty-centimetre gap on each side of the bed to get in or out of it. This was not satisfactory, and it was obvious that we had to move the bed right up to the wall on one side so that we could get in and out of it. Once the bed was assembled and positioned, we stepped back and sighed in awe. Few things in those days gave us as much happiness as the sight of a proper bed — fewer still could be compared with the feeling of sleeping on a cloud, which is what it felt like when we reacquainted ourselves with our old mattress. Now we were ready to face anything. Or so I thought.

Very soon after the furniture transport crew filled our garage with our possessions, we realized that we needed said garage to store the hundreds of pinewood planks and wooden beams that were to arrive from Granada. When we started the remodel in September, we decided to have high-vaulted ceilings throughout the second floor of the house. We both felt strongly that this particular design feature needed to be a part of our dream house. While our builder did not object to the vaulted ceilings when the idea was presented to him on paper, it was only after the roof was laid that he admitted to not having any idea how to clad the ceiling of the roof on the inside. I spent weeks walking around the construction and looking at the exposed concrete beams, steel mesh and polystyrene insulation staring me in the face. Whenever I asked our chief builder, an Englishman from Montefrio, what his plans were for the ugly ceiling, he would shrug and give me random suggestions in the second person.

'I don't know. You could paint it.'

I would look at him as if he had just cooked my cat for supper, which usually prompted more stupid ideas.

'You could put some MDF board on it and then plaster it.'

I gave him a look of horror and walked away silently. By that stage of the renovation, our relationship was already severely damaged, and I liked to think that he was a little bit afraid of me. A month or so earlier, when I was talking about wanting to kill our architect, who stole a significant amount of money from us and disappeared, the English builder asked me whether I was going to send the Polish mafia after the said architect. I didn't answer. It must have been the years of stereotypes and the result of the frictions between Polish and English builders in the UK that made this man believe that I had connections to the mafia, but I never disputed his misconceptions. In fact, I enjoyed imagining the Polish mafia coming to rural Spain to talk some sense to my Spanish architect and my English builder. But since I could not lay my hands on any mafia men of any nationality, I had to resolve the problem of cladding the ceiling myself.

In the two years that we prepared for the renovation, I had a habit of taking photographs of any design features that I liked when I saw them used in buildings in Spain. On a visit to the Alhambra, I took hundreds of photos of small design items that I thought were precious: the stairs clad with wood and tile inserts, delicate window shutters as if they had been crocheted from African hardwood, water cascading down a marble handrail, and beautiful symmetrically-laid rose gardens with fountains brimming with colourful fish and water lilies — none of these designs would be achievable at my house since they would require the sweat, tears, and labour of hundreds of slaves.

But they were inspirational; thinking of these beautiful designs, I remembered that many old Moorish houses in Granada and Cordoba had ceilings that were clad with wooden planks supported by thick, substantial wooden beams. I was determined that that was going to be the ceiling of our house. Of course, the wood in those old houses is very dark as it had been painted over the centuries and darkened over the passing years. To buy hardwood that was naturally quite dark and then to clad the whole ceiling with it would have been very costly. A cheaper alternative, which we chose, was to buy pine planks from Germany and then stain them with palisandro and walnut wood stain.

In early January, at the peak of our DIY efforts and enthusiasm, we measured the ceiling and placed the order with our carpenter. Optimists that we were, we expected that all the walls inside the house would be completely rendered and plastered when these planks arrived; in our mind, we did not want to waste any time by having to wait for them even a week or two. As it turned out, we only finished rendering and plastering the inside of the house by July, and that was with Dani's help.

Of course, the huge delivery of wooden planks and beams could not wait at the carpenter's yard until the summer. He called us at the end of February and told us that they couldn't store the planks and beams for us any longer. The problem was that we had no place to put the huge load of wooden planks, beams, and the wooden flooring that we ordered. The wood had to be stored indoors in a reasonably dry place; otherwise, it would bend out of shape and be impossible to use as cladding for the ceiling. The only solution that we could think of was to move the boxes that were hogging the garage space to different rooms in the house and to store the wood in the garage.

Since we had only two days to make space in the garage, there was no way that the two of us would be able to move all the boxes and furniture alone. The job would have killed us. As always, full of ideas on how to avoid doing something severely physical, I suggested that we hire a couple of lads from Montefrio to move the boxes. Robert called Juan, one of the guys who had previously worked for us on the construction, and he recommended a friend to assist him. They had both finished working with olives. As neither of them had a car or any other means of transport, early next morning, Robert collected them from the square outside the round church in Montefrio. They worked hard and fast, and it was a pleasure to watch the boxes disappear from the garage at a steady pace. All Robert had to do was show the workers where to put them.

We made sure that there was at least one metre of space from the walls in the new rooms so that Dani could have access to them when he re-joined the project. Manu and Juan worked so fast that they were finished in one day. Since we felt bad for making them think that there were more days of work, we asked them to come back the next day to start laying the rocks that we used to build a stone patio, and the day after that, they came to help us unload the wood delivery.

Overall, we used their help for several weeks. Having two young men around who are eager to work and willing to lift heavy objects is very motivating; without their presence, we might have found it difficult to get up on many cold winter mornings to work in the rain and mud. Because Robert had to collect them and give them directions, we got up early every morning — despite the cold and rain — and were ready for work. As we developed a routine, I noticed that the early morning darkness and the cold were not conducive to good communication.

One of the main jobs that I hoped that Juan and Manu might do and save me from sweat and tears was laying a stone patio outside the future rental apartment. As a result of knocking down the structurally unsound animal room, we ended up with a giant pile of good quality stone that we felt obliged to reuse somewhere in the house. Most of the stones had at least one flat surface, and since they were quite big and extremely heavy, I felt that they would be well-suited to use in a traditional stone patio floor. I also thought that this type of work would be a nice change for Juan and Manu, who hardly ever got to build anything creative and attractive-looking.

Their usual work was limited to carrying uninspiring concrete bricks around building sites to build carports, garages, and retaining walls around Montefrio. I felt that building something creative and out of stone would give them both a sense of achievement and satisfaction. As it turned out, they both hated every minute of the job. Juan was the first one who started sulking and complaining about laying the stones on the patio floor. At lunchtime, he took out his very dry piece of bread, cut it into small pieces, and opened a tin of fish. He looked at Robert seriously, as if chewing both his food and what he was about to say.

'*No estoy contento,*' he spat out as if it was perfectly clear why he was not happy.

Robert looked at him with a somewhat blank expression, assuming that the young man was talking about his life in general and not the specific job at hand. As it was, Juan just had a baby with a young girl whose family did not approve of him. Neither Juan nor his girlfriend had any prospects of getting full-time jobs, and they relied heavily on social security. They both suffered from alcohol abuse in their homes, and it was very likely that young Juan's child would follow his young parents' life path. His saying that he was not happy might have applied to a million things that were going wrong in his life. As neither Robert nor his friend Manu responded, Juan reiterated.

'A mí no me gusta,' he stated strongly.

It was clear that something was on his mind, but he did not seem to be able to explain the problem. It was his friend Manu who read his mind and explained that they did not enjoy laying the stone floor. In fact, they hated it. Had it not been for the money that they got paid at the end of the week, they would have walked off after the first hour of working with the stones.

In the evening, when Robert told me about this discontent in our troops, I was quite surprised. I myself was very pleased with the work that they were doing and thought that the stone floor was shaping up beautifully. It looked authentic and rustic; it was not a factory-cut tile where repeated patterns and a fake rustic charm were painted onto the tiles. I thought that the patio floor looked solid and real, and because it was made from real stone, it would only look better with time after it was walked on hundreds of times and polished by wind and weather. I was dissatisfied with their attitude, but I wanted the patio done.

I did not have enough Spanish to discuss any artistic differences with the men, but I wanted to encourage them. The next morning, as soon as I heard them coming, I left my work by the laptop and approached the stone patio. But instead of seeing men at work, I saw a pathetic display of *machismo*. The three of them, including Robert, seemed to have forgotten human language and chose to communicate in grunts and by nodding their heads and shrugging their arms. The guys were standing by the stone patio they were supposed to be working on, but instead of arranging stones, they were chain-smoking cigarettes. Robert was leaning on an olive tree and looked as if he was about to murder one of them.

'What's going on?' I asked. 'Why aren't they working?'

'I don't know. Ask them,' Robert barked.

I turned to the guys and asked them what was happening. They shrugged and told me that they didn't know what to do.

'They don't know what to do.' I turned to Robert and translated even though he had heard them clearly himself.

'I told them what to do,' Robert snapped.

I doubted that he did but chose not to argue the point.

'Let's finish the patio,' I suggested to Juan and Manu in Spanish.

I could see that they were almost halfway done and calculated that the work would take three more days. The reason it was taking longer than anticipated was that each stone was of a different thickness. For the floor to have an even surface, they had to either dig down into the soil before laying the stone or pad the space under the stone with sand.

'I don't like this floor,' Juan explained. 'It is not nice to walk on.'

'People will trip when they walk from the apartment to the pool.' Manu demonstrated a vacationer in his or her flip-flops tripping over the stone patio.

'Also, you can't walk on this with bare feet,' his buddy chimed in. 'Concrete is much better.'

It was disappointing to hear that the two of them would much rather slave all day by a cement mixer, mindlessly carrying buckets of concrete to be poured out as an uninspiring concrete floor, than do something creative. It made me think of the beautifully crafted stone pavements in Montefrio and other medieval towns and villages all over Andalusia. It was evident that respect for the art of using stone had left these two workers. The careful craftsmanship involved in laying a stone floor did not give these young wannabe builders any pleasure. As I started to doubt our decision to use real stone to create a patio floor, I suddenly realized that I was taking advice from people who considered a print of the Virgen de los Remedios — the patron saint of Montefrio — a work of art.

Thus, after careful consideration of my critics' credentials, I decided to follow my own taste and asked them to finish the stone patio. I decided to ignore their sulking and left them to do the job; unlike the people who slaved over the pavements of Andalusia eight hundred or so years before them, these two had a choice.

Once Dani re-joined us, the work started to move at a rapid pace. Robert became Dani's apprentice and labour hand again, and we kept Juan on to bring in the concrete, mix the plaster, and tidy the site at the end of each day. I couldn't be much help as I was still working on the app content, which took up most of my day. In June, our reformed bedroom upstairs was fully rendered and covered with sparkling-white *capa fina.* Even though the work progressed at a steady pace, it did not seem to come to an end. Once our happiness of having white walls in our soon-to-be-bedroom wore off, we realized that we had to paint the walls before installing the wooden ceiling. Before we could paint the walls, we had to lay down fresh floors with special self-levelling concrete. Then, we had to start staining the planks and the beams to clad the ceiling's surface.

In our optimism, we ordered a walk-in closet that was to be delivered and installed on a given day. Thus, we placed all our attention on finishing the ceiling and the walls inside the closet so that the furniture store workers could install the cupboards and shelving. We also realized that we had to put the floor in the closet before it was installed. It seemed that making one small step forward in the project required an array of jobs to be completed. The completion of the renovation project was starting to take forever, and having to remember what had to be done first for the next task to be completed became overwhelming. That's why I started to make lists of things to do and left them on sticky notes on our laptop. This was the only way for us to keep track of things that had to be done as a priority.

While I made the to-do lists — mostly for myself, in order then to tell Robert and Dani what to do each day — it appeared that my husband had internalized them subconsciously and would often tell us what had to be done next *as if he had just thought about it.* There was no time to claim ownership, and I was happy that it saved me from nagging. Now that I had turned my husband into a mindless robot who followed the set of memorized instructions, I was free to paint the walls as soon as Dani and Robert finished the *capa fina.*

By July, I had finished my work on the app and became chief painter and a labour hand. Robert, Dani, and I worked as slaves throughout July and August in forty-degree heat and with just a few breaks for food and drink. We'd start at seven a.m. when the air was still cool and fresh. Dani would finish around three and go home to spend summer afternoons with his teen kids. Robert and I would break for a dip in the pool and a snack, but there was hardly ever time for a proper siesta. When I wasn't painting the walls, I was staining the endless pile of wooden planks.

To prevent the wood from being eaten by insects or infected by fungus, each plank had to be properly painted with an insecticide and fungicide liquid called *fondo*. Using fondo in a small room in the heat of the Spanish summer may not have been the best idea — on a few occasions, I might have inadvertently inhaled too much of the fondo fumes and became slightly delusional. Once we identified the culprit of our episodic hallucinations, we thought it best to apply the chemical on the wooden planks outdoors. The smell still permeated the area, but it was not intoxicating our brains to the same degree. It would take a day for the fondo to be applied and dried and a day or two for two coats of the stain. Then the ready planks would be pinned to the ceiling to make room for the next batch.

We worked in this haphazard and exhausting way until there was one more week to go. A week before my family's arrival, we needed a much more focused action plan. Now for each day of the week, we had a clear task that had to be accomplished; otherwise, my sister and her children would be sleeping on a concrete floor surrounded by rubble and smelling toxic gases oozing from the freshly painted planks. On Monday, we had to put the ceiling in Amelia's room — that's what we called the room where my brother-in-law's daughter would sleep. On Tuesday — put the laminate floor in Amelia's room. Wednesday — put the laminate floor in our new bedroom. Thursday — make the celling in Beata's apartment. Friday — put the floor in Beata's apartment. And so it went — each day assigned to a heavy, almost never-ending task. To accomplish all this in one week, we worked very long hours, and despite our best efforts, it was clear that we wouldn't be ready on the day of their arrival.

Despite the stress of trying to do as much as possible, it was a fulfilling summer. Because I was now fully immersed in the renovation, I did not have time to second-guess the whole project. Few things in life will clear your mind of worry or anxiety, as well as a day full of manual labour. And each week that summer was a small step forward to making our simple abode into a liveable house. Each week transformed this wretched building site into my dream home. With each step finished, we would often sit back and look at it in wonder. First, the ceilings were finally clad with nogal stained wood. Then, the giant beams were put into place as a nod to the region's Moorish past. And at last, electricity was connected to the second floor. I remember the evening when I locked the gate after our electrician had finally left. I turned around and looked up to see our little cottage on the hill now with all the indoor and outdoor lights on. 'It finally looks like home,' I thought with a great sense of relief and went up the driveway to cook supper.

TWENTY

THEY'RE AN HOUR FROM MONTEFRIO

O n the morning of my family's arrival, I woke up at six with a clear action plan in mind. The bedroom where my sister, her partner, and their babies were to sleep was still filled, floor to ceiling, with about fifty moving boxes. Since this was an unacceptable set-up for visitors to sleep in, we had to move these boxes downstairs to the bedroom where we were still sleeping. To make space in that bedroom for the boxes, we had to move our own king-size bed upstairs to our newly finished bedroom. After a sleepless night in which I went over these puzzle pieces over and over again, I woke up ready for action. I expected that my sister would be leaving Valencia after breakfast, so I gave her about five hours to get to Montefrio. I did not expect to see the whole Polish expedition on my doorsteps before three p.m. As I rushed Robert out of bed, emphasizing several times that it was 'go time' and that we 'needed to move,' it became apparent that I had not run this action plan past him, and so he had no idea about the day's mad agenda.

'We need to move this bed upstairs quickly,' I said.

'Why?' Robert was still getting to grips with the plan.

'So, we can make space for the boxes from the apartment.' I sighed, annoyed with his slow rate of comprehension and compliance.

The rest of the puzzle pieces seemed to fall into place, and I collected our sheets and bedding and took it upstairs to our new bedroom. The mattress, as it turned out, was a completely different story. I had bought it five or six years prior as a gift to myself. In those days, I suffered from occasional but severe back pains, and instead of doing more exercise, I convinced myself and Robert that a top-of-the-line spring-based memory foam mattress would cure my ailments. As I looked at the giant king-size monstrosity now, I could not remember if it had ever helped alleviate the pains. But it was time to move the mattress and the bed frame to their final destination, which was upstairs.

The expression 'king-size' has held a certain allure for me since childhood. It is one of the first words I learned in English because it was written on my father's cigarettes packet. My father did not know much English and thus was unable to explain what it meant. He thought it had something to do with luxury and being expensive. It was more than twenty years later in the Gulf that I learned the true meaning of king-size. Being a carbon copy of the US, everything in the UAE is either supersized or king-sized. And not just any king-sized but *American* king-sized. The truth is that king-sized is not a specific size, but whatever a given population deems to be of extravagant or outrageous proportions. Were our mattress a Spanish or French king-sized mattress, we would not have had any problems carrying it up the stairs to our new bedroom. But, as it was, our mattress was 'a Gulf king-size', and it turned out to be a beast.

First, we put it sideways and managed to slide it under the doorway, scraping the paint off the top of the frame, but as we reached the stairs, it became apparent that the mattress would never make the bend at the top of the staircase. Our staircase is such that there is a ninety-degree turn to the left after the first three steps. Given that the staircase is only one metre wide, turning that mattress at that angle in such a narrow space was impossible.

As we stood holding the mattress on its side and looking at the narrow staircase, dark thoughts started to cloud my mind. It seemed that we were never going to sleep on a proper king-size mattress in our new bedroom. We were doomed to sleep on the *cama de matrimonio*. I did not know who to blame for this oversight — should we have built the house around the mattress? I was clearly losing my mind, and as we stood dumbfounded, the clock was ticking.

'Let's go.' Robert seemed oblivious of the mismatch between the size of the staircase and the size of the mattress.

Lacking a better idea, I decided to follow his direction. Since pulling is more physically demanding than pushing, I opted to be the pusher while Robert went to the front and tried to pull the mattress up the stairs. We got the monster up the first three steps and then, in our manic rush, pushed it halfway to the bathroom on the landing. After some heated debate about the usefulness of a mattress in the bathroom, Robert tried to bend it to turn the corner. He might as well have tried to bend spoons with his mind; the giant memory foam was not going to give in one inch. The thing with memory foam mattresses with a spring base is that they are soft and springy when you lie on them, but as a solid two-by-two-metre object that needs to be carried around, it is not very flexible.

We pushed and pulled, and leaned on it and kicked it, and shouted at each other, but the gargantuan mattress would not budge. I caught a glimpse of the wall clock behind me and saw that we'd spent two hours, so far, moving the bed upstairs and were nowhere near finishing. In fact, we had wasted time trying to do the impossible. As all the other jobs that had to be done by three p.m. rushed through my mind, I told Robert that we should leave it. There was no time to move this mattress.

'Let's move it through one of the balcony doors,' my genius husband announced.

It was not a bad idea. I did remember once in Amsterdam asking about the cranes located on top of the roofs of the townhouses that lined the canals. As I learned then, the cranes were used to move people's furniture in and out of their apartments because the staircases were too narrow to do so. And so now we were going to apply Dutch ingenuity in our Spanish *cortijo*.

We dragged the mattress down the three steps and out through the main door. We left it leaning against the wall below the upstairs terrace, and Robert went looking for a set of suitable ropes. We were lucky that there was a delay in the delivery of the terrace balustrades, and so there was no physical obstacle that would be in the way of the mattress. Once the mattress was lifted in the air and high enough, we simply had to flip it over to the terrace and drag it up.

Once Robert tied all the ropes, he went upstairs and I threw the ends of the ropes to him. It would have been impossible for one person to lift the giant bed using what looked like shoestrings, so I braced myself and went upstairs. As I held the polyester rope in my hand, a thought occurred to me that, should the mattress slip, we would end up with severe rope burns on our palms. So, to Robert's dismay, I rushed downstairs to get some work gloves for protection.

Now, armed with proper work gloves, we started to pull the thing up. I could see Robert appreciate my foresight when the rope started to cut into the gloves and squeeze the life out of our hands. With great effort and further shouts of matrimonial encouragement, we managed to lift the mattress to the level of the terrace, but then it got stuck on the edge of the tiles. Someone had to run downstairs and pull it away from the edge.

As it was clear that I was not going to be able to hold the mattress by myself, I handed the ropes to Robert and ran downstairs to pull the mattress away from the edge so that it could be lifted to the terrace. Once the mattress was unstuck, I realized that I might just as well lift it above my head and save myself running up and down. And so, I stood under this monstrous mattress and lifted it up while Robert pulled it upwards with the rope. A thought occurred to me that should the ropes break, my neck might snap from the heavy mass hanging over my head, but we moved swiftly, and in seconds the whole gargantuan mattress was on the terrace floor outside our new bedroom.

I ran back upstairs and saw exhausted Robert sitting on the terrace floor. The next thing I considered was the two French windows that led from the terrace to the bedroom. My heart sank.

'Were we really so foolish as to not check the size of the door opening before we dragged this heavy beast onto the terrace?' I could not believe our stupidity. In my mind, I tried to remember the exact height of the French windows from when I ordered them, but various numbers were rushing through my head and I could not decide whether it was one hundred and eighty or two hundred centimetres. The mattress was two hundred centimetres on all sides, and as we had just learned an hour before on the staircase, it would not bend or fold at all. I did not share these thoughts with Robert because they seemed too dark. And for a moment, it seemed that we would never have a proper king-size bed in our new bedroom.

Unaware of these issues, Robert got up and we picked up the mattress. When we pulled it up to the French window, it became apparent that we were just going to make it. Pushing and kicking, we pulled the stubborn mattress into the new bedroom, and it landed with gusto onto the floor. This was the trigger for the rest of the dominos. Now we were ready to follow my plan.

We moved the bed frame upstairs via the terrace, as it turned out to be the fastest route, and we were now ready to move boxes from the new guest bedroom to the room that had served as our bedroom throughout the whole renovation process. By now, it was well past nine a.m., and my carefully arranged action plan was at least three hours delayed. I opened the guest apartment and then the door to the guest bedroom. The boxes inside were stacked from floor to ceiling. There were also about thirty boxes of laminate flooring that was to be used elsewhere in the house and lots of other bits and pieces.

When presented with a Herculean task like this, one may be tempted to overthink it.

'Let's move these out first, and then we can get to the rest,' I felt like suggesting.

The truth is that such remarks are just a delaying tactic. What I was really thinking was: 'There is no damn way we can move all these boxes out before lunch.'

But there was no way of avoiding the job at hand — my sister and her family were in the car driving to Montefrio, blissfully unaware that they had no bed or place to sleep. I was sure that they would not feel like moving furniture the very day that they arrived. The thought of having them stay in the grotty hotel in Montefrio did not even occur to me. The point of their journey was to see us back in Europe. In the past ten years, I had only seen my sister four times, twice on her trips to Al Ain, once when I visited Poland alone, and two years prior when my nephew, Kosma, was born and we went to Poland to see the baby. More importantly, they were travelling with a one-year-old baby girl, Zoja, who was born the previous October. It would be the first time I would see my niece.

For a second, I thought that it might be easier to put them downstairs in our old bedroom, but then I realized that we wouldn't be able to survive with one bathroom. It was bad enough for Robert and me to have to share it — especially in the mornings when we both needed to use it urgently and at the same time. Many sharp exchanges had taken place over limited bathroom access, with one of us leaning on the bathroom door outside and rushing the other to finish their business.

A shared bathroom is not good for a marriage. It was definitely not going to improve family relations. I could not imagine having to compete with three adults and three children over a bathroom. To be fair, two of the children were wearing diapers and could sort out their 'business' outside the bathroom, but still.

For the next several hours, we worked like farm mules — walking at a steady pace, not too fast so as to get out of breath and not too slow so as to annoy each other, and, box by box, we moved all of them out of the guest bedroom and stacked them floor to ceiling in our old bedroom.

There is really not much that can describe this kind of monotonous heavy lifting, but to illustrate our effort that day, it should suffice to say that we each lost over three kilograms. It was probably mostly from dehydration. Even though it was the beginning of September, the temperature outside was well above thirty degrees centigrade. By two p.m., the guest room was clear of boxes and could provide my sister's family with a sleeping arrangement of sorts. That's when my brother-in-law called to inform me that they would be with us in less than an hour. According to him, they were only sixty kilometres, or thirty-seven miles, away from Montefrio.

'That's great!' I said, knowing well that sixty kilometres in Andalusia does not translate to sixty kilometres in Central Europe, where the roads are mostly on a flat plane and reasonably straight.

I put the phone down, knowing that we had at least two more hours before they would get to Montefrio.

'Who was that?' Robert asked.

'Michal. They think they will be here in an hour.'

'Where are there now?'

'An hour's drive outside Alcalá,' I said and rushed off to clean the apartments and prepare the bedrooms. At the same time, Robert decided to sort out the patio and the outdoors area, which were scattered with building materials and assorted debris.

An hour later, the phone rang again. Since neither Robert nor I expected my family to be anywhere near Montefrio, I answered it, knowing exactly what Michal was going to say next.

'The road is very narrow and twisty, so we had to slow down to twenty kilometres an hour — everyone is honking and overtaking us.'

'Really? What a surprise,' I thought to myself. 'No problem. Don't rush.' I encouraged their slow speed. Call me when you are at the petrol station in Montefrio.

'Which one?'

'There is only one,' I said. 'You won't miss it.'

In those days, we still had not figured out how to explain to visitors how to get to our place, so we often met with delivery drivers or couriers at the Repsol petrol station in Montefrio. The problem was that strangers to our village were often worried about finding the said petrol station, and even when I assured them that there was no way to miss it, they often remained doubtful. Until, of course, they would drive into Montefrio and see the petrol station immediately. It would take a severely chaotic personality to miss it. But, like others before him, my brother-in-law was sceptical about how easy it would be to find a petrol station in a village. Wisely, he decided to worry about it when in Montefrio, and we hung up.

'We have one more hour,' I shouted to Robert, who was dragging a giant piece of cardboard to the rubbish pit that Jaime had dug with his excavator in the middle of our olive field.

The problem was that the rubbish had to wait in that pit until the general countryside fire ban was lifted, usually in mid-October. Until then, everyone else could admire our pile of rubbish from the road as they drove past our house.

'Is there any water in the tank?' Robert asked.

'I'll check.'

I went behind the house and opened the lid off the three-thousand-litre water tank installed behind the house. There was just enough water there for two or three showers — hardly enough for seven people to shower, flush the toilets, and wash the dishes. I went back to report to Robert.

'There is not enough water for everyone. We'll need to take the trailer with us when we go pick them up.'

'OK. Let's hook it up, then.'

By then, we had mastered the routine of bringing water to the house in one-thousand-litre cubes on the back of the trailer from the communal source in Montefrio. It was two months earlier, on a hot July day, when I turned on the tap one morning, that my worst nightmare had come true — our well had run out of water.

TWENTY-ONE

THE CURSE OF THE CALIPHATE

As we wait for my sister and her family to arrive, let me explain our water situation. It was a hot summer day when the taps ran dry. Hoping that it was just a broken water pump, I walked down to our well and pressed the starter button for the electric pump, but nothing happened. There was no sudden rush of water being pumped up the hill to our house, just dead silence. Where we live, running short of water is in the back of everyone's mind all the time. Despite that, Robert and I decided to repress this fear, so neither of us checked the water level in the well from May onwards. The reason was that we both knew the truth — with no rain the previous months, we were going to run out of water; we just did not know when. And since we chose to live in blissful ignorance, we woke up on that fine July morning to find ourselves with no running water.

As I squatted inside the dingy well house, it was time to open the well's lid and check the water level. The water was so low that I had to use the torch on my phone to see exactly how low it was. What I saw at the bottom of the well were just muddy dregs.

The curators of the castle at Alcalá la Real display a short movie that illustrates the history of the area during the time of the Moors. The Moors ruled the land around Alcalá, then called Al Qalat — which in Arabic means *fort* — from the eighth century until the fourteenth century. The caliphate's border stretched all the way from Cordoba via Montefrio to Granada. According to the movie shown to tourists at the *fortaleza*, after several attempts by a Christian army, Al Qalat was finally seized in 1341. The reason why the 'undefeatable' fortress was captured was — according to the movie — a drought that left the Moors surrounded by the Christian army trapped inside the fort without water.

As I stared in panic into the muddy abyss of my own well, I recalled the exact same scene from the movie when the Moorish leader stares blankly into the empty hole in the ground that once was the source of life and power for his little dominion. The fortress's empty well was why the Moors of Al Qalat had to surrender to the Christian army seven hundred years ago.

Many thoughts may occur to a person when faced with the prospect of no water supply; the profound realization that human civilization, as we know it and like it, can't go on without it seems absurdly obvious. While the Moors of Al Qalat were faced with the prospect of either dying of dehydration or having their heads chopped off by Christians, my concerns were more twenty-first century and could be definitely classified as First World problems. We had plenty of bottled water to drink, including sparkling water and flavoured soda, so we were not going to fight for survival. Instead, I was concerned with what the Western world has taught us is a basic human right.

Flushing the toilet was my most immediate concern. While

urinating in the field and under the olive trees seemed acceptable, I did not think we could start doing number two in the field too. We had experienced that already when living in a yurt on the Mongolian steppes, and it was not fun!

Even when there is no one around, a European bottom is used to sitting down comfortably to do its business. With this concern in mind, I closed the well's lid and started to climb the hill back to the house. No sooner had I stepped onto the patio, I heard Robert shouting from the bathroom. While I went to the well to investigate the empty tap, he must have gotten up and gone straight to the toilet. The pitch of his voice told me that he had just discovered that there was no water in the toilet and was now stuck in the bathroom with a massive problem resting calmly in the toilet bowl.

I looked in the direction of the bathroom and then at the pool shimmering to the left. I got a bucket from the storage room and brought a bucketful of swimming pool water to the bathroom.

'Is that it?' dark thoughts were going through my mind. 'All the money, time, and effort spent on renovating and improving the house, and we were going to live like nineteenth-century Swedish peasants.' I passed Robert the bucket of water to flush the toilet and told him that the well was dry.

We spent the next two days in foul moods, mostly avoiding the topic. The kitchen wall was now lined with recycled five-litre water bottles filled with swimming pool water to wash the dishes. The toilet was guarded by a bucket of swimming pool water. Our personal hygiene was now on a steady decline as we could not use soap in the pool.

The water level in the pool started to decrease, and in a few days, it became apparent that this was not a permanent solution. We were going to lose the pool. The skimmers were no longer able to filter the water because the water level had dropped below the skimmer openings, so the surface of the water in the pool was covered in a layer of dust, pollen, dead insects, and leaves. It was also high time to wash our clothes since, in forty degrees heat, cotton T-shirts are changed at an alarming pace.

Being clean out of ideas, I found a giant bucket that was

reasonably clean inside, selected the most needed clothes and filled it with swimming pool water and some washing powder. I remembered that in the eighties, before my grandmother got her first washing machine, she used to soak the laundry for a few hours with soap before washing it. Whether soaking things in soap for several hours does anything good is yet to be proven, but it beats standing there in front of the giant bucket and acting like a human washing machine. I tried that for a minute and moved the wet clothes around in water and swirled them and spun them around, but wet fabric is extremely heavy, and after a minute of such a workout, I started to understand why the washing machine had been invented. Doing laundry by hand is a hard and ungrateful job. As I was struggling to rinse and wring our clothes by hand, my genius husband had an idea.

'We should connect the water tank behind the house to the house mains,' he announced.

I thought about it for a minute while fighting wet T-shirts. We had installed a three-thousand-litre water tank behind the house to reduce the work done by the water pump in the well. The original idea was to pump batches of three thousand litres from the well to the small tank, which would then feed the house and reduce the wear and tear on the main pump. Before that, each time anyone opened a tap, the water was being pumped all the way from the bottom of the hill to the tap, which is about two hundred metres uphill. Since we did not have any water in the well, we could not use the tank the way we had intended, but nothing could stop us from filling it up with water from the municipal source in Montefrio.

'I think it will work,' I said.

I hung the hand-washed laundry, and we drove with the trailer and the ubiquitous one-thousand-litre cube to Montefrio to get water and test our theory. The sense of relief that we might actually survive the summer in our new home was overwhelming, and on the way back, we stopped to buy a couple of bottles of cheap Crianza to celebrate. As we drove back, we were trying to figure out how we were going to transfer the water from the back of the trailer to the tank behind the house. We did not have another pump to transfer the water from the trailer in front of the house to the back; we also did not have a long enough hose.

As we approached the house, the solution presented itself. By the side of our fence was a dirt track that would lead past the back of our house to our neighbour's, José. Most of the year, the field next to our house was used to grow wheat or grass for animals and was thus inaccessible. But in the summer, the crop was harvested, and the ground was really hard and dry. In those months, José himself used it as a shortcut and drove up the field to their own house at the top of the hill. We drove up the dirt track and parked the car with the trailer right behind the water deposit. This was a better solution than we had anticipated. We now simply connected a hose pipe from the little cube on the back of the trailer to the tank behind the house, and the gravity did the rest of the job; we did not need to use a pump.

Because we used a regular gardening hose and because there was no water pump to speed up the process, it took almost an hour to transfer one thousand litres from the cube into the house tank. Taking into account the travel time to Montefrio and filling the cube there, the whole process of getting water would take up to two hours. That summer, Robert spent most of his time driving up and down — almost daily — to bring water to our cortijo.

It was not that we took so many showers, but each day the water would be needed for a different purpose. One day, he would bring a cube of water to water the tomatoes and peppers in the garden. The next day, the pool needed topping off because, on a hot day, it would lose about three hundred litres of water in one day. Then, on the third day, he would bring water to shower, flush the toilets, and use it in the washing machine. And so, without the regular trips to Montefrio to get a cube of water, we would not have been able to live in comfort.

TWENTY-TWO
YOUR DESTINATION IS ON THE RIGHT

O n the afternoon of my sister's arrival, we realized that we had to bring a cube of water so that we could all enjoy the use of the toilet and take a shower. At four p.m., my sister called me to announce that they were waiting for us at the petrol station in Montefrio.

'We're on our way,' I lied.

We needed another fifteen minutes to shower off the sweat of the day and then hook the trailer with the cube to the car. Soon, we were on our way to collect my family from Montefrio.

When we arrived in the village, we saw the five of them outside the rental car and admiring the Montefrio church that hangs from a distance on a dramatic cliff with the rocks underneath it. Apparently, Kosma and Zoja had slept all the way from Valencia, and Kosma just woke up when they entered the village — just in time for the award-winning view of Montefrio to make him go 'wow!'

That year, National Geographic recognized the view of Montefrio village, with its rows of traditional white houses lining its hills and its mediaeval sandstone church crowning the village at the top of a very steep hill as one of the top ten most picturesque views of villages in the world. Indeed, when you drive from Granada to Montefrio, the view of the hill, the white houses, and the round church is one that does make you want to stop and take a photo.

I was happy that my family was enjoying this scenery. They had spent the previous two days in a crazy drive down from Barcelona to reach us. Like many new mothers, my sister refused to relinquish her previous sense of freedom and planned their trip as if she and Michal were on their own and twenty-one years old. They landed in Barcelona, which is more than eight hours' drive from us, and hoped to walk around the city and see all the famous Gaudi buildings and enjoy the buzz of cafés and restaurants.

Then, after two days of frolicking in Catalonia's capital, they were to visit Valencia and spend a day enjoying that famous city. My sister had many great memories from her time working on a passenger cruise liner when they would moor in various Spanish harbours, such as Valencia, and the crew had a great time crawling local bars and eating tapas. Subconsciously she must have been hoping to re-live those days. After Valencia, my sister and her family were to come and relax in the Andalusian countryside with us.

One of the major flaws of this plan was that it was devised without thinking about the logistics of driving a rental car. When my sister travelled in her youth, she never had a car, and hence, had never encountered the problems of parking a car in a big European city. I believe that she planned her trip out of nostalgia rather than common sense. As Michal later reported, the first three days of their holidays — the two days in Barcelona and the one day in Valencia — were a complete nightmare. They spent most of the time in the rental car looking for a free place to park or just *any* place to park.

Because Kosma was two and Zoja just one, public transport was out of the question. To start with, 'the baby stuff' filled most of the trunk of the rental car. The number of things that modern babies need is out of proportion to their tiny sizes. I suspect that my sister didn't even see the famous Sagrada Familia on that trip — the photos from their first three days on the road consisted of children eating ice cream at various petrol stations.

On the evening of their arrival, we sat under a starry sky, and both my sister and her partner seemed suspiciously quiet about their road trip across Spain. There were no 'wows' and 'ahhs' and passing the phone around to show us the wonders of Barcelona and Valencia. It was only the following year, when they visited us for Christmas, that Michal told us all about the never-ending drive around Barcelona and Valencia — a nightmare that haunted his dreams for months. I could have forewarned them about the horrors of looking for parking in Spain, but knowing how angry my younger sister gets when given any piece of advice, I kept my mouth shut.

Hardly anyone ever believes me when I tell them how difficult it is to find parking in any big city in Spain. By now, I have probably spent weeks of my life driving around and doing nothing but looking for parking. It's one of the main reasons I had not yet visited the Picasso Museum in Malaga. When I tell friends that I could not see it because there was no parking, they think that I'm making excuses for being ignorant and refusing to allow any form of high culture to enter my life. But it's not true. It was the first spring after we moved to Spain.

One day, I told Robert that we should take a day off from construction and building and do something 'touristy'. Since Malaga is the famous painter's proud birthplace, I expected the museum to be quite interesting. We could see some artwork — we both like Picasso — and then walk over to the beach and have some beers and tapas while looking at the Med. It was a great plan.

It started to fall apart at the seams as soon as we entered the city. Apparently, there was a big football match about to start that day. The whole area around the stadium and up to the outskirts of the city was parked chock-a-block. There was literally not a square metre of free space anywhere as far as the eye could see. As any visitor to Andalusia will notice, the Spanish are extremely efficient when parking, and they are ready to use any centimetre available to park their car. They will squeeze in, bumper to bumper, in the narrowest and the steepest of medieval alleys; they will park on a lawn, in the park, and right next to a building's entrance. The zebra crossing is hardly ever off limits — unless the *guardia* or *tráficos* decide to get out of their air-conditioned four-by-fours and make some money for their precinct by fining people. But this only happens once in a while.

The "No Parking' and 'Don't park in front of the garage' signs are treated simply as gentle suggestions and are hardly ever respected. Spanish drivers assume that you will figure out how to get out of your garage, the entrance of which may be blocked in by one or two cars. They also have faith that you will manoeuvre your way out when they double-park and go away for a *desayuno*, usually a toast and a coffee, with a friend. As we entered the outskirts of Malaga, we saw nothing but cars parked tighter than proverbial sardines in a tin.

'Well, I'm sure there will be some empty spaces near the museum,' I said encouragingly.

As we drove towards the museum, I scanned the streets left and right, hoping to see an empty space. Soon the GPS started to indicate that we were a few metres from our destination, but I could not see a single place to park.

'Where can I park?' Robert asked.

'I don't see anything. Let's drive a bit further.'

Now we were driving away from the museum and toward the old town, which we knew would be inaccessible for non-residents.

'We need to turn back,' Robert said.

'Hmm, OK,' I said, still hoping to find a parking spot.

Going back was easier said than done. Because of the system of one-way streets, to get back where we came from, we have to drive on completely unfamiliar roads, and we have no clue where they would spit us out at the end. Following the GPS, we drove into one of the narrow one-way streets and then turned and turned until we had no idea which part of Malaga we were in. As we wound left and right, I noticed that both sides of the road were completely packed with parked vehicles.

'Oh, look. There is a spot over there.' I pointed to a spot under a highway bridge.

'Yes, but we are three kilometres from the museum,' Robert pointed out.

Yes, we were, by now, at the Costa del Sol Highway and a long walk from the museum.

'Let's try again,' I suggested.

We followed the GPS back to the museum, and once again, we heard the GPS voice tell us that the destination was on our right, and then we drove away from it and back into the narrow and fully packed backstreets of Malaga. Even though we took a different route each time, we ended by the same highway bridge that we were at thirty minutes before. It did not look like we were ever going to find a spot to park our car in Malaga, but we were determined to give it one more try.

We had driven all the way from Montefrio to see the Picasso Museum and have a fun day out, so we were not going to give in that easily. We repeated our route of doom, searching every alley and every corner, but half an hour later, we were back under the familiar bridge. I was very frustrated and disappointed by now. The trip was ruined and I was not going to see Picasso's work.

'OK. We've done this three times. Let's go to Torremolinos instead,' Robert suggested.

We went to Torremolinos, where, while not easy, it is still possible to find parking by the beach, and had a nice lunch in a restaurant overlooking the Med.

With that day in mind, I expected that my sister's driving tour of Spain looked very similar. After hours of driving around looking for parking, exhausted and emotionally distressed, they probably parked anywhere — even if it was another city — and enjoyed what they found there.

TWENTY-THREE
CALLE ALTA

The day after my sister's arrival, I took them on a family walkabout around Montefrio. It had now been a year since we moved to Andalusia to start a new life, and because of the endless renovations and work on the house, it was the first time that I was going to explore our little village in more detail, walk its streets and observe it from a tourist's perspective. In truth, it's not the most beautiful village in the world, especially when viewed from the inside, but like the rest of the region, it's down-to-earth and real.

The first thing that strikes any Central or Northern European when walking into a *pueblo blanco*, like Montefrio, is that everyone on the streets greets you, and if you greet them back and smile, they smile back at you. What's more, the people who you pass on the street like to comment on your current situation in life. If you're carrying a heavy bag, they will say, '¡Qué pesado!'. If it's a hot summer day, they will inform you, as if you were oblivious to the sweat pouring down your own face, '¡Qué calor!'. If it's a cold January day, strangers on the street will make you aware of it '¡Qué frío!'.

It makes you feel welcome and at home. You can walk up to any one of the old men who stand at the curb outside the bars in the village and strike up a conversation — and they will love nothing more than to chat to an outsider who is visiting their town. The Spaniard's talent for talking for hours to complete strangers about nothing should not be underappreciated. It is one of the qualities, I believe, that makes them one of the healthiest nations in Europe. Being able to look your neighbours or passers-by in the eye and talk openly about anything that comes to your mind creates a strong sense of community and makes you feel happy about your place in the world.

This attitude of Spanish villagers to outsiders stands in stark contrast to many Northern and Central European communities. Should a foreigner or an alien to the area ever dare to enter such a town, they would quickly be made to feel like Jesse James, who by mistake stumbled into a Midwestern town. Pedestrians won't dare look you in the eye, and the sound of window shutters closing will resonate with your every step. Should you smile and say 'hi' or 'good morning' to any of the inhabitants, you will be instantly prosecuted and thrown into a high-security cell in a local jail or a mental institution. Stories of the outlaw who came to town and harassed people on the streets with unrequested friendliness would become the stuff of legends, and teachers will tell the story to pre-schoolers to show them the difference between normal people and criminally insane outsiders.

As it were, my family quickly started to appreciate the Spanish openness, and they walked Calle Alta shouting '¡hola!' and '¡buenas!' to all the grannies and granddads standing in their doorways or walking home with their grocery bags. Kosma especially took it upon himself to run in front of us like a proclaimer of a new religion and scream '¡hola!' to anyone who passed him. In return, he got showered with '¡Qué guapo!' by all the old ladies of Montefrio. Being only two, he still had his golden baby locks, which he refused to have washed, combed, or cut; this resulted in the true seraph look which most Catholic ladies find irresistible. With our little angel up front paving our way to the town square and Zoja completely asleep in a baby carrier on her father's chest, we mused about the shops that we were passing by.

'A *droguería*?' my brother-in-law read, surprised.

'Yes. Like our Polish *drogeria*,' I confirmed.

A droguería is a classic shop from the 1980s. In English, it translates as *chemist's*, but really it is much more than that. The best definition of a *droguería* is a shop that has pretty much everything that is not edible. And there is a logical reason for it, for if you need sustenance, there is a vast array of shops to choose from.

If you want bread, you go to a *panadería* or a bread shop. If you want fruits or vegetables, you go to a *frutería* or a fruit store. Need meat? Go to *carnicero*. And for some fish, visit the *pescadero*. Since processed food did not exist in 1980s Spain and in most of Europe, these shops would have covered all your food needs. Anything else? Go to a droguería. There, they sell: soaps, washing powders, curtains, towels, bleach, plasters, paint, mosquito repellents, candles, and all the other small items that we don't notice but that make our lives bearable in the constant fight against bacteria, insects, and other mundane nuisances.

The simplicity of naming the shops by what they actually sell is one that we have lost in most Western shopping centres, malls, and gallerias — whatever you wish to call them. Modern shops have elusive names like *Stradivarius, Mango, Salsa, Pandora, Snipes, Botticelli, Oysho, Parfois*, and until you are right outside their shop window, you will struggle to guess what they might be selling. Some names are simply out there to confuse you. I always felt *Stradivarius* was a good name for a music shop — but, no, they sell clothes. Not even rock-and-roll clothes — just mundane, everyday fast fashion. *Mango* or *Salsa* would be great names for a restaurant or a fruit-and-vegetable store — but no, they sell the same garments as *Stradivarius*.

Pandora is an unfortunate name for any business and god only knows what they sell. *Snipes* does not sell weapons, and *Botticelli* doesn't sell art supplies. *Oysho* is not a Japanese clothing brand. And *Parfois* is simply confusing to anyone who knows French. *Sometimes?* What do they sell? It's no wonder that shoppers often feel overwhelmed by the mall experience. The shops go to great lengths to hide the true nature of their business. What we usually find in all of these different shops are the same things made in the same miserable East Asian factory but sold under a thousand different elusive guises.

In stark contrast to this, the Montefrio shopping experience is similar to travelling back in time. There is no shopping centre or mall in a sixty-kilometre radius. On Calle Alta, or High Street — the main street of Montefrio — the shops have honest and intelligible names. Need shoes? Go to the *Zapatero*. Need a hat? Visit the *Sombrerero*. Want some sports clothes? Go to *Deportivos*. Fancy a churro with chocolate? Oh, here is a *Churrería*. We have *Papelería* if you need things made of paper and a *Regalos*, if you need a gift for any occasion.

Of course, with growing consumerism, even Montefrio shoppers demand choice. If you wish to buy a bouquet of flowers, you can choose between *Floristería Loli* or *Floristería Mercedes*. Adding the shop owner's name to its generic noun is Montefrio's nod to the twenty-first century. The owner of the shop with Catholic devotional articles — a gentleman called Jesús — has been one businessman who benefits from this trend; *Devocionales Jesús* can't be missed.

As we passed these establishments saying *¡Hola!* to old ladies carrying shopping bags with bread, a pint of milk, and some fruit and veg for that day's meal, I dreaded the day when churros and chocolate would be sold in Starbucks, and fresh bread will be only available at Paul's. The good news is that the nearest McDonald's — the harbinger of ruthless consumerism — is still a one-hour drive from Montefrio, so I feel that we are safe here for the time being.

TWENTY-FOUR
TEETHING IN MONTEFRIO

B y the time we reached the round church, which is situated on the main square, Kosma started to insist that he was not able to walk anymore. We were all, in fact, getting hot and bothered, and single droplets of sweat started to appear on my sister's almost transparent — from months of sun deprivation — temples. Even though it was early September, the temperature in the direct sunlight must have been around thirty-five degrees or more. Despite the heat bearing down on us, Michal picked Kosma up and, like a modern-day St. Christopher, put him on his shoulders. With this load on his shoulders and my sister carrying sleeping Zoja in a baby carrier on her chest, we started the steep climb up the hill to see the ruins of the Moorish castle that acts as a sentinel for the peaceful village of Montefrio.

This was the second time that I was to visit the ruins since we had moved to Andalusia. The first time we went up the hill was the previous February when the temperatures outside were refreshing, and the wind cooled us off on the climb. At that time, the almond trees that cover most of the hill all the way up to the old castle were in full blossom, and it was a spectacular sight. Almond blossoms, I dare say, are far superior to cherry blossoms. While I love the sight of both — the cherry orchard near our house usually blossoms in April — I find almond blossoms much sturdier and more robust than the fluffy and fragile cherry blossoms.

As I was reminiscing on the beauty of different blossoms, I must have missed the correct turn, and I quickly realized that we were taking the longer and the steeper way up to the castle. I did not recall having to walk up through the very narrow and windy streets of the gipsy quarter called Solana. I vaguely remembered that this was the way *out* of the castle and not the castle's entrance. My doubts were quickly confirmed by an old man sitting on a tiny patio outside his house, listening to flamenco and mending an old potato sack.

'Are you going to the castle?' he shouted at us in Spanish.

Since I was the only one who understood the question, I confirmed. 'Si.'

'It's the wrong way. You should go back to the square and turn right.'

'Si, si.' I nodded at him in agreement and smiled as if we were just discussing the weather.

'What did he say?' My family was in awe that a Spanish native would speak to them on the street.

'He said that it's very hot today.'

My sister and her partner looked at the old man, smiled at him and repeated several 'si, sis' in a row.

'This is too steep to carry the children this way.' He seemed concerned.

'Yes, you're right.' I kept my sunny demeanour and turned to my sister to translate.

'He says that it's not far from here.'

Both Michal and Beata seemed relieved to hear this. The extra loads that they were carrying must have been weighing them down by now, but they didn't want to moan. Fortunately, Robert wasn't with us, or he would have felt compelled to argue with me about the correct route to the castle. I took my phone from my back pocket — the only thing I was carrying — and suggested a quick photoshoot on the narrow white streets. They both agreed as it offered a short break from the steady climb up the hill.

After a quick photo session and with their spirits lifted with the good news that the end of the climb was not too far, we continued for another twenty or so minutes. While the ruins were not far, the steep climb that we were following due to my mistake seemed interminable. After dodging dog poo and the disconcerting stares of several defensive gipsy housewives who did not seem too happy that their doorsteps were on the main tourist path, we reached a crossroad.

'Look, there's a chicken,' Amelia pointed in the direction of a lonely chicken wandering the street.

I hoped we did not have to cross paths with it, as I have a severe phobia of birds, and I would rather go down and choose a new path than have to walk past a chicken. We stood at the crossroads for a few minutes, wondering which way to go. We could see the castle walls hanging above us; we just did not know which way would be the least draining to get there. Amelia — our teenager —spotted a sign labelled 'Castillo'. It was about ten centimetres long and three centimetres wide and attached to a sidewall of a house.

'Thank God,' I thought. The sign was pointing to a different street than the one the chicken was patrolling.

I was beginning to worry that we would never find the entrance to the fortress. As we were nearing the fort's gate, Kosma fell asleep on his father's shoulders, and Zoja woke up and started to whimper in her carrier. I knew by now that she never whimpered for too long and that soon her soft cries were going to turn into a hysterical fit.

'We'll see you at the top,' I said, and on command, Amelia and I rushed to the top of the stone steps to escape the cries of the teething baby dragon.

It was an unfortunate coincidence that Zoja started to teethe as soon as they landed in Barcelona a few days before. It was her first tooth, and it was now coming out with a vengeance and making everyone's life miserable. While Amelia and I stood at the top of the old ruins admiring the spectacular panorama, we tried our best to ignore the screams that we heard in the distance.

Amelia was finishing a session of artistic selfies with cacti when her father and my sister appeared at the walls. Michal was now carrying the screaming Zoja, and Kosma was holding my sister's hand and sobbing because she woke him up and told him to walk by himself. Like any family travelling with small kids, they were all in foul moods, regretting ever leaving their apartment in Gdańsk. The sun was now blazing and burning their pale faces. The extreme hike made the sunblock stream down their faces and irritate their eyes. I was not sure if their eyes were watering from the fatigue, stress, or sunblock, but I decided not to broach the subject. I felt a bit guilty for putting them through this ordeal and thought that a short rest inside a cool stone church might lift their spirits.

'Let's see inside the church,' I suggested.

We walked inside and were greeted by a cold blast. It was like diving into an ice cube. My company marched directly to the benches set out for tourists to sit on and watch a film about the fortress. They all sat down, relieved to find a place in Andalusia that was not as hot as hell. I paid the exorbitant fee of five euros per person and thought of it as my penance for lying to everyone about the directions.

The cold air seemed to calm the babies down. Zoja was now just whimpering, and sobbing and Kosma was sulking. Because the Spanish love children — they are never bothered with how loud or obnoxious they are — the museum's caretaker was not bothered with such behaviour. In fact, since we were quite a large group of tourists for Montefrio, she decided that she should entertain us with the film about the Moorish ruins and the Christian church.

She dimmed the lights and turned the entertainment on. The darkness and the musical crescendo combined with the dramatic shouting from the Moors defending their besieged castle and fighting to save their lives seemed to exert a calming effect on my niece's tooth.

Kosma, on the other hand, became hysterical and had to be taken outside to calm down. While Kosma and Michal stayed outside, we enjoyed the rest of the drama in relative peace. The medieval mayhem, the yelps of the dying Christian knights, and the apocalyptic hollers of the Moors running away from the burning castle seemed nothing in comparison to Zoja's ability to create lachrymose chaos. The ten minutes of 'peace and quiet' seemed to rejuvenate my sister, and as the film ended, she suggested that we climb to the top of the church's tower.

With Kosma now fully calmed and Zoja asleep again, we ascended the church tower and admired the breathtaking views of Montefrio and the olive hills surrounding it. On the way back, we followed the route that we were supposed to have taken on the way up. It was created by centuries of villagers walking up to the church for Sunday Mass; it had a gradual incline and was well shaded by trees.

'This is a very nice route and easy to walk,' Michal observed and looked at me suspiciously.

I pretended that I didn't hear him, and we walked cheerfully down the hill.

TWENTY-FIVE

WHAT'S ON THE MENU?

A few days later was my sister's and Kosma's birthday. In her usual efficiency, my sister gave birth to her first baby on the same day as her own birthday. I have always suspected that she did that to save time in the future — as a mother of two and a businesswoman, time is a commodity she cherishes the most. With Kosma celebrating his birthday on the same day, she cut down the number of parties in our family. I also suspect that she tried to pull the same trick with her daughter, but Zoja, being of a stubborn and inflexible nature, did not give in and came out of her mother's womb two weeks after her brother's and her mother's birthday.

For Kosma and Beata's birthday, we decided to take a drive up the Sierra Nevada mountains, which are about an hour's drive from Montefrío. Robert and I had driven there the summer before and enjoyed using the cable car system that takes you to the very top of the mountain. I felt that the children would enjoy it too. The drive itself is picturesque, and there are a lot of roadside restaurants in the area. I hoped to find one which would serve us a giant paella for the whole family to share.

As we started to drive up the Sierra Nevada National Park, I noticed clouds gathered over the mountains, but I did not think much of it. We stopped in a few places and took some scenic photos of Granada and the water reservoirs located at the bottom of the Sierra Nevada range. As we travelled higher and higher, we were soon driving through dense fog or possibly the clouds and thus could not see much out the windows. When we arrived at the skiing village at the top of the Sierra Nevada, we might as well have been on a set of an eerie movie. The fog was so thick that all we could see were the wooden Swiss-style chalets and the few restaurants that were open in the summer for hikers and mountain bikers.

As we commented on the lack of creativity in ski-resort architecture, it became apparent that without the spectacular views that I had promised, we might as well have been anywhere. My sister remarked how the place reminded her of the snow park in the Mall of the Emirates in Dubai. I could not help but wonder about the inexplicable ability of the typical Swiss Alpine village to replicate itself all around the world. Now, without the view of a mountain in sight, we strolled through the foggy streets of this Alpine simulacrum. I caught a glimpse of the cable car ticket office and saw a big notice on the window saying that the cable cars had closed on the seventh of September. Not wanting to add fresh salt to her birthday wounds, I did not mention this and hoped that everyone had forgotten about the cable cars.

By now, we had left the narrow streets and wandered onto the grass area that is directly underneath the closed cable car line. Since none of us felt like a proper hike, we decided to walk all the way to a safety fence that was some way ahead of us and then go back to the car. Kosma seemed well pleased with the sight of a herd of cows and spent a few cheerful minutes shouting at them and then found a giant steel bolt in the grass, which took all his attention. He showed uncle Robert the bolt and asked what it was. The clues were obvious — I looked at the cable car line above and wondered whether we were obliged to report our find to the cable car operators. I could not help but wonder whether what Kosma was going to take as a souvenir was a crucial piece of the car so that when re-launched in the winter, the car would just fall apart.

'We should tell someone about this.' I decided to speak up, not wanting to be culpable for a horrific ski-resort accident.

It was the right thing to do, so we went back to the spooky village and wandered the streets searching for a cable car engineer or anyone with authority to tell us what to do with the giant bolt. But apart from a few disinterested waiters and restaurateurs, there was no one else to report to. Worried that I might be haunted by the unfortunate bolt, I decided that we should leave it on the counter at the cable car ticket office. I hoped that whoever found it would be diligent enough to report it. We explained to Kosma the importance of the bolt and left it on the counter, happy to pass the problem on to a stranger. We went back to the car and set off to search for that elusive family-size paella.

The Spanish paella is probably the most iconic of Spanish dishes and the most divisive one. Everyone knows about it, but not many people actually taste it when they go on holiday to Spain. The reason is that, unlike risotto or spaghetti, it's never cooked in small amounts. Paella is cooked in a paella pan, which is usually the size of a small satellite dish. It is hardly ever sold in single portions; you usually need two very hungry travellers to order a pan of paella. What's more, these two diners have to agree to like seafood because even though paella is composed of a variety of meats, they all end up tasting like shrimp.

Because Robert hates overcooked rice, I only ever get to taste paella when it's served as a tapa, which means it's at least a day old and most likely the restaurant's leftovers. But I don't mind. I find it very comforting and homely, and the few bits of unidentifiable meat that you might come across in your paella tapa are always a nice surprise and a challenge to one's senses. Whatever meat is used in a paella — be it chorizo, chicken, rabbit, duck, or pork — it all ends up looking like a grey used cotton ball. This may also be one reason many people either love paella or hate it.

Since Robert is definitely in the anti-paella league, I was surprised when he suggested that we take my family to eat paella. However, I suspected that it was the low cost of such a dish vis-á-vis its ability to feed the masses that was on his mind. I did not question his rationale and agreed that it was a great idea to eat a family-size paella. The thing about paella is not only that it's divisive, but it's also elusive. When you don't crave it, it seems to be available everywhere. In spring and summer, giant paellas are cooked up in the middle of villages and distributed to residents for free. On the coast, restaurants have special offers of paella and free beer. But now that we'd resolved to gorge on a giant paella, we could not find one.

At first, we drove past several roadside restaurants expecting to see paella advertised on the chalkboard outside the restaurant. Each time we saw a restaurant, Robert slowed down, stopped outside the menu board, and we engaged in a group speed reading competition. It was now past lunchtime, and we were quite hungry. In desperation, we stopped at every restaurant we saw, and I went inside each one to inquire personally about the availability of a big paella for a family of seven. All I got in return were shrugs and blank stares — it was as if the paella had not made it to Sierra Nevada mountains.

After almost an hour of searching for food, we decided to abandon the idea of a paella and go inside the next restaurant that we came across. We had to make a quick decision because if we continued our descent down the mountains, we would soon be back in Granada and get stuck searching for parking for another hour or two. As soon as Robert spotted a familiar sign of a knife and fork, we turned into a narrow country road, and after a few minutes, we were in front of a restaurant. The restaurant looked dark and dingy, and I regretted that we did not turn back to one of the livelier restaurants we left behind. But, by now, we were all very hungry, which obviously clouded our judgement.

Rabbits are a common sight in the Andalusian countryside. As soon as you go for a walk among the olive groves, you will spot their little white bunny tails running away from you or crossing a hill in front of you. In fact, rabbits are the pigeons of the *campo* and tend to annoy the farmers with their habits. One of them is that they gnaw on the black irrigation pipes that are sometimes laid out for the olive trees. I know about that because that very summer, I was asked to collect all used plastic water bottles and donate them to our builder, Dani, who then used them to protect the tips of his black irrigation pipes from the rabbits. Why do they eat the ends of the irrigation pipes? I'm not sure, perhaps, to gain access to water as Andalusia in the summer is as dry as the Sahara.

Another rabbit-related nuisance is that, for one reason or other, some rabbits have suicidal tendencies. There is one specific family of rabbits that lives in a short stretch of the forest by the road that leads from our house to Montefrio. Each time we drive past the forest, one of the rabbits dashes out in a kamikaze-like mode to escape with his life just a few centimetres away from the car wheels. For obvious reasons, I assume that these are mostly male rabbits who choose to engage in this silly challenge against the machine. What saves them, I believe, is the fact that the road on that stretch is narrow and windy, which makes most cars slow down, thereby giving the rabbits a chance to escape in one piece.

Because of their abundance, rabbit is a common meat on the Andalusian menu — especially near Sierra Nevada, where there is a lot of forest. I have read about local people eating rabbits and have seen Spanish rabbit dishes prepared on travel shows. Thus, it was not surprising when we looked at the Sierra Nevada restaurant's menu that we found rabbit featured in all forms, shapes, and sizes. There were rabbit stews of various blends and spices and imaginative pairings of meats, like rabbit with chorizo and rabbit with duck. Rabbit meat is one of those meats, I noticed, that is best served in a thick stew where the individual bits of meat are unrecognizable. A bunny leg on a grill does not sound like something that I would like to partake of.

I have never eaten rabbit meat before and have only seen it cooked and eaten on TV. To me, wild rabbit meat is in the same category as country pigeon, and thus my feelings towards consuming it are quite ambivalent. I don't have a problem with other people eating it, but I'm not crazy about eating it myself. On seeing it on the menu, I wasn't sure whether I should order a rabbit dish and be done with it or follow my instincts and try to avoid eating rabbit for the rest of my life. Don't we all want to be nonchalant and daring like the French?

The menu was only in Spanish, so I had to translate it and make some general suggestions to the whole table. I proposed the following culinary adventure to my family.

'They have some interesting rabbit dishes,' I said as if it was a normal thing for us to eat. I was confronted with a table of blank stares. Maybe they thought that I was 'lost in translation' and had confused rabbit with pork. I felt that the rabbit needed to be promoted more enthusiastically since I was not being successful in selling it to the rest of the table.

'This area is famous for rabbit dishes.' I was making stuff up. I felt it might have been famous, seeing all those varieties of rabbit on the menu. Or ... I thought, the chef drives to work on a road that is visited by a school of suicidal rabbits.

'Is there a pizza or spaghetti?' our teenager asked. I could see she was not having any of the rabbit meat. I browsed the menu, which was obviously a waste of my time. The words for *pizza* and *spaghetti* are the same in Spanish, as they are in any other language in the world, but the teenage mind is not always as quick as they make us all believe.

'No, there is nothing like that,' I told her truthfully. As I gathered from my quick read, the menu was full of very traditional Andalusian dishes — roasted chicken and pork with heavy sides of potatoes roasted in olive oil.

'Is there a vegetarian dish?' my vegetarian sister interrupted, hoping to get a meal too.

I scanned the menu again, but I knew very well that there would be no vegetarian or pescatarian dishes. I wanted to please my sister and made a show of searching for the vegetarian option between ten different versions of *pollo asado*, or roast chicken, and the next section that had a dozen versions of pork and rabbit. Since we were high in the mountains, there was no seafood or fish either.

Personally, I liked the menu; you could see it was honest home-cooking. The long ten-seater tables that dominated the restaurant told me that the place was often full of Spanish families enjoying a lovely home-cooked dinner. Frozen burgers, pizza, fried shrimp or calamari — the staple tourist diet on Costa del Sol — wouldn't be found here. Everything on the menu would be cooked in large pots and in large quantities.

'Do they have roasted chicken?' Robert saved the day. The meat-eaters settled on two chicken dishes to share. No one took up my offer of sharing a rabbit dish, and while we seemed somewhat happy, my sister insisted on having a main course too, apart from the potato side-dish. I went back to browsing the menu.

'They have some grilled mushrooms,' I told her. It was a side dish, and I was confident that the mushrooms would be cooked in a good amount of pork fat or chicken fat, but I did not share all this with my sister and let her believe that it was a vegetarian option on its own. As it often happens, the vegetarian option arrived very quickly, and since we were all starving by now, we started to chow down on the mushrooms accompanied with olive oil and bread. I could see my sister turning a piece of mushroom on her plate, inspecting it to see whether it had previously had any contact with meat. If only mushrooms could talk, she would have given each one of them a thorough cross-examination.

'Have you been fried on the same frying pan as Mr Pork Chop?' she would have said to start her interrogation.

'Was the frying pan washed before they put you onto it, or did they fry you in the bacon fat?'

'Did they use the same spoon to stir the meat stew and the mushrooms?' She would have tried to guess any scenario in which a microscopic amount of meat might have touched her vegetables. From the way my sister overdramatizes the possible contamination of her vegetables with a single molecule of meat, you may think that she is severely allergic to meat protein. The very thought of meat invokes a psychosomatic rash on her pale, iron-deprived cheeks. The mere notion that a cooking utensil had touched meat and then touched a piece of vegetable that she is eating might make her go into anaphylactic shock.

As it was evident that no care had been taken in the kitchen to separate the grilled mushrooms from the meat *plancha*, a flat grill on which pork chops are usually prepared, my sister went into a huff and told us that we could finish her mushrooms. I must admit that the pork fat gave the mushrooms a lovely taste! She ate a piece of dry bread dipped in olive oil and then went out to fume quietly outside in the small garden that was attached to the restaurant. It was all for the best, as she took the toddlers with her, so when the meat arrived, the four meat-eaters were able to enjoy the chicken and *patatas a lo pobre* feast all to ourselves.

A trampoline is catnip to most children. There is probably no child in the world who can't resist jumping onto one when they see it. Most Spanish establishments are extremely child-friendly, and this little rural restaurant was no exception. To allow adults to consume their hard-earned food in peace and quiet, they arranged a small playground in the garden by the restaurant entrance. The central piece of this playground was a trampoline suitable for small children. It was a lovely idea, I'm sure, until the restaurant owners realized how much noise such a contraption generates.

We were still chewing on the chicken bones when we heard the first screams of joy, which we all easily identified as happy Kosma. Curious as to what was causing the birthday boy such elation, I went outside to see him bouncing happily on the trampoline and screaming at the top of his lungs with each jump. Since his sister could not even walk, there was no way for her to join in, but she was quite content sitting cross-legged on the trampoline and being thrown in every which direction inside the trampoline whenever her brother landed on the bounce mat. Luckily, the trampoline was surrounded by a safety net to stop children from falling out and smashing their heads on the concrete slab underneath it.

I watched the kids for a couple of minutes and realized that this activity might take much longer — we now had to wait for the kids to get sick of jumping. I brought out some plastic chairs, and Robert and I sat down watching the blissful jumping and screaming. My sister recovered from her lunch upset and was now filming the happy moments and chatting to Kosma while he was incessantly jumping.

'Look, what a big cat!' Michal pointed behind us. As we all turned to look, I heard a loud thump. The whole scene slowed down, and after what seemed like a delay of several seconds, but could not have been, we heard the loudest burst of tears of pain that I could imagine. In the split second that it took for all of us to look at the cat, Kosma had managed to fly out of the trampoline and landed on the side of his head underneath it. In the most unfortunate way, he must have flown through the gap in the protective net designed to let the kids in and out of the enclosed space.

Seeing her brother cry, Zoja, who so far sat quietly inside the trampoline like a little angelic Buddha, decided to burst into tears too. In such situations, kids are always best left with their parents. To be of help, I went inside the restaurant and settled our bill, expecting that in a few minutes, we would be driving to a hospital in Granada to scan Kosma's head. A friendly waitress realized what had happened and gave me a small bag of ice to put on the child's face to stop it from swelling and bruising. She was not worried that we might sue the business for the lack of rubber flooring in the playground. And I would never dream of suing someone for such an accident. This type of attitude towards litigation has not made it to Andalusia yet.

In rural Spain, accidents happen all the time. People fall off ladders, drive off the road, get hit on the head with an olive-picking stick, or fall over in their gardens and lose their teeth. While people around you will empathize with you, they won't get too excited about it. They will nod and raise their eyebrows and wish you good health, but they won't discuss who to blame for it. You just get on with your life and fix it yourself.

On my return to the scene of the incident armed with ice, I was desperately trying to figure out what to do next. The problem was that we had only been in Spain for a year, so my medical Spanish was non-existent. Neither Robert nor I had ever been to any local hospitals or *centros de salud*, and I had no idea about the procedures and what to expect. In my head, I played with my limited Spanish vocabulary, but for the life of me, I could not figure out how to say: 'My nephew fell off the trampoline; can you check his head, please?'

I handed Michal the ice while I silently tried to piece together what to tell the doctor in Spanish. I took out my phone, which was very old and had limited internet options, and started to search for a hospital in Granada. I figured that soon we would be driving to the nearest emergency department and plea for their sense of humanity. I figured that since it was a child who was injured, they would try to help him before they brought out the red tape.

'What is *emergency* in Spanish?' I wondered while waiting for the search engine on my ancient phone to start up.

I knew that I had to take charge of the situation and that both Beata and Michal expected me to know what to do, but they would have been surprised if they knew how seldom I went to a doctor with my own health problems. It is not that I'm never sick, not at all. However, I prefer to leave my health problems as they are and hope they go away on their own. One year, I had a twitch in my eye for over six months — once or so, every hour, my eye would involuntarily shut for a split second. I told a colleague about it, and she was insistent that I should see a specialist. I told her I would and thanked her for her care, but I never did; I got so used to the eye twitch that I was surprised when it disappeared one day. An eye twitch, severe back pain, a trigger finger, swelling, sudden skin discolouration, leg cramps, and various abdominal cramps and pains — I assumed them to be regular ailments caused by stress and a lack of holidays.

I felt upset that I wasn't prepared for this part of our Spanish adventure. I didn't even know the words for the body parts, never mind how to describe different injuries, aches, and pains, or how to explain to a nurse what had happened. Being familiar with a country's health system is often a sign of being well-settled. I remember that it took me five years of living in Al Ain before I knew where all the hospitals were and what protocols they followed. I knew where to go in case of emergency, how the insurance worked, and who to ask for help. The problem is that the health system is often the last public service that foreigners in a new country become familiar with. We all hope for the best and hope we never get sick. It was only now that we urgently needed a doctor to look at Kosma's head that I realized a big gap in our preparedness for our new life in Spain. I really did not know what to do, where to go, or who to ask for help.

As I was looking at Kosma, who now calmed down a lot and was sobbing in his father's arms, I knew that we had to check his little skull for any fracture. I have devoted enough hours of my life to watching *House MD* and *ER* to know that a fractured skull is a serious injury. I suggested to Michal that we pack up and drive down the mountain to find a hospital in Granada. As it often is with experienced parents who have seen their precious offspring tumble down staircases and fall flat on their face numerous times, Beata and Michal were concerned but did not think that the fall warranted a visit to the emergency ward.

We decided to go home and keep a watchful eye on Kosma. That evening, after the children fell asleep, we spent a rather morose evening — no one drank anything, in case we had to make an emergency visit to the hospital in the middle of the night. We sat and chatted but mostly listened to the white noise of the child monitor. We ended the evening early and hoped for a quiet night.

And a quiet night it was. At breakfast, I was greeted by a smiling Kosma, who was ready to devour his body weight in eggs.

'How are you feeling today?' I asked him in Polish.

'Jajo,' he responded with the candour and vigour of a two-year-old whose vocabulary consisted of about thirty nouns.

As *jajo*, which means *an egg*, was his favourite Polish word and, not coincidently, his favourite food, I was assured that he was and would remain perfectly fine. I handed him the requested hard-boiled egg, and he grinned with delight. We all sat down to the alfresco breakfast and looked at Kosma, enjoying his first day as a three-year-old.

One of the main attractions of living in Andalusia is the outdoor lifestyle that can be enjoyed from late April until late October. Of course, this is not true for every day of these months, but for many months of each year, we have breakfast, lunch, and dinner outside on the patio. The patio, which is directly connected to the kitchen and the living room, has become the natural extension of our house and our main living space. Our old camping table, which served us well when camping in the desert and mountains in the UAE and Oman, was now the centre of this living space. We used it to eat our meals, watch TV on the laptop, do small carpentry projects; we'd prepare seeds for sowing, shell fresh fava beans, clean garlic, and do all manner of household chores that a normal kitchen table is usually used for. Being outdoors most of the time and having my own outdoor space was one of the things that I loved about our new home. It was only normal that, when my family arrived to visit us, I decided that we would eat all our meals together at this big table. This might not have been the best idea.

On their last morning in Andalusia, my sister and I prepared a lovely breakfast spread with meats, pâté, cheese, lots of boiled eggs for Kosma, jams and honey, and all the things that central Europeans love to have for a special breakfast. It does sound a bit over-the-top, but since we don't see one another often, we were all in festive and generous moods. As setting it all up and getting everyone together took some time, by the time we sat down, ready to enjoy a sumptuous breakfast, we realized that we were not the only ones who had received an invitation to the feast. All the wasps of Montefrio and the surrounding areas joined us at the table and started to help themselves to the meats and jams before any one of us could say 'bon appétit'.

We soon learned that nothing will stop a hungry wasp from having a bite to eat — they are rude, relentless, and impudent. A humble fly will simply buzz off when waved away or sprayed with insect repellent. A wasp sprayed with a citronella concoction simply laughs in your face. It's as if the chemical gives it more strength and fuels its hatred of humankind.

Our festive meal quickly became impossible to consume; wasps were just sitting in neat rows on our plates, enjoying their own private parties and tiny celebrations. My sister and I rushed to the kitchen and got all sorts of food nets, glass bowls, and large plates and started to cover the food to keep the wasps away. This, of course, spoiled the beautiful presentation since most of the food was now covered with plates. We kept asking one another what was under each plate before daring to lift it for a split second to snatch a slice of ham or a sliver of cheese. It was a race against time, as each time a plate was lifted, it created a scent signal for the wasps to return. And they were not far away. While most of the troops were sent away in search of another family of saps who thought that they could eat breakfast al fresco in early September, a squadron of diehards stayed behind, convinced that sooner or later we were going to slip.

And, indeed, very soon, we heard a horrific cry coming from Zoja. As a baby, Zoja was a very good eater, and mealtimes were usually the only time when she did not cry, whimper, or have hysterics. She was happy to sit on a sofa by the table and chew on a piece of delicious ham or something similar. A particularly cunning wasp must have spotted the clueless child sitting and smacking her lips as she was relishing a slice of ham.

Since little baby Zoja was now wailing like a mad Irish banshee — worse than she did when her first tooth was coming in — we realized that something terrible must have happened. Unable to gather verbal evidence from a one-year-old, we had to piece the clues together. Exhibit number one was a piece of what the Spanish call *jamón york* and what the Polish call just *ham*, which was held firmly in Zoja's hand. This type of ham is particularly sweet in taste and has a slightly slimy surface that can leave a sweet residue when touched by your hand. Exhibit number two was Zoja's lower lip, which was now starting to increase in size and colour right in front of our eyes.

'Is she allergic to wasps?' I asked Michal.

'I have no idea,' he replied. 'She's never been stung by one.'

'Did she swallow it?' Robert asked astutely since there was no wasp in sight.

'Either she swallowed it, or she scared the daylights out of it,' I thought as all the wasps that were previously hovering about now seemed to have disappeared. While the crying solved the wasp problem, it created a huge dilemma. Should we sit here and see whether Zoja was allergic to wasp bites, or should we already be in the car on the way to the *centro salud* in Montefrio?

'Give her some ice cream,' Robert said, taking command.

We all agreed that this was a great idea, as it would slow the rate of the swelling and calm her nerves while giving us time to think. As Beata gave her baby daughter an ice lolly to suck on, she noticed exhibit number three: a hole in the baby's lower lip.

'I think the wasp ate some of Zoja's lip,' Amelia summed up our findings out loud.

This statement now caught the attention of little Kosma, who, so far, had been sitting quietly busy peeling his third hard-boiled egg of the day and was deep in his egg-shaped daydreaming world.

'Jajo,' Kosma managed to whimper his favourite word and started to cry uncontrollably.

'Give him some ice cream, too.' Robert resorted to his tried-and-tested solution.

The ice cream seemed to calm both children down, and the crying scared the wasps away. For the rest of her holiday, Zoja's lower face resembled that of Muhammad Ali's after Joe Frazier beat him to a pulp in the Fight of the Century. It was not a good look on a baby girl and made it difficult for us all to look at her. Apart from her sister, Amelia, taking one photo of the deformed face to taunt her later in life, no more photos of Zoja were taken during this holiday.

Having my family come and see our new life in Andalusia was great. It was the first time since we had moved to Spain the year before, that Robert and I had a chance to enjoy the coveted Spanish lifestyle to the full. For three weeks, we put pause to the renovation project, and we had no writing and translation work to do either. I loved the long evening meals with the starry sky above our heads and midnight swims in the pool to cool off, hiking among the giant aloes and picking cactus fruit to taste. All of these experiences made me feel happy to be where I was. But as my family left and October started, we had to put our dirty clothes back on and go back to work to make the guest apartments rentable. Another hard year was ahead of us; oblivious to the fact that we had very little money left in the bank, we continued with the reform.

TWENTY-SIX
SUN-DRIED TOMATOES

You know you are poor when you stand in a Lidl supermarket in front of a display of discounted goods and wonder whether you can afford a forty-five-cent bag of tulip bulbs. Due to our lack of oversight, in the fall of 2015, we had almost no money left in our account. I looked at the bulbs, sighed in desperation, and decided that money could be better spent. I grabbed a seventy-cent bottle of red wine and went to the cashier.

I could look for many excuses to explain our financial downfall, but the simple truth was that, during the year of renovations, we forgot where money comes from. The last time I had to count my weekly expenses to the last cent was when I was an undergraduate student. Then, the main issue was that the allowance I received from my mother and the occasional scholarships that I secured barely covered the cost of living. But since my student lifestyle involved a lot of beer drinking and cigarette smoking, I was broke most of the time.

Being poor again reminded me of those days when at the end of the month, I would empty the contents of my handbag and fish out all the lost pennies. The tiny coins that seemed insignificant on any other day of the month became nuggets of gold that had to be cherished and saved. Often, once added together, I was able to use this pitiful change to buy a bread roll and a yoghurt, which would be my meal for the day.

This, of course, was not exactly Hamsun's tale of hunger and despair. My destitution and poor nutrition were self-inflicted; they were the result of long nights in the student pub, where most of my food allowance was wasted on pints of beer and expensive packets of cigarettes bought at midnight from the bartender. That was a normal student life in the late 1990s. Even though I lived in deprivation for most of that time, I quickly forgot about it once I joined the workforce and became a happy-go-lucky recipient of a monthly salary. As it turned out, being poor in my late thirties was not as entertaining as it used to be in my early twenties.

During the first year of the house renovation, I worked as a freelancer writing content for an app for students of English as a second language. Robert did occasional translation and editing work but was mostly focused on managing the project and doing as much of the reform as possible himself. My work provided us with a steady paycheck and covered many of our construction bills after our savings ran dry. When my writing project ended in June, I was not worried because I had a lot of work to do: helping with the house renovations, painting the walls and the wooden planks. I also needed a break from sitting in front of the laptop. We both worked hard throughout the summer to bring the rooms to some sort of completion and then took a break during my family's visit in September.

When my family left, I looked into our accounts for the first time in months and realized that we had barely a thousand euros left. Because my next freelancing project was getting significantly delayed, it started to look like these thousand euros would have to last us until next March. With all the bills to be paid at the end of each month, it was clear that we would be bankrupt very soon. But denial and delusion are the food of the poor, so we ignored the money issue until our account was completely dry.

That fall and winter, we made cuts everywhere. Our weekly grocery bill went down from one hundred euros a week to about sixty. Even Lidl's wine became a treat, and pork chops rarely appeared on the table. What saved us from malnutrition and aided our budget cuts were all the fruit and vegetables that we had harvested in the summer.

In our enthusiasm to become subsistence horticulturists, the previous spring, we planted over one hundred different vegetable plants. We both love growing vegetables, even though the cost of doing it hardly covers the expenses, and now that we had all this land that we could do what we wanted with, we created a giant vegetable garden. Throughout the summer, we collected kilograms of tomatoes, peppers, and cucumbers every day. The peppers were not a big problem as we had only ten or so plants, and we were able to eat the peppers as fast as they grew.

The cucumbers did become a temporary problem. After the initial excitement of having our own cucumbers, we quickly realized that we could not eat them fast enough. To prevent them from rotting and to give ourselves time to consume them at our own leisure, I started to pickle them. Two pickle recipes helped us save the cucumber crop from going to waste. The Polish recipe created a traditional pickled cucumber that goes well on a sandwich or as a snack with a cold beer. Unfortunately, one of the key ingredients of this recipe is radish root, which is unknown in our part of Spain. I could not complain about the lack of the other key ingredient, which is dill seed.

Wild dill grows in our area like a weed; you can find it on the side of the road and scattered in meadows and between the olive trees. It's often two metres high and has thick, fragrant stalks. It was a great addition to the traditional Polish recipe. While the Polish pickles are delicious, their shelf life is limited, so we served them to all our guests on all occasions and ate them ourselves with every meal. But even I was getting sick and tired of pickled cucumbers.

Then I remembered a Swedish style of cucumber pickles that calls for a lot of sugar and vinegar. This turned out to be a huge hit with all our Spanish friends and neighbours. Knowing how much sugar goes into one jar of Swedish pickles, I avoided them myself, but they were such a hit that Dani would take whole jars of this sweet pickle from me and then come back the next day and ask for more. I was more than happy to meet popular demand as I hate wasting food. As soon as I thought that I had the cucumbers under control, our tomatoes started to mature.

While we only had about twenty or so cucumber plants, we did overplant the tomatoes and had at one point sixty or more plants. When I saw our first mature tomato in early August, I was delighted. Because no other vegetable tastes as good as a homegrown tomato, we planted all the varieties we liked to eat; we had cherry tomatoes, beef tomatoes, bell tomatoes, and finally Roma tomatoes. The last one was planted with the specific purpose of making sun-dried tomatoes, but as it turned out, one can sun-dry all of the different varieties of tomato with great success.

Throughout the spring, we couldn't wait for our tomatoes to start to flower, so we were thrilled when the first little yellow flowers turned into fruit and then when the fruit started to ripen. The first two weeks of a tomato harvest in August were idyllic. Before cooking supper, we would take a cardboard box. I wish I could say we took a woven basket to add more pastoral charm to this story, but no, we used what was at hand — and we would wander to our massive vegetable garden and get a head of lettuce, dig some potatoes, and pick the ripened tomatoes. In those early days, there were usually just enough tomatoes for a salad for two people. We would then stroll back through the tall grass and stray wheat stalks glistening in the sunset and prepare our homemade meal.

The food was beyond delicious. The quality that fresh homegrown vegetables add to your meal is impossible to replicate with any store-bought vegetable. We lived in this bucolic paradise for a couple of weeks in August until it was impossible to eat the number of tomatoes that we would collect each evening. The first solution was to start gifting boxes of tomatoes to friends, neighbours, and anyone who passed by our house. While a person from a big city living far away from farmland might have appreciated such 'generosity', the local people simply refused to take the unwanted gift. The reason was that they themselves were inundated with a massive tomato harvest and probably feared what their wives and mothers would do to them should they bring more tomatoes home.

Our plumber, Paco, was the kindest in his rejection. He looked at my offering and tasted a few cherry tomatoes and a bell pepper and told me that he would take the cherry tomatoes but not the others. I promptly ran to the kitchen, spilt the contents of the box into the sink, and selected the cherry tomatoes, hiding a few innocent beef tomatoes among them. I was desperate to get rid of the tomatoes.

I had always been keen on sun-drying our own tomatoes, and this time the conditions could not have been more perfect. I had gazillion tomatoes, and the temperature outside was over forty degrees, with the direct sun scorching the soil most of the day. Soon the patio, the areas around the pool and everywhere else where there was minimal dust and dirt were covered in trays with tomatoes drying in the sun. I set them out on plastic tables, baking trays, and cutting boards. You could not move around the place without having sun-drying tomatoes in sight. And while this was a great idea, it was not fast enough for us to process the tomato production in the garden.

For every ten kilograms that I would set out in the sun, I would go out and collect another ten. As I'm not the most devoted horticulturist, I would often get tired and leave the harvest in the crate for a couple of days until I summoned some energy to do something with it. Unfortunately, as I found out, fruit flies are not very picky eaters and don't care whether they sink their teeth into a peach or a tomato, so the ignored crates of tomatoes would start to rot and release a terrible odour.

This experience taught me that tomatoes must not be left unattended for more than a day. In desperation, I remembered a YouTube video that showed an American housewife freezing whole tomatoes. Upon quick investigation, I found out that tomatoes can be easily frozen when fresh and then used for sauces and soups. I contemplated freezing whole tomatoes, but that would mean that the freezer would be unusable for other foods. The most space-efficient way was to peel them and then chop them for future use in pasta sauces. I was able to fit over a kilogram of tomatoes into each small freezer bag.

The tomato-preserving job continued until late October when we had English friends from a nearby village come and pick whole bags for their own use, and then we left the last of the tomatoes to rot on the vine. It was a shame, but we learned our lesson about overplanting. While my production of sun-dried tomatoes went on throughout August and most of September, the tomato trays around our house were soon joined by trays of dried figs.

The fig tree is a familiar sight in the Andalusian landscape. Most fig trees are very old and have strong, thick trunks and slightly contorted branches that resemble the rheumatic fingers of a cartoon witch. Being one of the few trees around our house that is not evergreen, a fig tree is a sad sight in the winter; its spooky fingers cast uncanny shadows in the full moon. But in the summer, the fig trees recover their lush foliage and start producing the most delicious fruit.

The first thing that we learned about the fig was that we should not burn its branches because, when burned, the fumes of the burning fig wood create a toxic smoke that can give you a strong headache or make you feel dizzy. It was young Gabi, the previous owner of our house, who chose to share this piece of valuable advice as a parting gift to the new owners. He told us about it because when we bought the house, there was a large pile of tree cuttings in the middle of our antique threshing floor. We understood that open fires were prohibited in Andalusia throughout the summer months and so pointed to the pile of wood and said that we would burn it in the fall.

The look of panic on his face was as if we had suggested that he put his firstborn son onto the pile. Since he did not know enough English and we did not understand a lot of Spanish, he used his best mime technique to explain to us the severe brain damage that the smoke from burning fig wood would cause. His performance of feigning dizziness and collapsing, and losing consciousness was extremely convincing. Since he was an Andalusian farmer by birth, he repeated it a few times with a few slight variations to make sure the knowledge sank in.

As a result, for years afterwards, we were convinced that should the fig wood get into our fire, we would all die a terrible silent death. The toxic gas emitted by burning fig wood would spread across our valley and take down everyone in its path: the stray cats on the trees, the dogs chained to the houses, the children playing on the patios, the busy housewives sticking their heads out from the kitchen, the olive pickers drinking bottles of San Miguel, and the innocent visitors from the city. When the Guardia Civil would come to investigate the mystery of 'death valley', as it would soon become known, they would discover the charred fig wood outside our house, nod their heads in disbelief, and summarize the case in one word: *¡extranjeros!*. As we learned later by chance, you *can* burn fig wood — just do it far away from your house, and don't stay too close to it when it burns, or, simply, don't stay nowhere near it when it burns.

Burning its wood is one part of the fig tree mystery; the other one is its fruit. When we first stayed in Andalusia, we rented a cottage in Campo Nubes, a small hamlet outside Priego de Cordoba. In the village, there was a very ancient fig tree growing next to the ruins of an abandoned farmhouse. One morning, as we were getting into our car, I saw a teenage boy 'stealing' the fruit from that tree and then taking it to his own house. 'What a wonderful breakfast,' I thought, but since we were not part of the community, I did not dare to do the same.

Because you can't buy green figs in any supermarket, I had no idea what they would taste like or what they would look like inside. Unlike the black or dark-purple figs that we buy in European supermarkets at a ridiculous price, the green figs that grow in abundance in Andalusia are semi-wild. Why they are not harvested, packed, and sold in small quantities of four for £1 has remained a mystery to me. They taste just as good, if not better, than their dark cousins and seem much more resilient to extreme climate and drought.

Because figs were new to us, we had no idea when to pick them. Unlike most fruit, which changes colour when ripe, the green fig stays green throughout its maturation process. The first summer, when we stayed in our new home, I inspected our fig trees several times. The fruit was big and looked ripe, but then when cut in half, the inside revealed a hard, white sponge. This clearly was not edible. Throughout our first August at the house, I attempted to eat the figs a few more times, but each time the fruit was hard and unappetizing. As I learned the following year, when we finally moved to Andalusia for good, the figs only ripen at the end of August. You can tell when they are ready to eat because they become soft and start drooping on the branches.

The trees next to our house are quite old and yield a spectacular harvest every year. The first ripe figs are always a treat - you pluck them straight from the tree and eat them directly, not worrying too much about washing them. The green figs, fresh from the tree, are sweet and delicate in taste. They go very well with our local goat cheese from Montefrio, but any type of Spanish goat cheese will do; unlike the French goat cheese, which is soft and smelly, the Spanish variety is hard but is musky enough to complement the figs.

While we were happy to have this delicious fruit at our disposal in large quantities, after a few weeks, the figs became a problem. Once they start falling off the tree and rot on the ground, they attract wasps from far and beyond. To control this, I would go out with baskets and pick around ten kilograms of figs every day. Just as with our tomatoes, the figs turned on us. From the sweet delight, they became a nuisance.

Not being able to control the production on the trees, I started to sun-dry them. I was surprised how quickly the green fruit started to resemble the dried figs that my family used to buy in packets for Christmas. Because of their high sugar content, they only needed a few days in the sun and were ready to be stored in jars and plastic bags for winter.

By the end of October, we had a freezer full of tomatoes, and the cupboards were stashed with sun-dried tomatoes and figs. I even made huge jars of tomato sauces which survived a few months in the cupboard. Little did we know how useful these food supplies would become. We lived on tomatoes throughout that fall and winter; for lunch, we would have the weekly special — tomato soup and bread — and for supper, pasta with tomato sauce. As a treat, we would munch on dried figs and our own walnuts and almonds.

An unexpected bonus was that the dried figs that I had stored in plastic bags in the fridge had become very boozy — I did not understand what chemical reaction happened or what steps were taken to cause this. The sun-dried figs started to sweat sugar, which turned into a sugary brandy-like syrup. We loved the 'boozy figs,' as they were the only type of dessert that we could afford for many months.

TWENTY-SEVEN

CORTIJO BERRUGUILLA CASA RURAL

Becuse living on sun-dried tomatoes and figs and checking our empty bank account every day, expecting some miracle to occur, started to lose its charm, I decided that it was time for us to speed up our grand project of renting rural apartments to tourists. We decided to open our casa rural to guests for Christmas 2015. It was going to be a soft launch to help us prepare for the summer season. It was still early November when we decided, and we had almost two months to get things ready for our first guests. Even though the place was a total pit with building materials and tools scattered around and with no proper furniture in the apartments, I felt confident that we would be able to pull it off for the holiday season.

Neither of us had any freelancing work in sight, so we could devote all our time and energy to opening the new business.

There is nothing in life that motivates me more than a looming deadline. The first step, of course, was to start advertising online. Because machines and the internet have an inexplicable grudge against Robert and tend to break down as soon as he sits in front of a laptop, it was my job to write up the postings and list our casa rural, or rural guesthouse, online. I chose two websites: one that I had used myself in the past and another recommended by a friend who had his own casa rural outside Alcalá.

The first problem that I encountered when setting up our property page on these sites was that we had to settle on a name for our rental business. The second problem was the lack of attractive photos. Both an appealing name and alluring photos seemed essential to launching our casa rural on the internet. We discussed the issue of a name on several occasions since we had bought the house. Most houses in Andalusia have a name that starts with either *casa* or *cortijo*. Having grand plans for our rural rental, we considered different name combinations with the word *casa*. *Casa Roberto* was a strong contestant, as suggested by Robert.

Since moving to Spain, Robert had been introducing himself to Spaniards as *Roberto Carlos*, which often creates a lot of confusion and consternation. Despite this, I was soon presented with Robert's second suggestion, the even more self-aggrandizing, *Casa Roberto Carlos*. Both of these suggestions left me blank. *Casa Robert y Sabina* or *Casa Sabina y Robert* were both quite unacceptable to anyone's ear and would look out of place, as I imagined the plaque on our gate. While I can see why many expats desire to plaster their name on the gate to their Spanish 'mansion', *Casa John* or *Casa Charles* always catch me off guard when driving through a Spanish village.

Personally, I felt that linking your house name with plants that surround it was a particularly inviting and pleasant way to name a house. A neighbour's house is called *Casa Membrillo* — The Quince House. I liked this idea so much that I got the dictionary out and started to experiment with options. *Casa Almendras*, The Almond House, was a strong contestant, as we have many almond trees around the house. *Casa Nogal,* The Walnut House, had a nice sound to it, but it also gave a false idea that the house is made of walnut. *Casa Granada,* The Pomegranate House, was lovely, but we had only one puny pomegranate tree to substantiate the claim.

As I was rather enchanted by our fig trees, I played with *Casa Higos,* but somehow when written on paper, the *h* and the *g* in one word looked rather sinister to my untrained eye. *Casa Higos* did not sound like an inviting place, and, to make it sound worse, anyone who does not have a passing knowledge of Spanish might inadvertently pronounce it *Casa He Goes.* I liked the idea of a *House of Figs,* but it did not seem practical.

In desperation, as always, I turned to the internet and Googled *the most popular bed and breakfast names in Spanish. Paraiso* and *Buena Vista* turned out equally popular in Spain and South America. While I loved our place, I felt that *paraíso* might overpromise and underdeliver; I was not confident enough to call our little rental apartments *paradise. Buena Vista* seemed appropriate as we do have lots of amazing views on the way to our house and from the house itself, but it did appear clichéd.

As I ran out of ideas regarding where to look for inspiration, I started to warm up to our house's traditional name — no country house in Spain is nameless. The name that features on our title deeds and which is incredibly difficult to pronounce if your Spanish is below intermediate level is *Cortijo Berruguilla.* In fact, the name is such a mouthful that, for the first year after the purchase, I did not even identify it in any legal documents as the name of our house. Mixed in with a lot of legalese Spanish, I assumed it to be the name of a special law for rural properties. It was only after we received our architect's renovation plans, which clearly stated the name of the house on the cover, that we realized that *Cortijo Berruguilla* was the name of our house.

The meaning of *berruguilla* is elusive, and until now, I have not found it in any dictionary. However, many Andalusians have heard this word and have some idea of its meaning. We thought that the word might be part of the dialect that my neighbours speak and hence not appear in a contemporary Spanish dictionary, but we were proven wrong when Robert called a car insurance company in Barcelona and, when asked for his home address, the female agent started to giggle. As she explained, *berruguilla* means 'little nipple', or so it did in her interpretation.

My neighbours, whose houses are also called Cortijo Berruguilla, tell me that it means 'little wart'. Other interpretations vary from 'wart' to 'growth on your skin'. While the exact translation remains unclear, the origin of the name is self-evident once you look at our house from the road. In the middle of the green hill covered in symmetrically planted olives, you see a little white wart sticking its head out from amid the greenery. It only felt right to keep the old name of the house given to it more than a century ago by someone much more sensitive to nature and its beauty than us. We decided to use the name as it should be and soon gave it an online presence as *Cortijo Berruguilla Casa Rural*.

I chose the *Casa Rural* ending because of its whimsical versatility. We planned to launch our hospitality business as a B&B because the two guest apartments did not have the kitchens ready, so we had to serve our guests breakfast. Once the kitchens were installed, we would transition to self-catering rural apartments. I felt that the term *Casa Rural* allowed us some creative space to define our business idea later on in time.

While we settled on the name and submitted that as our establishment's official name, we still had to entice prospective clients with photos. I could hardly photograph the mattresses on which my sister and her family had slept during their stay. Even though one man's mattress is another man's futon, I was convinced that paying guests would expect a proper bed, which we were going to build but needed more time to do so.

Having some past experience with photography, I understood the art of visual deception. I decided that, from the right angle and with the right focus, a nicely made mattress may appear to be a proper bed. The key to our success was staging, and so I put all my other work on hold and devoted a day to careful staging and doing a photo session of the new apartments.

I learned about home staging from American real-estate TV shows.

Realtors in the US often set up the interior to attract prospective buyers to purchase the property. To do so, estate agents hire companies specialising in making a dull and empty house look appealing to house viewers. The day before an open house, home staging experts will arrive with their truck full of stage props: antique furniture, bone china, crystal wine glasses, oil paintings, plants, fresh flowers, scented candles, fluffy towels, oriental carpets, and loads of hand-embroidered cushions. In short: a huge assortment of home decor touches that we have been conditioned to interpret as 'cosy' and 'welcoming', but also 'aspirational' and 'desirable'.

Because our own living quarters were still quite messy and unfinished, I first had to scavenge through our unpacked boxes for items that would make the empty and half-finished apartments look appealing to prospective guests. After a couple of hours of sifting through the boxes, I had managed to assemble a good collection of cushions of various shapes and sizes. Cushions, as I have witnessed in various hotel-makeover shows, are the life and soul of hospitality. I also found a box with our own bone china, some wine glasses, decorative throws, and some pretty Arabic side lamps. I looked at this booty and was confident that my staging would be a success.

As it turned out, transforming an empty bedroom with nothing but a mattress on the floor into a snug and inviting boudoir was not a problem. The mountain of cushions on the bed and the throws confused the perspective, and in the photos, it appeared to be a proper bed. With some inspired lighting created by the Arabic lanterns and the exposed stone walls, the bedrooms looked very stylish and artsy and in keeping with the Moorish history of the region.

After I photographed the first bedroom, I moved all the cushions and lamps to the second bedroom and, after slightly rearranging the set, I photographed that. I was well pleased with the final result of the bedroom staging. It was the living rooms that turned out to be problematic; they were large empty rooms with no furniture and with large vacant spaces left open and awaiting the future installation of the kitchens. Since we were hoping to bring the first guests in the winter, I thought that I might bring the camera focus onto the fireplace to create a Christmassy atmosphere.

I hauled up my own armchair and coffee table from the main house and positioned them in front of the fireplace. I spent a few minutes looking for a book with a hard cover and placed it face open on the coffee table next to a bowl of walnuts. Because we did not have any red wine or spirits at home, I had to think out of the box; water with a dash of iodine had the most inviting colour, so I poured this impromptu mixture into a wine glass and placed it between the book and the walnuts. The surface of the coffee table was, of course, quite cluttered, and the way the items were placed on the tabletop would make using any of them very awkward, if not impossible, but that's how they had to stay for the sake of artistry.

I looked at my masterpiece. If you just focused on the fireplace and its immediate surroundings, it did look as if someone had been reading a book by the fire while enjoying the nuts, albeit still in their shells, and drinking a lovely glass of some dark liquor, presumable old port, or brandy. What did not make sense in my installation was that there was no fire in the fireplace. In fact, we had yet to light the apartment fireplaces, and I was not even sure if they would work properly. Despite it being November, the weather was almost thirty degrees with blue skies; hence I was not looking forward to the next step in my master creation, but it had to be done to complete the illusion.

I collected a pile of firewood and started the fire. Either because it was the first fire in that fireplace or because I left the vent closed by mistake, all it did was create a great deal of smoke. I hoped that, with time, it would develop into the blazing fire that I needed for the photo, and so I walked away to start staging breakfast on the terrace. When I got back thirty minutes later, the fire had gone out and the wood was not even charred. I did not have time for this, so I got a whole bunch of paraffin sticks that we used to start fires and placed them behind the wood. I reckoned that I would only have a few minutes for the sticks to burn out, so I had to make sure that everything was ready for the shoot.

As I scanned the set, it occurred to me that with the sun blazing through the glass terrace door, I wouldn't be able to photograph the fire even if there was one. As there were no curtains on the windows, I went to the main house and fetched a bunch of blankets and bedsheets. I then spent a good twenty minutes fastening the rags to the windows so that the room was dark enough to photograph this wintery scene. With all this in place, I lit the paraffin sticks, closed the fireplace, and started shooting. I had only taken some photos of the walnut bowl and the 'wine' with the fire in the background before the fireplace started to smoke again. But I was happy with what I captured — all I really needed was a photo that would tell the prospective guests that there was a living room with a fireplace.

Upon accomplishing this, I went to photograph my grand oeuvre — the alfresco meal on the terrace. Because I was not planning on cooking a real meal and presenting it — plating is not my forte, so even the most delicious meal would be wasted for a photograph — I decided to focus on the table setting, which is also not my strength but it did not require any actual cooking.

First, I found an empty bottle of red wine and half-filled it with water. I placed it in the centre next to a wooden board with a frozen baguette, a bottle of olive oil, and a jar of sun-dried tomatoes with rosemary and garlic. It was a random assembly of things that I found in the kitchen and that had some sort of Mediterranean connotation — a seasoned food critic might question what kind of meal this ensemble might foreshadow. Still, I was focused more on invoking cultural associations rather than culinary cohesion.

I polished the cutlery and placed it in a way that suggested that someone had been using it just a second ago — presumably to cut the frozen baguette with; I then stood back to admire my work. I was enchanted by the staging. It was clear to me that the wine glasses and fancy plates were positioned so that the diners would have to be ambidextrous to use them. The table was moved so close to the terrace wall that no one could sit at it. But it was so positioned to include the mountain view in the background of the dinner setting.

With a final spark of creative genius, I went downstairs and cut three beautiful roses and placed them nonchalantly between the olive oil and the wine bottle; the tableau was complete. If this image did not entice customers, I did not know what would. With another day spent on some judicious Photoshopping of the images, I uploaded them to the websites we had chosen to advertise on. Encouraged by the progress made in the photos, I created a Facebook site for the business and shared it with friends. While friends who had never seen or been near our property congratulated us on the swift completion of the B&B project, our close neighbours and friends were more astounded and shocked than congratulatory.

'OMG! How did you finish it all in two weeks?' wrote an English friend from a nearby village who had been to a barbecue at our house just recently.

'Well, if Keith was fooled, and he knows the state of our house, then hopefully we will lure some hapless travellers into booking their stay with us for this winter,' I thought that evening while sipping a glass of real red wine and grinning like a Cheshire cat.

And, sure enough, a couple of weeks later, we received our first booking for New Year's Eve 2015. We now had a deadline written in stone. All we had to do was 'put on the finishing touches.'

TWENTY-EIGHT

THE CRINKLE CRANKLE WALL

T he list of finishing touches was long. I posted it on the fridge
to help us not lose sight of the jobs at hand.

'We should do the staircase first,' I suggested as we sat
down one evening and decided to write it all down.

It was November, and we did not have much time to waste. The
aforementioned staircase was inside one of the apartments and needed
to be clad with something. At that moment, it consisted of ugly, grey
concrete bricks — hardly a stylish detail in what I advertised as a
traditional Andalusian cottage.

'Build chimney stacks,' Robert suggested, and I added the item to the list. We did not want the guests to admire the night sky through a large hole in their bedroom ceiling.

'What about a balustrade outside and the steps to the apartment,' I said and wrote these two tasks down. At the time, the steps ended abruptly, about half a metre above the ground. We had to climb up or jump down this obstacle when going in and out of the rooms.

'Oh, and connect the electricity to the Granero' — that was the name we gave one of the apartments so that we could distinguish which one we were talking about.

'Call Rufi,' I wrote down. Rufi was our electrician who had to be forewarned weeks in advance of any impending job.

'What about beds?' Robert suggested.

I added beds and nightstands, and tables to the list of essential furniture that had to be made or obtained in some way. To the list, we added cladding a bathroom ceiling, putting up skirting boards, and grouting.

The next morning, we went to the Granero to assess the job of cladding the staircase inside.

'Do you know how to tile?' I asked Robert.

'I watched Dani closely and intently,' was his response.

And there was some truth in that. Robert had helped Dani finish off all the bathrooms and some floors in the house. I just hoped that he had paid attention. Since we did not have any money left to pay anyone to do it, we had to do it ourselves. Robert would now be Dani, and I would be the builder's assistant. However, the problem remained regarding the materials we could use to cover the ugly concrete bricks that the internal staircase was built with.

I walked around the house — which at this stage could easily be described as a builder's scrapyard — and brought some samples of some of the different materials that we had left over from previous jobs. There were some tiles that local builders call *peldaños* that could be used on the steps. There were some surplus pine cladding and wood scraps that we used on the ceilings and a random assortment of different tiles from different bathrooms. We first counted the *peldaños* and, to our delight, discovered that we had just enough to cover the tread of each step. But we did not have any material to cover the riser of each step.

One idea was to cover the face with stained pine planks, but I was not convinced. The planks seemed dark and charmless. What I would have liked to see was a type of Andalusian staircase cladding that I have seen in some old houses. The face of each step has tiles with colourful and lively hunting and forest scenes. The tiles have a piece of wood above them meant to protect them from getting chipped. The flat surface of each step is usually dark red or brown *gres* or stoneware.

I knew that we would not be able to mimic this style exactly, but the idea of mixing wood and tiles had become an *idée fixe*. So, while Robert started laying the first steps with the *peldaños* that we already had, I stood by my strange collection of materials and kept on matching different leftover tiles to the stained pine planks. The juxtaposition of wood and decorative tiles was lovely, but I had no idea how to combine the two materials.

'It would be nice to combine the wood with the tiles,' I told Robert as I was passing him the *peldaños*.

'Look.' I put a lovely decorative tile in one hand and put it against a piece of wood.

'It's nice,' Robert admitted, 'but you need a router.'

'What's that?' I had just recently figured out how to distinguish between a table saw and a circular saw.

'It's a tool that makes grooves, then you can lay the tiles inside the recessed wood,' Robert explained.

That was exactly what I needed, and I was quite amazed to find out that someone had invented such a tool. I have always admired the variety of power tools that exist. It seemed that there was a power tool for any job, no matter how minuscule or unimportant. I blame this on men's inherent need to either delegate work to others or to spend countless hours thinking about how not to do a job. It is one of the reasons why our garage is filled with tools for any event or occasion. Some of them have only been used once — for one particular job. Many tools had been purchased while browsing the aisles of Leroy Merlin and bought in case they might be needed one day. Others had been on sale at Lidl — the concept of a 'loss leader' means nothing to my husband — and impulsively purchased in disbelief that such a great tool was on sale for only €5.99. They all sit together on the dusty garage shelves, hoping that their master will need them one day and remember where they are. When a new box of drill bits arrives fresh from the middle aisle, they all stick their heads out curiously. The drill bits box gives them a dirty look, confident that he won't end up like these washed-up losers.

'How long have you been here?' the newcomer would ask the soldering iron smugly.

'I've been with them for many years. First, in the storage room in their house in Al Ain, and then they brought me here,' the soldering iron would justify his place in the world through the window in the unopened plastic box.

'We'll be out of this box soon. I'm sure,' the individual drill bits would reassure themselves, not aware that several other drill bit sets were yet to be opened.

Even though our garage is filled with tools, any new job starts with a prerequisite trip to the hardware store to buy tools that are absolutely indispensable to this specific job. When we were students, we decided to paint our second-hand furniture to give it a breath of new life. This job required a purchase of a professional sander; sanding furniture by hand was out of the question. When we lived in Al Ain, one of our internal wooden doors expanded in the summer and had to be trimmed down to be able to close it again. We could not use the old sander for this job; we had to acquire a professional-grade DeWalt power planer. When I asked why we didn't buy the cheapest planer, since it was just one set of doors and the price difference between the unknown brand and the well-known brand was outrageous, I was informed that when it comes to power tools, you should always buy the best quality. Once, I asked Robert to sweep leaves around the house; this had swiftly ended in him browsing the Stihl catalogue, searching for a leaf blower. Drawing on these experiences, as soon as I heard the word *router*, I just asked about the price.

'I can get a *fresadora* for about two hundred euros.' I was surprised that he knew not only the Spanish word for a wood router but also the price; it clearly wasn't the first time Robert had thought of this power tool.

'But we don't have any money,' I tried to reason.

'Yes, but I can use it to make furniture.' This, in his mind, seemed to be the winning argument. He said it as he cleaned his hands from tile glue and ran to his laptop to search Amazon.

'Well, we need to finish the steps, so we may as well try the router,' I thought to myself. 'We might use it again one day in the distant future.'

While the acquisition of the router helped us create quite unique risers for the staircase, the job itself was slow. Because we had to lay the tiles from the bottom up, we could only lay two steps a day. We would do this straight after breakfast, then go work on the outside staircase leading to the second-floor apartment on the other side of the house.

Our English builder, who had been tasked to build these a year before, left us with steps that were somewhat suspended in the air. As I mentioned, anyone taking the stairs down had to jump off the last step to the ground; a leap of one metre. A certain flexibility in one's legs was demanded on the return trip to the apartment. The reason for this Gehry-like design was that the English contractor had built the steps from the top down. Being mathematically challenged, he did not measure the exact width and height of each step but rather used an old technique of 'hope for the best.'

Unfortunately for him, the Fates were not interested in his project, and with every step closer to the ground, it was obvious to all of us that he was not going to be able to finish the stairs. To start with, because he started at the top, his stairs had no proper foundation. Secondly, his poor calculations meant that any additional steps would come right in front of the garage entrance, thereby blocking the entrance to the garage and rendering it unusable to store the car. We asked him to stop where he was before he blocked the garage with the stairs — a few days later, he was finally asked to pack his tools and go, as his blunders were countless and evident even to the untrained eye. It was now almost a year later that we were forced to resolve these stairs ourselves.

The solution was quite simple: we decided to make the stairs turn right, away from the garage. We would then build a foundation and measure out the distance necessary to have a generously curved staircase that would connect with the existing steps a metre and a half above the ground level. It all may sound complicated, but the idea was simple in itself. The problem was that immediately to the right of the garage was a small hill that needed to be excavated to provide sufficient space to build the steps. We would not have been able to excavate the hill by hand, so we called our neighbour Jaime who owned an excavator.

It is always difficult to ask a neighbour for a favour in the middle of the olive season. They are usually working hard every day from dawn to dusk, trying to collect as many olives as possible before the heavy winds and storms that can occur in the winter damage the crop. But despite being busy, one Sunday morning, Jaime arrived with his excavator. We could see him leave his house almost an hour before he got to our place.

A tracked excavator is an excruciatingly slow form of transportation. But once he got to our house, the digging out of the hill went unbelievably fast. In two hours, the hill by the garage was gone and the soil distributed evenly over the surface of the driveway, which now increased its average elevation by half a metre.

'Don't worry about this,' Jaime assured me as he saw concern in my face over loose rock and soil being spread all over the driveway. 'It will compact itself.'

In two hours, the job was done, and Jaime was ready to commence his long journey home, which was not more than a kilometre away. As he crawled down our hill, we stood for the first five minutes waving good-bye and thanking him, but we soon realized that he could not hear us over the noise of the excavator engine. We went back to admire the blank canvas that we were now given.

'Why didn't he excavate further back?' I asked upon seeing the exposed rock that we were now left with. 'Don't we need space to build a retaining wall?'

'He said it's OK. The rock will not cave in.' Robert assured me that there was no need for a retaining wall.

We spent the rest of the afternoon planning where to lay the concrete foundation for the stairs and doing exact measurements of the steps' width and high. We were going to start building the steps first thing the next morning.

It might have been two o'clock in the morning that I was woken up by the sound of a storm raging outside. Since the last years' experience of living without our roof, I still had slight PTSD every time I heard the raindrops. This time was no different, and I woke up in a panic, only to realize that we had a roof over our heads. As the torrential rains continued for a week, we could not build the stairs and simply watched the driveway, which consisted of newly excavated soil, turn into a giant mud bath. With our list of things to do, we were busy working inside anyway.

As soon as the router arrived, we finished the stairs inside the Granero and started building the bed frames. Robert even used the router to make decorative grooves on the bed frame, which convinced me that it was a good purchase. But with the storms raging outside, there was one thing that we did not take into account, and that was the newly excavated side of the hill adjacent to the garage.

As I walked to the garage to get tools one sombre and wet morning, I saw that the whole side of the hill that Jaime had excavated for us just a week ago had caved in and collapsed. It clearly was not as stable as he had thought it would be. With the first guests arriving in two weeks, there was no point in delaying the dirty work. Since the roads were now completely soaked and clayey, it was impossible to get the excavator to our house, so I went to the garage and got us two spades, a hoe, a pickaxe, and some black rubber buckets to put the rocks and soil into. And thus armed, we started a long, cold, and wet labour of clearing the debris away so that we could build these god-damn steps.

As I hacked with the pickaxe through the never-ending layers of rock and clay, I could remember a distinct image of a Mickey Mouse hammering endlessly at some stubborn rocks in a prison quarry. His companions were all dressed in prison stripes and tied to one another with a chain. A realization came to me why for centuries, prisoners of all sorts were often tasked with smashing stones, building tunnels through rocks, and digging earth to make roads. The fight against nature and its hard surface is mindless and does not seem to have an end. Only someone who had been deprived of choice and free will would be able to do it. It took us several days of labouring to clear the rock and soil that continually fell down off the side of the hill.

'It looks good,' I commented.

'Yes, but we need a retaining wall,' Robert announced.

To do that, we had to smash some more rock away to make space for a foundation for the retaining wall. I went to get a sledgehammer, and for the next few days, we spent our days smashing impossibly hard compacted rock from the side of the hill, gradually making space for the foundation of the wall. Smashing rock is a mindless job in that it sucks all the life and joy out of you and leaves you numb and empty. The job itself requires some thinking, but it has to be done by someone who has abandoned all hope and does not care about life's complexities as they while away the day, hitting hard things. Initially, the plan was to build a wall in a straight line next to the foundation of the proposed staircase. We stretched a piece of string from the steps and along the rock wall to the oak tree to know how deep into the rock face we had to dig.

After two days of cartoonish labour, we managed to clear a metre in a straight line to make a foundation for part of the wall. There were four more metres to go, and if we worked at this pace, the wall would not be finished before the guests came … or ever, as we were both losing our will to live.

'Why don't we make a curved wall,' I suggested, looking at the rocks that protruded past the section that we had cleared.

'You mean bulge it out here.' Robert pointed at the rock that was sticking out.

'Yeah.' I was hoping to sell this idea as if it was a perfectly normal thing to have a bulging wall.

'You can't do it,' Robert stated with the authority of an engineering architect telling a builder that you can't have an upside-down chimney.

'Why not?' I knew that I was not going to sell this shortcut on a nihilistic platform. So, I had to dig deep for ideas. 'It's art deco,' I announced.

'How?' I piqued his interest with the art deco reference.

'They have curved walls in art deco architecture.' I also reminded him of a *Grand Designs* episode in which the family built a house with a curved wall in art deco style.

'Oh, yes.' Robert seemed to have a vague memory of what I was talking about. 'I need to see it.' He went inside the house to look at the images online.

I dropped the sledgehammer into the mud hoping never to have to use it again, and followed Robert inside.

'We can have a crinkle crankle wall,' he announced from behind the laptop.

'A what?' He might as well have said 'a Humpty Dumpty wall.'

'It's a wall that curves,' he said, generously mansplaining the term *crinkle crankle* to me.

I did not mind being mansplained about something that I had just dreamed of twenty minutes before and turned out to have a properly established architectural term which means *a curvy wall*. As long as we were going to build around the bulging rocks and stop trying to straighten out a palaeolithic feature, I was happy to sit in a warm and dry room for a few minutes and contemplate the time this would save us.

'Ok, let's get the bricks and start the cement mixer,' Robert commandeered, and we were out again in the cold, but this time with some hope of finishing the stairs before the guests arrived.

We went out and cranked up the cement mixer and spent our second Christmas in Berruguilla out in the rain and mud, building a crinkle crankle wall and steps to the rental apartment.

TWENTY-NINE
TWELVE GRAPES

T he day before our first guests were to arrive could not have been more stressful. We started the day by taking the pieces of the wooden bed frame that Robert had made in the garage and assembled them in the bedroom. We screwed and glued them together, and we were both surprised by the great result. The handmade wooden bed frame looked imposing and very rustic. It matched the other wood features and the beams in the room

because it was made with the wood scraps left from cladding the ceiling. The legs of the bed were also made from scraps of the ceiling beams. The installation of a proper bed was a huge relief. Until then, I had been constantly worried that we would not be able to pull it off and would have to offer our first paying guests a mattress on the floor.

As soon as the bed was in place, I went out of the bedroom and looked at the empty living room. There was a large oriental rug in the middle of the room, which I had placed there to cosy up the room when my sister's family stayed in September. But it was hardly a homely space with no chairs, tables, armchairs, or cupboards. It reminded me of the flat that we had occupied for a few days in Ulan Bator, where we stayed with a family of displaced nomads (one of whom was a student taught by Robert in the UAE). This branch of the family had sold their cattle and decided to move to the capital to take advantage of the luxuries of modern living. With the money obtained from the sale of their livestock, they bought a one-bedroom flat in a decidedly Soviet-looking block of flats in a suburb near the city centre.

While they had swapped the green steppes of Uliastai for the hustle and bustle of Ulan Bator, the interior of their new home was an exact replica of the yurt that they had left behind. The living-room-cum-guest bedroom consisted of a carpet with thick fleece covers decorating the walls. The kitchen was equipped with a carpet, a traditional stove, and two cupboards set on the floor. The bedroom consisted of a carpet and rolled-up mats that were put away during the day.

On arrival, we all sat in a circle on the living room's carpet as if we were in a yurt in the middle of the green steppes. Bojo, the student who had invited us to her home, sat with us and interpreted while her mum offered us extremely hot cups of weak tea with yak milk. The goblets from which we drank were imitations of the silver cups that Genghis Khan might have drunk from himself; these made of tin, however. Tin conducts heat very well, as anyone will learn as soon as they try to take a sip of the impossibly hot brew from a tin cup. Bojo explained that it is a Mongolian custom not to put the cup down until one has a proper first sip. And so, not wanting to be rude, a visitor is forced to decide whether to burn their hand by holding a cup of volcanic tea or burn their mouth with the molten liquid.

Robert thought a quick sip might do it and took one small gulp, only to start whining and cursing as the lava touched his lips. On seeing this, I decided to go against Mongolian savoir-vivre, and I put my tea down on the carpet to let it cool. This was the beginning of a long journey where we unwittingly insulted Mongolian customs and sensibilities on a daily basis. But that is another story.

Right now, I was staring at an empty carpet laid in the middle of the spartan living room and realized that in our frenzy to create steps, we forgot that a European-born person would not want to consume his meals on a carpet. I came to realize that there were a thousand and one bits and pieces that modern Homo sapiens deems essential to a comfortable existence; I got a notebook and started writing them down. In addition to a table and two chairs, we needed two armchairs, a rubbish bin, toilet paper holders, towel pegs, coat hangers, shower curtains, blinds, dish drying racks, silverware containers, knife blocks, soap dispensers, a shower mat, a small fridge, a water kettle, etc. I made a long list, and we rushed off to search Alcalá's second-hand shops for these essentials.

Many traders in Northern Europe and the UK have turned second-hand shop-keeping into an art and a prosperous trade. Once I visited friends in North Wales, and as a pastime, we wandered from one second-hand shop to another. In Wales, second-hand shops are treated like free museums of modern private life. There you can admire the living arrangements of times past, see the different styles of chairs and tables, and marvel at changing tastes in crockery and wall decorations. The antiques are neatly arranged and organized by their mode of use, and the prices are not exorbitant.

The second-hand shop in Alcalá — run by a kind but not business savvy Englishman — was quite the opposite. It was used by the local people, both Spaniards and expats, as a dumping place for their unwanted stuff and soon became a memorial of rampant consumerism. Most modern people are no longer satisfied with old-fashioned window-shopping where one can fulfil one's needs with aspirational daydreaming. A modern man or woman has to actually purchase the desirable object, or a shopping expedition won't be satisfying.

And thus, we fill our homes with new objects while the old ones are still in good use but fail to satisfy our social aspirations. Most people are conflicted and don't like to throw away things that are not broken even when they don't use them anymore. As a result, we end up hoarding the stuff, shoving items into the back of wardrobes and cupboards and hiding them in overflowing basements. Some of us convince ourselves that the moment we throw away the unused bikes, rollerblades, skis, badminton rackets, PCs, old TV screens, printers and various radios, we will need them the following day.

Because most of us share his philosophy, we struggle as things take over our living space. Thus, the second-hand shop in Alcalá was a perfect solution for getting rid of things. The owner of the shop, who was not an entrepreneurial genius, would accept any trash. He promised to pay people once their unwanted item was sold. This was a win-win for the people who got rid of the lumber from their flats and a lose-lose for the shopkeeper who was storing old-fashioned goods for free in the hope to make a few euros on an unlikely sale. Because of this business model, the shop overflowed with unwanted drinking glasses, novelty mugs, chipped plates and washed-out crockery sets, vases, chandeliers, old dolls, old toys, broken toilet seats, used washbasins, kitsch horse portraits, greying baby clothes, bicycles with flat tires, greasy fridges, and a surprising number of yellowing mattresses and accompanying steel bed frames.

Tat is an English word that is quite impossible to translate into other Indo-European languages. It encompasses the idea of being cheap, shoddy and tasteless, but at the same time, it carries the notion of being still of use in the form of a possible gift or a souvenir. When something is not in its prime but not complete rubbish or junk, it's *tat*. When an object is somewhat eye-catching and seems like it might be of use to someone, just not me in this lifetime, it's *tat* too. 'Tat shop' would have been a better name for the second-hand shop in Alcalá, but since we had no money to spend and a long list of things to make the rental apartment seem liveable, we had no choice.

We grabbed a simple table, three chairs, and an armchair that did not have any (visible) stains on it. We got some bathroom 'essentials', such as a shower curtain and a bathroom bin, at a local *ferreteria*, and we rushed back home to assemble the items to fulfil the idea that I alluded to with my cleverly staged photography a few months earlier.

We worked on the apartment until midnight, bringing all sorts of finishing touches to the room.

I searched through the boxes that had not yet been unpacked and found all sorts of household treasures, like candle holders, cushions, colourful coffee mugs, and an assortment of pretty Arabic and Indian shawls. We pinned the exotic fabric to the walls to stop the somewhat empty room from echoing. In the morning, I went to inspect our work and was quite pleased with the results of our rushed labours. The outside, on the other hand, was still a bit of a tip. The crinkle crankle wall right outside the apartment had not been plastered, and the steps leading to the rental were just bare concrete bricks; we had no time to finish them. There were random building materials gathered in small piles in different places around the property, and the driveway consisted of finely blended mud.

I asked Robert to put the building materials into the greenhouse to get them out of the guests' sight and went upstairs to check everything. As I looked inside the bedroom, I realized the obvious; there were no pillows or sheets on the bed. I had been so focused on making the whole apartment seem lively and inviting that I had forgotten to buy new duvets, pillows, and sheets.

It was already ten a.m., so there was no time to go to the shops. I gathered an assembly of unused pillows and blankets from our own wardrobe. This was very unfortunate but had to be done. I then searched our own laundry cabinet for a set of bed linen that was acceptable to present to strangers or paying guests. While a perfect TV housewife would not have any problem fishing out a lavender-scented and pink-ribbon-tied bed linen set from her linen cabinet, I had to throw out all the contents of the said cabinet onto the floor to be able to appraise it.

First, I set aside mismatched pieces of linen that had lost their partners over the years. Even I understood that the bedsheets in a B&B should match. I then rolled out the sheets that were previously jammed into balls and stashed in the cabinet, and inspected them for irremovable stains. Those joined the mismatched lot on the side of the bed. Finally, I narrowed down my audition to two sets. One had a tiny yellow stain on the pillow. The other had a rip on the side. As the clock was ticking and the sets had to be ironed, I had to think quickly. I decided that a rip was more forgiving than a stain and chose the bed linen set with the slightly ripped duvet cover.

I set up my ironing station next to the window, and as I clumsily ironed the bed set, I kept on looking out of the window expecting the guests to arrive at any minute. It was the first time in my life that I had to iron bed linen, and it seemed to take forever.

Once I was done, it was almost noon, and I kept obsessing that the guests would show up at any minute. They informed me that they would arrive *después comida*, which Google Translate told me meant 'after food.'

'But what time is *después comida?*' I kept wondering as I was making their bed in a hurry.

When I finished, I looked at my work and was very disappointed. I wanted the bed to look lush and inviting, just as you see beds in hotel advertisements. But my bed-making skills were subpar, and the whole thing looked like a guest bed in a friend's house. It was acceptable but really not worthy of the classy B&B or a guesthouse that I aspired to become. I looked at it for a long time but could not figure out what was lacking. While I may have had some sense of style and design in some aspects of life, bed-making is not my forte.

I took out my phone from the back pocket and searched 'how to make a bed in a hotel'. I expected to find some useful insider tips or a secret life hack, but all I got was a Wikihow that explained — presumably for aliens wanting to adapt to our earthly lifestyle — in twelve steps how to make a regular bed. I tweaked my search to 'how to make a bed nice' my English was clearly failing me, and the results were coming out gibberish too. I looked at the clock — it was almost one. There was no more time to brush up on housekeeping for dummies. I made a mental note to figure out how professional hoteliers make their beds appear so luxurious and left the room.

The guests arrived after four p.m., which made sense since Spanish lunch is at two o'clock. They were a lovely couple from Cádiz who must have been overwhelmed by our overexcited welcome and too much information, but they did not show it. It was New Year's Eve, and they wanted to have a quiet evening with a glass of wine by a fireplace in a rural setting, and that's what we managed to deliver.

As they enjoyed the complimentary bottle of cava by the fireplace, Robert and I sat down exhausted to our markedly un-festive supper. It was just eight o'clock when I heard a knock on the door. The woman was holding a small basket with grapes in her hand and was handing it to me. I thought it was a strange gift but received it graciously while stating what was right in front of me.

'Oh, grapes, how nice, thank you,' I mumbled.

'It's twelve grapes,' she explained as a matter of fact.

I thought it very bizarre to give someone an exact number of grapes.

'Oh, thank you,' I said, despite my surprise. I accepted the gift humbly.

'It's for New Year's Eve,' she said.

She could see from the blank expression on my face that I was unfamiliar with this custom. As it turned out, we were supposed to eat twelve grapes at midnight to ward off evil for the next twelve months, one grape for each anticipated month of prosperity.

I nodded my head in understanding and thanked her profusely for saving us from an ill-fated year. As with any superstition, several exact rules inform you how, when, and at what pace you should eat the twelve grapes. I could not be bothered following them in any detail. To start with, I had not managed to stay up until midnight for many years. To do so would be long and torturous. Instead, I decided to eat the grapes after supper.

Logically speaking, there was no reason to wait for the Puerta del Sol clock in Madrid to strike twelve; it must have been midnight somewhere that December 31st/January 1st. I also wondered about these goddesses of good Fate travelling the night and checking everyone's stomach for the consumption of the lucky grapes. Many poor people in South America follow the Spanish custom, and they are not exactly living in the lap of luxury. Even though logic told me that the twelve grapes were a con that made the grape producers rich in the winter, I decided not to tempt my own Fate.

So, on the last evening of 2016, watching online videos, chowing down the twelve grapes, I hoped that the next year might bring us some good luck and some much-needed money. We set off on this adventure to 'live deep' and to taste the marrow of life, and so we did. Our first year and a half in Andalusia was hard and often brutal, but it was real, and few things in life are as precious as real, authentic experiences. As it was, we had just planted the seed for our future in this new and wonderful place. More hardships were to come. If I had a glass ball that evening, I'd see many disasters that were yet to come. Would that have made me turn my back on this place? The answer is a definite *no*. I was home, and the adventure had just begun.

ABOUT THE AUTHOR

Sabina is a non-fiction writer. She has lived and taught English in Poland, Sweden, the Netherlands, the UAE, and Spain. Her memoir series depicts her and her husband's adventures of starting a new life in rural Andalusia.

She currently lives in the middle of olive groves outside the picturesque village of Montefrio and runs a language school in the town of Alcalá la Real.

For the occasional glimpse of Cortijo Berruguilla and the nature around Montefrio, follow us on Instagram or Facebook:

Facebook @cortijoberruguilla

To get updates about new books, subscribe to her website or social media:

www.sabinaostrowska.com

Facebook @sabinawriter

For the occasional glimpse of Cortijo Berruguilla and nature around Montefrio, follow Sabina on Instagram or Facebook:
Instagram @cortijob
Facebook @cortijoberruguilla

Chat with Sabina and other memoir authors
and readers in the Facebook group,
WE LOVE MEMOIRS:
https://www.facebook.com/groups/welovememoirs/

A REQUEST

If you enjoyed *The Crinkle Crankle Wall*, please do leave a review.

To get updates about the next books in this series and to read other free stories, subscribe to my website or follow me on social media:

www.sabinaostrowska.com

Facebook @sabinawriter

Instagram @cortijob

ACKNOWLEDGMENTS

I started my journey as a self-published writer in the summer of 2020 while incapacitated for weeks by a broken leg. Even though a solid draft of *The Crinkle Crankle Wall* had been ready for years, I had no clue what to do with it and how to get it in front of readers. I also doubted whether anyone would like to read this story, which slowed down the process of getting my it out there. Now, almost a year after I published my first non-fiction book, I'd like to thank everyone who has contributed to its success.

First and foremost, my writing would have never taken off if it were not for good friends all over the world who didn't hesitate to purchase my book as soon as it was released even though they had no idea whether it was any good. Thank you: Jeff, Julie, Christine and Aidan, Claudia, Joanna, Zosia, Livia and Sachin, Janusz, Jim, Mariette, and many others who remain anonymous. Thank you all for reading it and getting the snowball rolling by recommending it to your friends and family.

Secondly, I'd like to thank the readers and other authors from the We Love Memoirs Facebook group for being so enthusiastic and encouraging along the way. Thanks to this group, I've met readers all the way from Melbourne in Australia to rural North Carolina. It's always a humbling experience to hear from readers from parts of the world I have never visited. It's also gratifying to learn that I've managed to bring a slice of Andalusia and a little bit of adventure to their lives through my writing. And thank you to other self-published authors for sharing not only your victories but also your downfalls.

And finally, a huge thank you to readers in Andalusia and other expats in Spain who have embraced this tale of trial and tribulation.

Thank you for the lovely messages and e-mails that told me how relatable my story is and how much you enjoyed it. It's always a treat to hear from local readers, so please don't hesitate to reach out. Thank you, Alison and Lynda — you are my two biggest fans in Alcalá la Real and the neighbouring villages — for all the support and for spreading the word in the local community and beyond.

To have my story reach people beyond my circle of friends is more than I could have ever imagined. So thank you for reading it.

Cortijo Berruguilla, December 2021

Made in the USA
Las Vegas, NV
07 August 2022

52870668R00173